COUNSELING AND
THE THERAPEUTIC STATE

COUNSELING AND THE THERAPEUTIC STATE

James J. Chriss
Editor

ALDINE DE GRUYTER
New York

About the Editor

James J. Chriss is Associate Professor of Sociology at Newman University, where he also serves as Chair of the Social Sciences. His main areas of research are sociological theory, law, management and organizations, and the social organization of the helping professions. His latest book is *Alvin W. Gouldner: Sociologist and Outlaw Marxist* (Ashgate, 1999).

ALDINE DE GRUYTER
A division of Walter de Gruyter, Inc.
200 Saw Mill River Road
Hawthorne, New York 10532

This publication is printed on acid-free paper ∞

Library of Congress Cataloging-in-Publication Data
Counseling and the therapeutic state / James J. Chriss, editor
      p.   cm. — (Social problems and social issues)
  Includes bibliographical references and index.
   ISBN 0-202-30623-2 (alk. paper). — ISBN 0-202-30624-0 (pbk. : alk. paper)
    1. Counseling—Government policy—United States.
  2. Psychotherapy—Government policy—United States. 3. Public welfare—United States. 4. Welfare state. I. Chriss, James J., 1955–   . II. Series.
  HV95.C675 1999
  361'.02—dc21   99-19052
                                         CIP

Manufactured in the United States of America

10 9 8 7 6 5 4 3 2 1

Table of Contents ──────────────────────────

Preface

There are many indications that in modern western society the utility and efficacy of counseling and psychotherapy are taken for granted. Examples from the past few years abound. Everybody knows of the infamous boxing match in which Mike Tyson was disqualified for biting off a chunk of Evander Holyfield's ear. News and sports commentators advocated "help" in the form of anger management counseling for Tyson as a viable option for him to redeem himself. This sentiment seemed to be shared by the general public. For example, appearing on the Larry King show, Tyson was peppered with questions from the call-in audience about whether he had received, or was seeking, counseling.

Tyson later applied for reinstatement of his boxing license to the Nevada Athletic Commission. As a condition of possible reinstatement, Tyson was ordered to take a battery of psychological tests and undergo examination by a team of three psychiatrists at Massachusetts General Hospital. The assumption made was that the explanation for Tyson's behavior was buried deep in his psyche, and hence psychological tests would need to be conducted to ascertain the "truth" regarding his condition.

The team of psychiatrists concluded that Tyson is "mentally fit to return to boxing" but that he should undergo additional psychotherapy for a "constellation of neurobehavioral deficits," including problems with attention span, memory, reading, spelling, and impulse control. Ronald Schouten, the lead psychiatrist, suggested that Tyson suffered from depression as well, and if the prescribed therapy did not work, medication would probably be required. And the saga continues.[1]

A string of school shootings that occurred in 1997 and 1998 in Kentucky, Mississippi, Arkansas, and Oregon focused public attention on the horrors of such imponderable acts. Many were left bewildered, asking why our children were engaging in such senseless, violent acts, and what we as a society could do to stop it. Throughout these ordeals, media coverage caught images of phalanxes of counselors descending on the schools to provide grief therapy and whatever additional services shell-shocked students, parents, and school personnel needed.

After President Clinton admitted to the nation that he had indeed had improper sexual relations with Monica Lewinsky, he hurriedly gathered together members of his cabinet, top-ranking democrats, and other legislators in a closed-door session to air grievances and to allow Mr. Clinton to personally apologize to those he had misled over the previous seven months. Again, the therapeutic ethos was quite in evidence here; by all accounts the meeting was described as something akin to a group counseling session.

Whether such counseling services or orientations do any "good," in the sense of helping people make adjustments so that they can lead healthy, productive lives, is not the most important issue here. Rather, for purposes of this volume, what is important to note is the fact that almost everyone— parents, students, the mass media, teachers and administrators, managers and businesspersons, lawyers, doctors, and of course everyone involved in the "helping professions"—assumes that counseling is an appropriate avenue for ameliorating all sorts of disturbances in people's lives. Somehow, we as a society have arrived at a point at which we are willing to give our lives over to these "physicians of the soul," either voluntarily or as mandated by some institutional concern (be it government, the courts, business, schools, or the church).

This volume examines the reasons why modern society and culture appear thoroughly saturated with this psychotherapeutic ethos. The issues of counseling and the therapeutic state involve a host of connected substantive topics, including the social organization of counseling and psychotherapeutic practice; theories and conceptualizations of state and government; work, the professions, and professionalization; the rise of the service sector in industrial economies; the sociology of knowledge, particularly medical knowledge; credentialism and schooling; and the nature of social solidarity in modern society.

Because the therapeutic ethos has permeated the everyday operation and understanding of society and its citizens, the analysis of this phenomenon extends beyond the borders of any particular discipline. As a result, this book is relevant to a vast number of college courses and programs, both at the undergraduate and graduate level. A list of major programs would include sociology, psychology, political science, government, policy analysis, decision sciences, history, corrections and criminal justice, religious studies and theology, law and legal studies, philosophy, business and management, and of course the whole array of helping professions (including social work, nursing, occupational therapy, mental health counseling, drug and alcohol addiction counseling, and pastoral counseling, to name a few).

It is hoped that through this systematic examination of counseling itself, as well as the role that government and professional organizations play in attempting to legitimate psychotherapeutic knowledge and practice, students and professors will engage in honest and open discussion about the vision of the good life that the counseling professions champion as we approach the twenty-first century. Only with a well-informed citizenry can we hope to conceptualize alternatives to the status quo and also be aware of whose interests are being served by current arrangements, and how we arrived there in the first place.

James J. Chriss

NOTE

1.   Information gathered from "Tyson Is Deemed 'Fit' to Fight, But Questions Remain," *The Wichita Eagle*, Wednesday, September 14, 1998, p. 4C; and "Back in the Ring; After Humbling Hearing, Tyson Gets License Back," *The Wichita Eagle*, Tuesday, October 20, 1998, pp. 1–2C.

Introduction

1

James J. Chriss

One of the most exasperating experiences of my recent marriage was dealing with the church requirements for premarital counseling. Because I was Greek Orthodox and my fiancée was Muslim, we were unable to get married in the Greek Orthodox church. We contacted a number of churches of various denominations and were surprised to find that all of them required marriage counseling before they would conduct the wedding ceremony.[1]

I made it clear to each of the priests with whom we met that we expected to receive, and even welcomed, traditional rounds of pastoral counseling. Here, the emphasis would be on the awesome obligation that a man and a woman accept when they enter into marriage, and the acknowledgment of the sanctity of such a union as it takes place under the watchful presence of the Lord.

What we did *not* expect, however, and what we strongly objected to, was the requirement that we receive our counseling from an on-staff therapist, typically a social worker or marriage and family therapist. This amounted to a standard six-week counseling session with fees ranging anywhere from $125 on up. These so-called "licensed" therapists usually had only a masters degree or less, and it seemed odd to entrust the sustenance and care of our mental and spiritual lives to such a person, especially considering that I hold a Ph.D. and two masters degrees in sociology. What was this person going to tell me about marriage, family, relationships, caring, forgiveness, or spirituality that I did not already know? As a matter of fact, I had taught sociology of marriage and family for years, and had also studied issues involving counseling and the therapeutic state. If anything, I would be teaching our "therapist" a thing or two about the empirical social world.

This situation was untenable for me and my fiancée (now my wife), and we eventually decided to forego a church service in favor of a civil ceremony. This experience was another example of what I argue to be the illegitimate encroachment of counseling and the therapeutic mentality into areas of life in which such services are not warranted.

Although this introduction focuses on the particular ways in which counseling and therapeutic discourse continue to inundate and dominate the daily workings of modern society, it should be noted that the therapeutic state goes beyond any particular set of practices or professional ideologies.

1

As Nolan (1998b:6) notes, the therapeutic ethos "has become a taken-for-granted part of everyday life. It provides culture with a set of symbols and codes that determine the boundaries of moral life." Noting the pervasiveness of the therapeutic ethos, this volume will seek answers to the following questions: Why are the assumptions of the utility and even appropriateness of the therapeutic model so pervasive and such a part of people's taken-for-granted, everyday reality? Why are so many institutional concerns—business, religion, the polity, education, the courts and criminal justice, mass media, and even the family—giving over access to or control over the lives of people to these so-called "certified" or "licensed" experts? Why are so many people running around calling themselves therapists? Why do so many people want a piece of the therapy pie? What is behind this "democratization" of counseling and therapy? How and why have we arrived at this state of affairs, which Jurgen Habermas (1987:363) has aptly dubbed the "therapeutocracy"?

These questions are not merely idle speculations or the misgivings of a group of researchers whom some might accuse of overestimating the presence and influence of therapeutic practices and thinking on modern society. By all accounts, psychotherapy is indeed big business. As Rowe (1994:8) explains,

> Psychiatrists do psychotherapy, so do psychologists, nurses, social workers and occupational therapists. If people feel that "psychotherapy" is too pretentious a word to apply to what they do, they describe what they do as counselling, and so we have student counsellors, marriage guidance counsellors, Samaritan counsellors, alcohol counsellors, drug counsellors, tranquilizer counsellors, clergy counsellors, policewoman counsellors, counsellors at day care centres and drop-in centres, counsellors on radio and television. More recently, many of these psychotherapists have turned into experts.

In the United States there are now over 700,000 practicing physicians, with some 130,000 of these specializing in psychiatry. In addition, there is a growing tide of nonpsychiatrist mental "healers"—practicing psychologists, clinical social workers, marriage and family counselors, mental health counselors, substance abuse counselors, group psychotherapy facilitators, and others—whose numbers are now estimated at around 650,000, or about five times the number of psychiatrists (see Ivey et al. 1998; Nolan 1998a; Pallone 1997).

To understand this increasing emphasis on counseling and therapeutic discourse (Labov and Fanshel 1977; Silverman 1997) across an ever-expanding array of practices and social settings, we must carefully trace the historical, cultural, legal, and sociological factors giving rise to state support and mandating of such services. In the next few sections I present a broad overview of trends associated with the rise of, and increasing emphasis on, counseling and therapeutic discourse in modern society. Later, I will summarize the contributions of each author to the volume.

TOWARD THE THERAPEUTOCRACY

The "helping professions"—social work, occupational therapy, marriage and family therapy, school counseling, nursing, psychiatry, psychology, educational psychology, mental health counseling, Alcoholics Anonymous and other 12-step programs, and correctional counseling—represent a wide array of disciplines and practices ostensibly geared to providing services to marginal groups and an assortment of distressed individuals. In effect, the helping professions attempt to instill prosocial adjustment in individuals who, for whatever reason, have taken a wrong turn in life, whether the result of addictive behavior, crime, delinquency, aggression or violence, problems in marital or interpersonal relations, mental illness, social or physical stigma, poverty, youthfulness or old age, or simply "odd" behavior more generally (see Kennedy 1984; Kittrie 1971; Murphy 1979).

Because the helping professions are competing to provide services to governments in a climate of shrinking public funding and decreasing confidence in such services, turf wars have been ignited, as each profession has had to justify its knowledge base and therapeutic efficacy in relation to others. For example, over the last decade mental health counseling has become overtly concerned with defining itself as a distinct profession within the health care system and in the eyes of legislators. As Rigazio-DiGilio (1996:291) explains, "Scholars are working to establish an epistemological framework that more ably identifies mental health counseling as a discipline that offers preventive and treatment services distinct from those of psychology, psychiatry, social work, marriage and family therapy, and nursing."

The emphasis on therapy, and the continuing proliferation of various helping professions involved in one way or another with providing counseling to patients—or rather "clients" [see Frans (1994) for an explanation of this terminological shift]—can be understood as arising out of the transition from folk (or communal) to modern (or associational) society (Giddens 1990; Hillery 1968; Redfield 1947; Toennies 1957). Durkheim [1951 (1897); 1984 (1933)] has perhaps best described the ways in which sources of social solidarity or integration shifted concomitant to this societal transition.

In primitive societies, the basis of social solidarity is homogeneity, meaning that for the most part all members of society share a common culture, including a common set of beliefs, life experiences, everyday practices, and orientations toward the sacred. Since folk societies tend to be small, attachments between members of society are deep and abiding, grounded in large measure along kinship lines and familiarity arising out of everyday face-to-face interaction and co-presence.

Because of the high level of intimacy and knowledge that each member possesses of others, group solidarity is strong. Durkheim (1984), in fact, used the term *mechanical solidarity* to describe the overriding importance of the group over the individual in primitive society. Individuals are held in check because violations of the normative order are interpreted as an assault on the collective consciousness or sensibilities of the group, and hence sanctions or punishments against violators tend to be swift, harsh, and retributive.

With the advent of industrialization and the democratic revolutions occurring across Western society beginning in the late 1700s, central cities experienced increases in population density as productivity increased and as more and more persons from a variety of countries immigrated to these cities in hopes of finding work in the newly burgeoning industrial economy. As populations grow denser, the social solidarity previously ensured through likeness, familiarity, and face-to-face contact is imperiled as the urban metropolis now becomes characterized by anonymity, heterogeneity, and temporal and spatial distancing between members.

THE SOURCES OF SOCIAL SOLIDARITY

Durkheim and other mass society theorists were worried that in this new associational society, the quality and quantity of attachments would become increasingly superficial and impoverished as persons are set adrift amidst a sea of faceless and anonymous others. Durkheim's (1951) pessimism about modern society was fueled by data that indicated that social pathologies—suicide, divorce, poverty, homelessness, mental illness, crime, violence, and drug and alcohol abuse—were occurring at higher rates, per capita, in these urban, metropolitan communities.

The assumption was that the city was a dysfunctional place that threatened the socialization process, the unity of the family, and the development of secure and stable attachments and selves. The modern trend toward individualism creates greater awareness about selves and especially self-esteem (Hewitt 1998). Lasch (1979:7), for example, argues that the earlier religious sensibility has given way to the modern therapeutic sensibility, wherein "people today hunger not for personal salvation, let alone for the restoration of an earlier golden age, but for the feeling, the momentary illusion, of personal well-being, health, and psychic security." In the past few years we have witnessed a proliferation of self-help and self-esteem gurus seemingly playing on the insecurities of modern persons' senses of self

(Giddens 1990; Jenkins 1997). Indeed, Bauman (1997:178) suggests that "Postmodernity is the era of experts in 'identity problems,' of personality healers, of marriage guides, of writers of 'how to reassert yourself' books; it is the era of the 'counselling boom.'"

Consider how this emphasis on the self and self-concept arises as a concomitant to the transition from mechanical to organic solidarity, as delineated by Durkheim. In earlier times, societies are typified by mechanical solidarity where individuals mechanically acquiesce to the will of the group. In modern society, in contrast, individuals slowly cast off the constraints of family and family background, community, tradition, ascription, and other forms of informal social control and monitoring, and are judged more as individuals via their achievements in the world and by virtue of the unique attributes constituting status, self, and personality.

As Kreuger (1997) points out, in earlier times individuals were assured a supportive institutional fabric made up of families, schools, churches, and various voluntary associations. Today, with the increasing emphasis on anonymity, contracts and other formal relations, and other mechanisms of distancing and isolation (such as television or video games, which tend to replace human contact with technology; see Putnam 1996), individuals are left with few guides or cues regarding how to get on with day-to-day life. This perception of a lack of guidance and insight among the average citizen sets the stage for the encroachment of "experts" into virtually all walks of life, an ideology that serves the economic interests of therapists and others in the helping professions especially well.

Hence, a prominent feature of modern societies is the impact of the "professional complex" (Parsons 1978:35–65) on persons' routine definitions of the situation. Conditions of anonymity and increasing population densities lead to a greater array of social situations in which persons must interact with and rely on nonfamiliar others for their day-to-day necessities. Trust, which used to be ensured through familiarity and routine face-to-face contact, must now be formalized within more or less impersonal client–professional relationships. In other words, in modern society a wide range of professionals emerge to offer services and provisions to persons who, because of the highly refined division of labor and task specialization characteristic of modern society, simply cannot do everything for themselves.

MEDICINE AND THE ADVENT OF THE HELPING PROFESSIONS

With respect to issues involving the therapeutic state, certainly the most relevant profession impacting the lives of citizens is medicine. As used here and elsewhere, the term "therapeutic state" refers to the ascendancy of the medical model as the prevailing ideology of the modern welfare state (see Cloud 1998; Leifer 1990). This section discusses how and why the medical terminology of "wellness," "sickness," "syndrome," "addiction," "disease," "healing," and "therapy" has come to dominate social, political, and policy discourse (for important discussions of psychotherapy and the therapeutic welfare state, see Albee 1990; Barney 1994; Farber 1990; Gergen 1990; Nolan 1998a, 1998b; Peele 1990; Polsky 1991; Sternberg 1977; Szasz 1990; Vatz and Weinberg 1990).

As Neustadter (1991–92:29) notes, "it is clear that medicine has become the central restitutive agent in modern society" (see also Farber 1995; Illich 1977a, 1977b; McKnight 1995). Like other professions, individuals acquiring medical degrees have conferred on them a "cloak of competence" (Fox 1959), which, as long as they do not make glaring or egregious errors in diagnosis or treatment, effectively render them "experts" in their chosen fields. The expertise accruing to medical professionals tends to be accepted by patients (or clients) seeking their services, for physicians' training, skills, bedside manner, and other related competencies are presumed to be ensured by their acquisition of a medical certificate or diploma.

These medical experts were of course originally empowered to make professional claims about the physical and biological condition of patients. But discourses and narratives that find legitimacy in one arena of social life often expand into other, perhaps (initially) unrelated areas of the human condition (see Foucault 1973; Habermas 1971). Hence the ideas of disease, sickness, and wellness eventually expanded beyond the proper object of medical discourse and practice—the body—to any and all areas that conceivably could be subsumed under the rubric of medical expertise (Dineen 1996; Kendall 1996; Turner 1992).

Professional organizations—whether organized around medicine, law, business, social science, or the burgeoning array of helping professions—always seek to expand the range of objects and phenomena to which their members' expertise may arguably be applied, primarily because it is in their own economic interests to do so. This is especially noticeable in the case of the myriad practitioners fancying themselves as therapists, whose collective efforts have resulted in what can best be described as a sort of "psychological expansionism." For example, each new edition of the *Diagnostic and Statistical Manual of Mental Disorders* (*DSM*) has grown dramatically as new mental disorders or pathologies are "discovered" and codified (see Conrad 1975; Kirk and Kutchins 1992; Schissel 1997).

Before physicians could begin to apply their training and expertise about the body to other areas of inquiry, they had to overcome, or at least challenge, the philosophical basis of modern Enlightenment thinking, namely the Cartesian dualism of mind and body. As early as the 1770s, for example, German physician Franz Mesmer was applying magnets to patients on the theory that the mind and body could simultaneously be healed of disorders if the body's magnetic fields were properly realigned (Hunt 1993:98). Although this particular research was nonsensical, Mesmer nevertheless became a medical and psychological pioneer, as other physicians and investigators followed suit and began to apply the tools and ideas of medicine to the human mind.

Eventually, of course, medical expertise and definitions of wellness expanded not only to the province of the mind, but also to society. By the late 1800s psychiatrists and psychoanalysts, informed and inspired primarily by the theories of Sigmund Freud, were the first group of medical professionals to apply everyday discourse and counseling techniques to describing, diagnosing, and ameliorating the mental illnesses and pathologies of their patients.

These medical practitioners began making great strides in gaining legitimacy in the eyes of individual patients, state governments, and even social scientists. For example, by the 1920s, anthropology, sociology, and social work had taken to the psychiatric notion of viewing whole societies as "patients," and to the belief that psychiatric techniques could be marshaled to better understand and perhaps cure "sick societies" (Edgerton 1992; Frank 1948).

Social workers became especially enamored of Freud by the late 1920s, primarily because out in the field, during their day-to-day casework with clients, they came to realize that they could not very easily predict the behavior of their clients (see Hale 1995:93–95; Polsky 1991:111–115; Shorter 1997:293–295; Sibeon 1991; Specht and Courtney 1994). This led many social workers of that era to believe that to go beyond the surface appearances of the client–provider relationship, Freudian psychotherapeutic techniques and theories could be employed to uncover the "true" factors contributing to clients' maladjustment problems. Although Freudian theories of intrapsychic process have been severely challenged since World War II, within social work and various other helping professions—especially occupational therapy, nursing, drug and alcohol counseling, and marriage and family therapy—the percentage of practitioners engaging in psychiatric or psychotherapeutic professional practice nevertheless continues to increase (see Thomas 1996). Emblematic of this "triumph of the therapeutic" (Rieff 1966) at the societal level was the establishment of the United Nations' World Health Organization (WHO) in the 1940s. As Lasch (1977:98) explains, the establishment of WHO "provided the mental health profession with a forum from which to preach the new gospel of 'complete physical, mental and social well-being.'"

The expansion and acceptance of a world organization defining health to encompass physical, mental, and social well-being meant that the medical and health professions' constituency now included not only the clinic and the hospital, but also the home, churches, schools, prisons, business, and government (Lasch 1977:99). With evidence of the increasing numbers of social pathologies besetting modern society and the difficulties modern citizens were facing in their everyday lives, psychiatrists, and later groups of health and social science practitioners emulating psychiatric counseling techniques, became emboldened to translate everything human into medical terms of illness. Hence, bad social conditions, bad families, and bad schools were producing maladjusted individuals who needed the services of doctors who could "cure" them.

The problem with this "medicalization" of everyday life is simply that when expertise in one area expands into other areas of understanding and reality—as has happened with the extension of the disease model (Peele 1995) and the encroachment of medical expertise into virtually every facet of modern social life—persons are disempowered within the contexts of their everyday life, because they systematically lose the ability to discuss and negotiate definitions of the situation informally among themselves, that is, within the contexts of family and community (Herman 1995). If indeed state legislators see increasing evidence that social pathologies are on the rise and that many persons—especially the indigent—are seemingly unable to cope with the day-to-day rigors of modern living, they are apt to subscribe to certain prevailing social narratives that have been shown to be efficacious within limited professional contexts. Several of these social narratives, or "discourses," in Foucault's (1973) terminology, are the disease model, the service-delivery model, and the legal model.

More and more these days, law and medicine are implicated in social and government policies, the ultimate purpose of which is to ensure the social order in light of a fragmented postmodern world in which shared understandings of the "good life" no longer seem to hold and in which informal consensus formation by the citizenry on difficult social issues is stymied by expert systems embedded in the legal-bureaucratic structures and institutions of government. The service-delivery model of business is implicated as well in many government policies, as illustrated in the assumption that governments are in the business of delivering "products" to "customers" in the form of services and provisions, and ensuring positive social "outcomes" or "goods" such as stable families, low levels of crime and delinquency, and an overall well-adjusted citizenry (see Pegnato 1997).

It is interesting to note that this ongoing monetarization of social policy is adversely affecting social work in Britain, for example, as explained by Dominelli (1996:156): "Case management techniques have facilitated the penetration of market forces into a hitherto sacrosanct professional arena—the 'client-worker relationship', through the implementation of the purchase-provider split in service organization and delivery." As part of the broader process of rationalization, monetarization also leads toward an emphasis on outcome-based or performance-based evaluation of the services provided by the helping professions, another factor that has led to the "deprofessionalization" of social work. Dominelli (1996:163) explains that "Competencies represent the Taylorisation of professional tasks, that is, their reduction to discrete elements which can be undertaken by less highly qualified individuals lower in the labour hierarchy at lower rates of pay."

DEMOCRATIZATION AND THE MODERN WELFARE STATE

In earlier times, when the social order was held together by informal group consensus, government—whatever there was of it—represented an intact collective conscience that acted on behalf of the people, often punitively and harshly against those who dared to violate the moral order. Preindustrial governments or societies could not be characterized as compassionate in their treatment of, and attitude toward, citizens. In fact, such governments often acted oppressively, wielding their coercive powers arbitrarily against the citizenry to stifle dissent and to ensure social order.

It was not until the late 1700s that the modern democratic state first came into view. Social movements such as the French Revolution of 1789 and the American democratic revolution against the British sovereign (1775–1783) marked a mass repudiation of the concentration of power in the hands of a few government elites. As Habermas (1987:360) argues, this third wave of juridification, which he calls the *democratic constitutional state*, sees the idea of freedom already incipient in the concept of law given *constitutional* force. Here, constitutionalized state power was democratized, and citizens, as citizens of the state, were provided with rights of political participation.

The idea of the monarchy or the traditional authority residing in the notion of the "divine right of kings" was overthrown and rendered illegitimate, as we have seen. Citizens' rights are no longer defined only on the basis of property rights and economic status. Now, laws come into force only when there is a democratically backed presumption that they express a general interest (the "general will") to which all those affected could agree. Also, the lifeworld—the realm of everyday life—is incorporated more meaningfully into the operation of the polity that once dominated the lifeworld through generalized, delinguistified media such as power (seated in the polity) and money (seated in the economy). Power is more structurally dispersed away from the sovereign by way of the creation of differential governmental institutions, namely the legislature, the executive branch, and the judiciary.

Although the polity acts more compassionately toward its citizens in the democratic constitutional state, it is not until the emergence of the *democratic welfare state*, beginning in the 1920s, that we see the full institutionalization of policies and social roles dedicated to enacting and carrying out the work of amelioration. The modern welfare state, illustrated by the struggles of the European workers' movement and especially by the emergence in the United States of President Roosevelt's New Deal in the 1930s, represents the latest in a line of *freedom-guaranteeing juridifications* occurring across western society. As Habermas (1987:361–373) argues, this can be understood as the institutionalization in legal form of a social power relation anchored in the lifeworld and in class structure. Here, constitutionally guaranteed protections are being made explicit with regard not only to one's occupational status or citizenship status, but also to virtually all other statuses comprising a person's status-set, whether gender, age, disability, race, ethnicity, sexual orientation, marital status, etc.

Originally, the movements that gave rise to the early welfare state were aimed at ameliorating problems besetting the economic institution, illustrated by policies such as placing limitations on working hours, ensuring the freedom to organize unions and bargain for wages, social security, and protection from layoffs. In effect, these movements represented efforts by the citizenry to create protection from economic harm and the problems associated with the unequal distribution of resources. Thus, initially, welfare state guarantees were meant to cushion the external effects of a production process based on wage labor that, although creating prosperity for some and a higher standard of living for the citizenry as a whole, also produced in some pockets of western society levels of poverty, disadvantage, and despair theretofore unseen.

Eventually, of course, the idea of freedom-guaranteeing juridification burst out of the confines of the economic realm (in terms of one's status as, say, "worker") or claims against the sovereign into virtually all areas of social life. In other words, the force of law as a guarantor of rights is now being used as a wedge to provide relief to citizens claiming damage based on any number of possible statuses. In connection with social welfare law, it has been shown that although legal entitlements to monetary income in case of illness, old age, and the like definitely signaled historical progress, "this juridification of life-risks exacts a noteworthy price in the form of *restructuring interventions in the lifeworlds* of those who are so entitled. These costs ensue from the bureaucratic implementation and monetary redemption of welfare entitlements" (Habermas 1987:362).

Surely one of the greatest paradoxes of this latest phase of freedom-guaranteeing juridification is that the welfare state is more likely than ever to invoke the claim of *parens patriae*, namely, the "state as parent." As Kittrie (1971:3) explains, in this new therapeutic state,

> little or no emphasis is placed upon an individual's guilt of a particular crime; but much weight is given to physical, mental, or social shortcomings. In dealing with the deviant, under the new system, society is said to be acting in a parental role (*parens patriae*)—seeking not to punish but to change or socialize the nonconformist through treatment and therapy.

As Habermas (1987:364) points out, in this new therapeutocracy, the polity spreads a net of client relationships across society in order to pacify the class conflict and limited life chances some persons experience as a result of the operation of a capitalist system that appears to favor some groups (white males in particular) while disvaluing others (especially females and minorities).

Of course, the polity or state is certainly not the only social institution mandating counseling for various purposes. For example, much debate has arisen over the issue of mandatory counseling of university students (see, e.g., Amada 1995; Gilbert and Sheiman 1995). Beyond traditional pastoral counseling, more and more churches have certified marriage counselors on staff, and couples seeking to get married in the church are expected or even required to receive this extra level of secular or "professional" marriage counseling (see Varacalli 1997). And even in this current age of pessimism concerning the effectiveness of rehabilitation of prisoners, the criminal justice system is nevertheless rife with mandatory counseling and psychotherapy programs for accused or indicted offenders. For example, judges are more likely to suggest diversion into mandatory anger management or marriage counseling programs for men accused of domestic violence than even social service providers working in women's shelters (see Davis 1984). This is because the legal field has largely incorporated (thereby reifying) the "certainties" of the welfare sciences that appear in the form of the expert testimony of psychiatrists, psychologists, and occasionally social workers working in fields such as child protection, homeless or poor advocacy, alcohol or drug addiction, marital and family counseling, and corrections and parole (White 1998).

Additionally, a growing number of states are requiring diversion into drug therapy or counseling for first time driving under the influence offenders as a condition of parole. Claims of effectiveness of treatment for clients coming out of voluntary therapy programs are dubious enough because of the ever present placebo effect; when persons are mandated or coerced into therapy, such as is the case of diversion into drug treatment (for example, Alcoholics Anonymous), outcomes are even worse (see Peyrot 1985).

THE IDEOLOGY OF COMPASSION: SEEKING "PROFESSIONAL" HELP

To keep such marginalized persons and groups in check, agents of the therapeutic state are made available—initially through public programs and agencies, but now more and more through private practice providers—to a wide range of persons adversely affected by the rigors of modern living, especially criminals, the poor, the mentally ill, drug and alcohol addicts, adolescents, those in family distress (as a result of divorce, abandonment, or child or spouse abuse), the homeless, and even the temporarily distressed (in the form of bereavement counseling, anger and tension management, life skills counseling and training, dating and relationships counseling, and so forth).

Hence we see a continuing proliferation of helping professions and programs coming into existence in order to tap into the largess of the welfare state through the procurement of services and treatment to "clients." What is important to keep in mind is that the prevailing piece of wisdom driving the entire therapeutic and helping professions paradigm is a truism that sociologists and the early mass society theorists (such as Durkheim) had put forth years ago, even before the advent of psychotherapy, namely, that the transition from agricultural to industrial society tends to erode the quantity and quality of attachments between members of society, leading to anomie, alienation, despair, a reduction of group consensus, heightened mistrust of others, egoistic individualism, and an overall uncertainty about the meaning of life.

As we have seen, psychiatrists discovered early that many persons suffering such problems could be helped if they simply had someone with whom they could speak and to whom they could communicate their anguish and uncertainties about life. Psychiatrists were able to connect themselves and their services to people in need because of the power and legitimacy conferred on them by their medical degrees. Many psychiatrists, even as early as the late 1800s, had private practices or, at the very least, had ready access to hospital facilities or mental asylums that provided relatively easy access to those patients seeking help (see Hunt 1993:559–598).

The occupational prestige of physicians has always been high, and over time many persons in various lines of work have attempted to emulate the work, style, or rhetoric of physicians in hopes of capitalizing on that prestige. Additionally, with regard to counseling and therapy per se, many observers questioned the legitimacy of applying medical training to something as seemingly simple and straightforward as "talking," "discussing," or "counseling." For example, even Freud (1947) believed that the training a physician received was of little value in actually doing psychotherapy. Indeed, psychotherapy has often been described as the "talking cure" because it appears to be little more than a licensed "expert" sitting down with a client and talking through his or her problems (see McLaughlin 1998:117).

To defend themselves against the ongoing encroachment of non-medically trained personnel into psychotherapy, medical doctors and psychiatrists such as Vaughan (1997), drawing on alleged evidence from cognitive science, have attempted to establish that psychiatry actually brings about physiological changes in the brain, thereby once again recasting psychiatry as a legitimate medical procedure that should be performed only by licensed physicians. Along these same lines, a rift has occurred between proponents of drug treatment in psychotherapy (whose practice is of course monopolized by psychiatrists) and all others who have only the talking cure to offer. This has led to a variety of non-M.D.-trained personnel (mainly psychologists, nurses, social workers, and occupational therapists) seeking the right to prescribe drugs to their clients on a limited basis (see Ivey et al. 1998; Lomas 1997; Pallone 1997). Indeed, Fromm (1970) views this democratization of counseling as a major aspect of the overall "crisis of psychoanalysis" plaguing the modern therapeutic state.

In any event, what people began to realize was that a good number of distressed persons simply needed someone to talk to, so initially the state hired social workers to engage in nontherapeutic case management so that such persons could count on someone being available to them on a regular or semiregular basis (Sibeon 1991). Evidence concerning the effectiveness of professional therapists versus lay or informal approaches in alleviating clients' distress, however, is sketchy. A recent study reports that although the average client undergoing psychotherapy appears to be better off than 79% of the members of a nontreatment group, it is also the case that the average client undergoing a placebo treatment (that is, treatments by untrained therapists who simply "talk," in more or less laymen's terms, with their clients) is better off than 66% of the members of a nontreatment group (Lambert and Bergin 1994). So simply making persons available to other persons in distress is better than doing nothing at all, regardless of the training or expertise of the helper. (For a summary of the spotty evidence of psychotherapy's efficacy, as well as the generally coercive nature of psychotherapy and mental health institutions, see Albee 1990; Bergmann 1992; Dawes 1994; Goffman 1961; and Kennedy 1984.)

Agents of the therapeutic state, then, are institutionalized through government programs and policies to connect with distressed persons who otherwise have few or no opportunities to form attachments with conventional others. As Gouldner (1973:50) states, "It is the ultimate function of the federally based programmes to win or maintain the attachment of urban lower and working classes to the political symbols and machinery of the American state in general, and of the Democratic Party in particular."

Unfortunately, the legal-bureaucratic structure of the therapeutic state obviates against the simple solution of hiring persons coming out of various service provision programs (such as social work) to be there and monitor the progress of persons coming to the attention of the state. The trend toward professionalization of the myriad therapeutic practices and "disciplines" that have followed on the heels of psychiatry serves ostensibly two purposes. First, professionalization of the human services in the form of codification of procedures, including licensing and certification requirements (see Jenkins 1997; Sibeon 1991; Sweeney 1995), attempts to ensure that only certain programs or practitioners are able to monopolize interventions into the lives of distraught persons. Second, from the perspective of the state, in having personnel go through such certification and licensing training, social workers and other helping professionals learn the intricacies of bureaucracy with regard to filling out forms properly as well as the procedures for procurement of services to clients under the auspices of state-operated programs. In effect, states are concerned with protecting themselves and their agents from legal action in case something goes wrong with a client. By requiring that persons working with particular clients in state-sponsored programs be licensed to perform W or X according to guidelines Y or Z, the state can more easily trace out lines of accountability via the creation of quasilegal administrative structures. Hence, although it is certainly a noble and honorable idea for states to connect helping agents to members of marginal populations for purposes of shoring up attachments, these acts of compassion often produce less than desirable outcomes as they pass through the bureaucratic structures and legal mazes endemic to the operation of public agencies.[2]

The therapeutocracy of the public realm is also alive and well in the private realm of counseling and therapeutic practice. Perhaps even more important in the realm of private provision of therapeutic services is the emphasis on the therapist's credentials. Certainly, the rhetoric of private practice counselors is that they are "experts" in their chosen specialties. But unlike M.D.-trained psychiatrists or Ph.D.-trained clinical psychologists, later generations of nonmedically trained therapists must offer evidence of their training that may appear substandard or dubious to laypersons, especially if such therapists hold only bachelors degrees (e.g., B.S.W or B.A.), masters degrees (e.g., M.S.W, L.M.S.W., M.F.T.), or perhaps no degree (which can be the case for Alcoholics Anonymous and other 12-step programs, as well as other types of volunteer counseling). In this era of the counseling boom, more and more persons with only masters degrees or less are opening private therapy practices in the wake of the perception that funding for public service agencies is drying up, and especially because of the move by a growing list of states to privatize certain public programs and services (for example, Social and Rehabilitative Services in Kansas).

The rise of managed care also has implications regarding the partnership between the state and the helping professions under the old welfare regime. For example, clinical (psychiatric) social work continues to place an increasing emphasis on private and short-term practice (see Goldstein 1996; Reid 1997; Specht and Courtney 1994), primarily because brief therapy costs less than traditional therapy. With regard to the future of the helping professions and the sustainability of their partnership with public welfare agencies, Kreuger (1997) believes that the therapeutic state as we know it is coming to an end, and with it, the end of social work as well. As Kreuger (1997:19) explains, "radical dislocations in the social structure—brought on by the decline of nation-states, the emergence of a borderless business world, and the subsequent loss of public-sector accountability—will completely obviate traditional service delivery systems."

Echoing Kreuger's sentiments on privatization and monetarization, Dominelli (1996:164) suggests that the therapeutic state, driven largely by the assumptions of the service-delivery model and competency-based evaluation, "must be understood within the context of the privatization of the welfare state—a need engendered by the globalization of capital with its voracious appetite for decreasing the costs of production whilst seeking to maintain high prices at the point of consumption to maximize profits."

Regardless, what this illustrates is that the actual cognitive or intellectual bases of counseling practice and, hence, whatever special skills are supposedly acquired within the course of such training, are of less relevance to therapeutic practice than the practitioner's simply being available to distressed persons as an attachment replacement or substitution, all of this supported of course by the successful dissemination of an ideology that tells people that they ought to seek "professional" help during periods of transition or disturbance. (This last point will be returned to shortly.)

Trends in certification and licensing requirements in counseling and psychotherapy, then, are better explained by external factors (that is, sociological and economic) rather than factors internal to the profession (such as the cognitive and intellectual bases of such practices). As London (1964) explains, psychotherapy can be likened to a service guild in which the typical issue of concern is restricting candidacy and membership to a limited number of persons who satisfy the requirements for "competent" performance. What happens, though, when the craft the guild members practice is so vague or easy that competition emerges from sources outside of the original guild (as has happened with the continuing erosion of medicine's monopoly on psychotherapy)? In this case, the guild will attempt to sustain itself by seeking formal social sanctions. As London (1964:151) states:

> The nature of the bargain struck is that the society restricts title or function of the craft in question to individuals who, in effect, are either members of the guild or approved by it; in so doing, it extends de facto permission to those approved persons to accept gainful employment and collect fees for the hire of their services in that craft. In return, the guild guarantees the society that it will perform its services faithfully (by implication asserting that it has a valuable service to dispense) and that it will police or oversee the activities of its members in this connection.[3]

The turf battles that continue to be waged between medical psychiatry and the helping professions, as well as between the helping professions themselves, are simply efforts to gain competitive advantage over other practitioners and disciplines offering the same or similar services. They are acting like guilds in that they are seeking from the polity economic protection for their own interests. But unlike guilds that produce tangible products (e.g., bicycles) or services (e.g., electrical or plumbing), counselors cannot readily illustrate the efficaciousness of the services they provide, or even that such services require the expertise that guild members are claiming for their craft in the first place.

Returning to the issue of counselors or therapists as attachment replacements, a good example of private practice therapists seeing themselves as providing attachments to clients in need is Cathleen Gray's marriage and family therapy practice. Gray (1996) suggests that in the early stages of divorce, the therapist ought to take the role of "expert-consultant." In the first stage of the divorce process, clients often face a broad range of legal, social, and psychological issues as they attempt to deal with the trauma of separation from their spouse. As Gray (1996:120) explains,

> The most critical factor in this framework is the clinician, or expert-consultant, as the "constant object," beginning at the time of attachment rupture. The clinician enters the system at an early point in the dissolution of the marriage and begins to form a relationship with the client in which the clinician is the constant object that the client can use over a long period of time.

In the later stages of the divorce process, the clinician may then take on the more conventional role of therapist. What is important to note, however, is Gray's suggestion that in the first stage of divorce conventional therapy may be inappropriate. Instead, the clinician should be available to the client to serve ostensibly as a stand-in for the lost spouse so as to manage the attachment deprivation that he or she is suffering as a result of the divorce. This of course assumes that persons' group affiliations and attachments to others are so impoverished and tenuous that any transitional or disruptive events, such as divorce, are matters that must be attended to by a helping professional (see Gerstl 1969).

ESOTERIC KNOWLEDGE AND THE PROFESSIONS

One of the defining characteristics of a "profession" is the control or utilization of some esoteric body of knowledge that is unavailable to others not trained in the particular field of study. As modern industrial societies continue to experience a transformation in their economic productive base—that is, from manufacturing and "working hard" to service provision and "working smart"—more and more emphasis is being placed on the "expertise" of professionals who are "licensed" to guide laypersons through the treacherous affairs of everyday life. As we have seen, the therapeutic helping professions have historically serviced clients who are basically wards of the state, such as the indigent, the mentally ill, the criminal, and the disabled. One way of improving the occupational status of these helping professions is by expanding their client base from marginal groups to more mainstream clientele. The ideology of "seeking professional help" allows the helping professions to thrive in private practice as greater numbers of more or less "normal" or "well-adjusted" persons seek guidance for even minor disturbances or transitions in their lives.

As the helping professions continue to expand their services to all members of society, they must also attempt to appropriate heretofore mundane or lay knowledge and repackage it as esoteric knowledge, such as what is happening in the "wellness" or "caring" professions. A good example of this is the "Carenotes" series of information pamphlets being produced by One Caring Place, a wellness organization based in Indiana. One pamphlet in the series, titled "Visiting a Seriously Ill Friend," provides guidelines for persons who must confront the "difficult" business of visiting a sick friend or relative (Stout 1994). Because it is assumed by the author of the pamphlet that many persons do not always know what to do, how to act, or what to say during such visits, guidelines are offered to reduce the embarrassment or discomfort that presumably both parties may experience. Some of these guidelines are "be sensitive to your friend's routine," "follow your friend's lead," "make concrete suggestions of assistance," and "be yourself."

My point in all this is to underscore and highlight the assumption that the helping professions make about the fragility of persons' self-esteem and the uncertainty about life that confronts us in virtually everything we do, even something as simple as visiting a sick friend (Gergen 1990). And unfortunately, state legislators and policy analysts seemed, at least until recently, to be buying into the therapeutic vision of society held by the helping and medical professions. We are, however, witness to a backlash of sorts against the cult of "self-esteem" and the assumptions of the fragility of the self that are the lifeblood of the helping professions. As we have seen, there has been a move to privatize certain public welfare programs as federal and state legislatures attempt to get their fiscal houses in order, some of which involves reducing support or funding of counseling and rehabilitation programs that have not proven to be efficacious or "cost effective." As a result, more therapeutic resources are being shifted to private practice where the emphasis now is to secure third-party payment and reimbursement allowances from state regulatory agencies and medical and health insurers. This has led to a continuing proliferation of various helping professions waiting in line to garner the right of third-party pay, whether marriage and family therapy, social work, occupational therapy, nursing, or drug and alcohol addiction counseling.

To bring sanity to the claims of professional expertise being made by an exploding number of helping professionals seeking the golden ring of third-party pay through the provision of therapeutic counseling, I believe that the right to perform such therapeutic practice will need to be seriously curtailed in the future and limited to three groups: M.D.-trained psychiatrists, Ph.D.-trained clinical psychologists, and pastors.[4] There is simply no need for persons in other fields to provide therapeutic interventions in the lives of distraught persons, and certainly not to receive third-party reimbursement for such services. This will be viewed as a radical policy suggestion, and certainly one that will be seen as a threat to the livelihood of the other helping professions discussed here. We still need persons to perform the type of nontherapeutic case management that social workers used to perform, and to be available as attachment replacements for persons who are legitimately marginalized or cut off from conventional society in one way or the other. For example, mentor programs by such public service and volunteer agencies as Big Brothers/Big Sisters are paradigmatic of such a nontherapeutic approach. This will probably be a solution that many state and local governments will consider as we approach the end of the millennium.

We have touched on a number of points concerning the social organization of counseling and psychotherapeutic practice in modern society. Any overview and analysis of this issue invariably brings us into an examination of the "state" and the extent to which it may indeed be characterized as "therapeutic." Part I of this volume deals more directly with this latter issue, namely, the theory and conceptualization of the state. After laying this essential groundwork, Part II examines counseling and psychotherapeutic practice more directly.

PART I: CONCEPTUALIZING THE STATE

In "Children and the Civic State: A Covenant Model of Welfare," John O'Neill presents a theory of the stages of evolution of the modern liberal state. The way children are treated in society—generally badly, according to O'Neill—reflects earlier, and now antiquated "state of nature" or "naturalistic" views of children and the family. This state of nature view—in essence, the social contract theory of Hume, Locke, and Rousseau—suggests that children are the "property" of parents and entirely under the power of the father. Simultaneously the mother is rendered powerless as well, relegated to the private domains of household and community. As a result, the state, as overseer of the citizenry, acts punitively toward its citizens, while the father, as head of the family, acts punitively toward both mothers and children.

To move beyond this defective contractarian view of the state and family, O'Neill argues for a *covenant* model of family and state, one that insists on the intergenerational and communal bases of life. Instead of conceptualizing a state of nature and granting dominance and authority of some groups of people over others, in the covenant model of the state, *justice* and *care* perspectives come to the fore, ensuring that women and children are treated with the same respect and given the same opportunities or life chances as males had been granted exclusively under the social contract. As children and women are now pulled under the umbrella of a more caring and compassionate state (as depicted in the transition from Welfare State #1 to Welfare State #2 to the Civic State; see Figure 2.1), citizens as a whole benefit as well.

Welfare State #1 was grounded in a so-called gendered social compact (GSC), in which the breadwinner–homemaker (father as provider, mother as nurturer) family form is prominent, and in which a social wage (father's earnings) structures exchanges between church, state, and the economy. In this first stage, "welfare" is administered informally in the form of a social wage with the support of church, state, and community (the reproduction of *moral capital*). In Welfare State #2, more and more professionals are designated in the roles of caring and helping those persons who cannot meet the expectations of a middle-class life-style. In this second phase of the welfare state (GMC), the state and therapeutic helping professions secure conformity to middle-class values through the reproduction of *human capital*.

One of the dangers of this second welfare state (GMC) is that a state of domination is maintained, merely being transferred from fathers (under GSC) to a cognitive elite of therapeutic "professionals" armed with the coercive powers of the state. That is why today there are pressures to once again transform the state by returning power to the community and emphasizing civic attachments rather than attachments between individuals. In this third evolution of the state (ICC), the civic state is concerned with the reproduction of *social capital*, thereby sustaining a *civic income* in the new context of globalization of consumption and production.

In "Power and Social Action beyond the State," Roger Sibeon takes the position that most attempts to deal with the monolithic entity known as the "state" are poorly conceived and misguided, primarily because of the problematic nature of the concept of the "state" itself. Most attempts at dealing with the state reflect the error of reductionism, namely, the attempt to explain social life in terms of one unifying or central concept. Often when such central concepts are employed—be it the "state," "globalization," "control," or what have you—little attention is devoted to the actual central concept itself, insofar as it is so central and so taken for granted in the analysis or theoretical system. Sibeon suggests that we need to move beyond positing the state in such an unreflective, uncritical way.

Most analyses of the state suffer as well from a variety of additional maladies, including reification, essentialism, and functional teleology. Reification, the mistake of attributing agency to entities that are not actors or agents, is especially problematic when it comes to conceptualizations of the state, because the state is often posited as an actor whose activities and aims transcend, and even become detached from, the willful intervention of real human beings. Hence, traditional approaches view most of the important decisions that are made in society, be it welfare policy, or law, or the way money is allocated for the building of bridges or the paving of highways, as emanating from the power of the state. But Sibeon argues that attributing unbridled power to a monolithic state in this way is illegitimate, insofar as this neglects the willful agency of individuals and groups in fashioning visions of the good life. Rather, many of the important decisions in social life are settled in forums that exist "beyond the state."

Rather than falling back on standard theories of the state such as pluralism, elite theory, Marxism, or corporatism, Sibeon argues for a version of policy network analysis mixed with a dose of the critical theory of Foucault and "governmentality" (although these latter two approaches possess weaknesses as well). Although the nation-state "still matters," Sibeon suggests that careful attention to the way the state is conceptualized leads to the ultimate conclusion that social life is much more fluid and indeterminate than state theories have previously allowed, thereby illustrating how social affairs exist and are decided "beyond the state."

In "Therapy, Organizations, and the State: A Blackian Perspective," James Tucker agrees in spirit with Sibeon that, as a reified concept, the "therapeutic state" does not really exist. That is, no group or person is therapeutic all the time. Following the theories of Donald Black, Tucker argues that in order to explain how social control is initiated and maintained, it is necessary to take into account social structural factors, such as the amount of inequality and social distance between parties.

Therapy is a form of social control insofar as it is used as a means of defining and responding to deviant behavior. Therapy can indeed be quite coercive, and may reflect simply one coercive mechanism the state uses against its citizens (for example, in the case of Soviet "psychoprisons"). As social space and distances expand between persons, wherein intimacy is reduced and anonymity increases, therapy, or punishment more generally, tends to become more authoritative and retributive. Conversely, in closer or more intimate settings persons provide each other with lay or informal therapy. Therapy thrives, in fact, in decentralized communal settings in which the ethic of egalitarianism is high, such as in communes and modern "post-bureaucratic" corporations.

Tucker documents the modern therapeutic corporation via his case study of HelpCo. What is important to note, however, is that corporations or states are not automatically "therapeutic"; rather, certain factors must be in place for such a characterization to be accurate (see also Cloud 1998).

Blackian theory, according to Tucker, accurately predicts the degree to which an organization will be therapeutic, nontherapeutic, or even authoritarian.

Although Sibeon and Tucker argue that power and therapeutic social control exist beyond the state, we nevertheless can find good examples of nation-states being involved in social engineering through central planning and administration of both nature and society. In his book *Seeing Like a State*, James Scott (1998) documents a variety of such efforts, for example, collectivization in Russia, urban planning in Brazilia, Franklin D. Roosevelt's New Deal welfare program, the Great Leap Forward in China, agricultural modernization in the Tropics, and rational planning of monoculture forests in the United States and elsewhere. These and other attempts at state planning and administration reflect the "high modernism" characteristic of western industrial society beginning in the late 1700s (Torpey 1998). As Scott (1998:4) explains, the ideology of high modernism is best conceived

> as a strong, one might even say muscle-bound, version of the self-confidence about scientific and technical progress, the expansion of production, the growing satisfaction of human needs, the mastery of nature (including human nature), and, above all, the rational design of social order commensurate with the scientific understanding of natural laws. It originated, of course, in the West, as a by-product of unprecedented progress in science and industry.

With the rise of psychiatry and the application of the medical model in psychology and the other helping professions, the state started taking on greater responsibilities regarding the control and supervision of all its citizens, including the mentally ill. In "The Institutionalization and Deinstitutionalization of the Mentally Ill: Lessons from Goffman," Philip Manning describes the rise of the "total institution, " in this case, the large sanitarium or asylum that housed the mentally ill, namely, those persons felt to be both incapable of looking after themselves and a threat to the community (see Grob 1983; Sutton 1991).

Beginning in the late 1950s and early 1960s, a countermovement arose, namely, the "antipsychiatry" movement, embodied in the writings of critics such as Ivan Illich, Thomas Szasz, Michel Foucault, Christopher Lasch, and of course Erving Goffman. These authors were opposed to the warehousing of the mentally ill in total institutions, as well as to the free reign the state gave to psychiatrists and other mental health practitioners in determining the life chances of those labeled "mentally ill." Manning analyzes the extent to which Goffman's writings may have contributed to the deinstitutionalization movement that began in the early 1960s (for example, in 1955 there were 559,000 persons in mental hospitals, but today that figure has dropped to 110,000).

PART II: COUNSELING AND THERAPY
IN INSTITUTIONAL SETTINGS

The first chapter of Part II, James Nolan's "Acquiescence or Consensus? Consenting to Therapeutic Pedagogy," analyzes the extent to which the American educational system is influenced and informed by the therapeutic culture. Especially emblematic of the therapeutic ethos in schools are school counselors and psychologists. Most states mandate a certain number of these therapeutic practitioners per number of students in the schools. Counselors are not only present to work through the difficulties students may be facing at school and at home, however; they also more than ever are actively involved in what goes on in the classroom—in terms of teacher–student interaction, for example—but also in terms of developing curriculum. The continuing presence of counselors and therapists in the schools, many of whom typically graduate from programs in educational psychology, creates and serves to legitimate the taken-for-granted therapeutic assumptions that schools are akin to mental health institutions—with teachers and parents acting as "co-therapists" along with school counselors—and that students are fragile therapy clients. Nolan goes on to suggest that even those who object to the therapeutic approach of school counselors invariably invoke these same categories as when, for example, claims are made about the "psychological" harm that students suffer at their hands.

Shifting focus somewhat, in "The Emergence of Recovered Memory as a Social Problem," Roger Neustadter examines how the recent issue of recovered memory has arisen as a social problem in the last few years as characterized both within the mass media and American culture more generally. Drawing primarily on the theoretical traditions of symbolic interactionism and social constructionism, Neustadter argues that the problem of recovered memory was literally "created," that is, socially constructed, out of a complex interplay of forces and events, including heightened concerns over reports of child abuse; the rise of an aggressive child protection system in reaction to these reports, which gave rise in turn to an even more aggressive "child abuse industry"; this industry being led by "moral entrepreneurs," chiefly concerned parents and educators, psychotherapists, developmental psychologists, and social workers, working with perceived child victims to help them deal with the trauma of their victimization but also to recover their deeply buried memories of "repressed" events; and a more recent oppositional movement led by scholars, lawyers, and other concerned parties who argue that the child abuse industry is running amok and falsely accusing many innocent persons of child abuse.

Although many of the arguments for and against the extent of child abuse and recovered memory of abuse are being played out and negotiated by "experts" and other antagonists in courts of law across the country, there is also intense media interest in the phenomenon, especially as represented in feature stories in magazines such as *Newsweek* and *Time*, and also television news and entertainment programs such as "20/20," "Turning Point," and a series of PBS documentaries. On a variety of levels, then, parties come together as "claimsmakers," employing a variety of rhetorical devices to actively negotiate and construct the meaning of recovered memory.

The next two chapters diverge somewhat from the generally critical tone of the preceding chapters, suggesting ways in which psychotherapeutic assumptions and practice may be improved or modified. In "The Concept of a 'Healthy Person': A Sociological Contribution toward a Truly Revolutionary Psychotherapy," John Kovach argues that prevailing psychotherapeutic perspectives overwhelmingly conceive of the healthy person in asocial, individualistic terms. The implications are that psychotherapeutic practitioners tend to view individuals themselves, or their primary groups, as the source of whatever mental maladjustments or pathologies their clients may be suffering, thereby neglecting to take into account social structure and the broader social forces (power, sexism, racism, stratification, ageism, lookism, etc.) operating beyond the scope of the individual's immediate experience.

A promising development in psychotherapy has been the emergence of "radical therapy," a perspective that rejects individualistic, medicalized views of human behavior in favor of the sort of social structurally informed views mentioned above. However, even with this advance, most radical therapists did not have an adequate conceptualization of *praxis*, namely, the practices or actions clients engage in to change their material conditions of existence for the better. A critical sociology, informed primarily by Karl Marx and Lev Vygotsky, can provide such resources to the client, insofar as the client is no longer perceived as the passive recipient of treatment, but as an active agent who is empowered to establish the material conditions and the modes of consciousness that are consistent with the notion of a healthy person.

In "Toward a Critical Social Interactionism for Counselors," Sydney Carroll Thomas draws on symbolic interactionism, the linguistic theory of Basil Bernstein, and interactionist strands within counseling theory in an attempt to fashion a counseling practice that takes both the social construction of reality and social structure seriously. To realize the ideal of a critically informed social interactionism for counseling, it is imperative to move beyond the microrealm of the individual client or the client–counselor relationship, and connect this level of reality to the broader system within which such activities are occurring. Once the nature of the micro–macrolink is understood, the interactional realm, where counseling practice typically remains, can be linked to the macrorealm, whereby resources can be drawn from such macrotheories as Marx's critical theory or even functionalist systems theory. According to Thomas, it is Bernstein's linguistic theory of symbolic control that provides the bridge between the otherwise disparate traditions of micro- and macrotheory, thereby creating a counseling practice that maintains fidelity to both the micro- and macrorealities of a client's situation.

In the book's final chapter "The Family under Siege," I offer a broad discussion of how the proliferation of experts in our modern information-driven society may be eroding the autonomy of our most important social institution, the family. This intrusion of experts into the family and other social institutions, which Jurgen Habermas refers to as the "expertocracy," coincides with the rise of the therapeutic state, and is one of the more pressing issues that modern industrial society is facing as we approach the millennium. (This issue is dealt with by other authors in this volume as well. For example, James Nolan deals with the encroachment by school counselors into the educational and family institutions. Roger Neustadter examines how experts in so-called recovered memory are attempting to use the rhetoric of therapy and medicine to define reality in the area of child abuse and victimization through the courts and the mass media.)

CONCLUSION

In summary, then, this book offers a wide-ranging examination of the ways in which counseling and psychotherapeutic practices operate and are organized in modern society, and how assumptions about the efficacy or the utility of counseling by citizens of the modern state (the "therapeutic ethos") impact our everyday lives. This is by no means the definitive statement on the way psychotherapy is practiced or the nature of the relationship between the state and therapy. No single book could hope to address all the topics of relevance about something as complex as counseling and the therapeutic state. Nevertheless, what we hope to have accomplished is a presentation of a select range of pertinent issues that will stimulate discussion and new ways of thinking about counseling, therapy, and the state.

NOTES

1. Similar requirements for premarital counseling have been instituted at the state level with regard to Louisiana's "covenant marriage" option. The odd thing about this statute is that priests and other religious ministers are prohibited from fulfilling the law's counseling requirements. Unless the priest has gone through the state's credentialing procedures, thereby being able to claim the title "licensed" or "certified" therapist, the state simply will not recognize such priests as marriage counselors. So for many couples opting for the covenant marriage option, they typically go through two rounds of required counseling, the first being the "informal"

marriage preparation conducted by the church, and the second the "formal" marriage counseling conducted by a state-certified "professional" therapist.

2.   Habermas (1987:363) states that "The form of the administratively prescribed treatment by an expert is for the most part in contradiction with the aim of the therapy, namely, that of promoting the client's independence and self-reliance" (see also Armstrong 1993; Funiciello 1993; Masson 1994; and Szasz 1963, 1978, 1984, 1994).

3.   This credentials race taking place in and among the counseling professions is certainly not unique to counseling and therapy alone. More than ever these days our higher education system is emphasizing the service delivery model of education where students are "customers" and knowledge is treated as a commodity. Student-customers seeking certification in any number of counseling programs connected with the helping professions are emblematic of the broader educational trend of viewing education and knowledge as a private, rather than a public, good. For more on the problems of conceptualizing education as a private good and the credentials race it spawns, see Labaree (1997).

4.   Religious pastors were of course the primordial counseling professionals. Because their authority has always been based on biblical scripture and the word of God, pastors have never needed to subscribe to or heed secular or humanistic counseling world views. Unfortunately, however, many pastors have given in to the therapeutic vision of the counseling professions. This has facilitated the therapeutic invasion of the private spheres of everyday life, including the family, insofar as the doctrine of religious confession assumed that such matters were private, to be discussed only between a person, his or her pastor, and God (Varacalli 1997). The three-tiered reworking of counseling suggested here makes sense only if pastors remain free from the influence of psychiatry and other secular counseling traditions.

REFERENCES

Albee, George W. 1990. "The Futility of Psychotherapy." *Journal of Mind and Behavior* 11 (3–4):369–384.

Amada, Gerald. 1995. "Mandatory Psychotherapy: A Commentary on 'Mandatory Counseling of University Students: An Oxymoron?' and 'Anger and Aggression Groups: Expanding the Scope of College Mental Health Provider Services.'" *Journal of College Student Psychotherapy* 9 (4):33–44.

Armstrong, Louise. 1993. *And They Call It Help: The Psychiatric Policing of America's Children*. Reading, MA: Addison-Wesley.

Barney, Ken. 1994. "Limitations of the Critique of the Medical Model." *Journal of Mind and Behavior* 15 (1–2):19–34.

Bauman, Zygmunt. 1997. *Postmodernity and its Discontents*. New York: New York University Press.

Bergmann, Jorg R. 1992. "Veiled Morality: Notes on Discretion in Psychiatry." Pp. 137–162 in *Talk at Work: Interaction in Institutional Settings*, edited by P. Drew and J. Heritage. Cambridge, UK: Cambridge University Press.

Cloud, Dana L. 1998. *Control and Consolation in American Culture and Politics: Rhetorics of Therapy.* Thousand Oaks, CA: Sage.

Conrad, Peter. 1975. "The Discovery of Hyperkinesis: Notes on the Medicalization of Deviant Behavior." *Social Problems* 23:12–21.

Davis, L. V. 1984. "Beliefs of Social Service Providers About Abused Women and Abusing Men." *Social Work* 29:243–250.

Dawes, Robyn M. 1994. *House of Cards: Psychology and Psychotherapy Built on Myth.* New York: Free Press.

Dineen, Tana. 1996. *Manufacturing Victims: What the Psychology Industry Is Doing to People.* Montreal: Robert Davies.

Dominelli, Lena. 1996. "Deprofessionalizing Social Work: Anti-Oppressive Practice, Competencies and Postmodernism." *British Journal of Social Work* 26:153–175.

Durkheim, Emile. 1951 [1897]. *Suicide,* translated by J. A. Spaulding and G. Simpson. New York: Free Press.

Durkheim, Emile. 1984 [1933]. *The Division of Labor in Society,* translated by W. D. Halls. New York: Free Press.

Edgerton, Robert B. 1992. *Sick Societies: Challenging the Myth of Primitive Harmony.* New York: Free Press.

Farber, Seth. 1990. "Institutional Mental Health and Social Control: The Ravages of Epistemological Hubris." *Journal of Mind and Behavior* 11 (3–4):285–299.

Farber, Seth. 1995. "Undermining Community." Review of John McKnight's *The Careless Society. Telos* 102:177–192.

Foucault, Michel. 1973. *The Birth of the Clinic: An Archaeology of Medical Perception,* translated by A. M. Sheridan Smith. New York: Pantheon.

Fox, Renee C. 1959. *Experiment Perilous: Physicians and Patients Facing the Unknown.* Glencoe, IL: Free Press.

Frank, Lawrence K. 1948. *Society as the Patient: Essays on Culture and Personality.* Port Washington, NY: Kennikat Press.

Frans, Douglas. 1994. "Social Work, Social Science and the Disease Concept: New Directions for Addiction Treatment." *Journal of Sociology and Social Welfare* 21 (2):71–89.

Freud, Sigmund. 1947. *The Question of Lay Analysis,* translated by N. Proctor-Gregg. London: Imago.

Fromm, Erich. 1970. *The Crisis of Psychoanalysis: Essays on Freud, Marx, and Social Psychology.* New York: Henry Holt.

Funiciello, Theresa. 1993. *Tyranny of Kindness: Dismantling the Welfare System to End Poverty in America.* New York: Atlantic Monthly Press.

Gergen, Kenneth J. 1990. "Therapeutic Professions and the Diffusion of Deficit." *Journal of Mind and Behavior* 11 (3–4):353–367.

Gerstl, Joel E. 1969. "Counseling and Psychotherapy Today: Role Specialization and Diversity." Pp. 1–23 in *Explorations in Sociology and Counseling,* edited by D. A. Hansen. Boston: Houghton Mifflin.

Giddens, Anthony. 1990. *The Consequences of Modernity.* Stanford, CA: Stanford University Press.

Gilbert, Steven P. and Judith A. Sheiman. 1995. "Mandatory Counseling of University Students: An Oxymoron?" *Journal of College Student Psychotherapy* 9 (4):3–21.

Goffman, Erving. 1961. *Asylums.* Garden City, NY: Doubleday Anchor.

Goldstein, Eda G. 1996. "What is Clinical Social Work? Looking Back to Move Ahead." *Clinical Social Work Journal* 24 (1):89–104.

Gouldner, Alvin W. 1973. *For Sociology.* New York: Basic Books.

Gray, Cathleen. 1996. "When Therapy Is Not in the Client's Best Interest: Adapting Clinical Interventions to the Stages of Divorce." *Journal of Divorce and Remarriage* 26 (1/2):117–127.

Grob, Gerald N. 1983. *Mental Illness and American Society, 1875-1940.* Princeton, NJ: Princeton University Press.

Habermas, Jurgen. 1971. *Knowledge and Human Interests,* translated by J. Shapiro. Boston: Beacon.

Habermas, Jurgen. 1987. *The Theory of Communicative Action,* Vol. 2, translated by T. McCarthy. Boston: Beacon.

Hale, Nathan G., Jr. 1995. *The Rise and Crisis of Psychoanalysis in the United States: Freud and the Americans, 1917–1985.* Oxford: Oxford University Press.

Herman, Ellen. 1995. *The Romance of American Psychology: Political Culture in the Age of Experts.* Berkeley: University of California Press.

Hewitt, John P. 1998. *The Myth of Self-Esteem.* New York: St. Martin's Press.

Hillery, George A., Jr. 1968. *Communal Organizations: A Study of Local Societies.* Chicago: University of Chicago Press.

Hunt, Morton. 1993. *The Story of Psychology.* New York: Doubleday.

Illich, Ivan. 1977a. *Medical Nemesis.* New York: Bantam.

Illich, Ivan. 1977b. *Toward a History of Needs.* New York: Pantheon.

Ivey, Susan L., Richard Scheffler, and James L. Zazzali. 1998. "Supply Dynamics of the Mental Health Workforce: Implications for Health Policy." *Milbank Quarterly* 76 (1):25–58.

Jenkins, Peter. 1997. *Counselling, Psychotherapy and the Law.* London: Sage.

Kendall, Kathleen. 1996. "Mental Illness—Tales of Madness: From the Asylum to 'Oprah.'" Pp. 129–148 in *Social Control in Canada: Issues in the Social Construction of Deviance,* edited by B. Schissel and L. Mahood. Oxford: Oxford University Press.

Kennedy, Daniel B. 1984. "Clinical Sociology and Correctional Counseling." *Crime and Delinquency* 30 (2):269-292.

Kirk, S. and H. Kutchins. 1992. *The Selling of DSM: The Rhetoric of Science in Psychiatry.* New York: Aldine de Gruyter.

Kittrie, Nicholas N. 1971. *The Right to be Different: Deviance and Enforced Therapy.* Baltimore: Penguin Books.

Kreuger, Larry W. 1997. "The End of Social Work." *Journal of Social Work Education* 33 (1):19–27.

Labaree, David F. 1997. *How to Succeed in School Without Really Learning: The Credentials Race in American Education.* New Haven, CT: Yale University Press.

Labov, William and David Fanshel. 1977. *Therapeutic Discourse: Psychotherapy as Conversation.* New York: Academic Press.

Lambert, M. J. and A. E. Bergin. 1994. "The Effectiveness of Psychotherapy." Pp. 143–189 in *Handbook of Psychotherapy and Behavior Change,* 3rd ed., edited by S. L. Garfield and A. E. Bergin. New York: Wiley.

Lasch, Christopher. 1977. *Haven in a Heartless World.* New York: Norton.

Lasch, Christopher. 1979. *The Culture of Narcissism.* New York: Norton.

Leifer, Ronald. 1990. "Introduction: The Medical Model as the Ideology of the Thera-peutic State." *Journal of Mind and Behavior* 11 (3–4):247–258.

Lomas, Peter. 1997. "The Durability of the Talking Cure." *Society* 35 (1):17–19.

London, Perry. 1964. *The Modes and Morals of Psychotherapy.* New York: Holt, Rinehart & Winston.

Masson, Jeffrey Moussaieff. 1994. *Against Therapy.* Monroe, ME: Common Courage Press.

McKnight, John. 1995. *The Careless Society: Community and its Counterfeits.* New York: Basic Books.

McLaughlin, Neil G. 1998. "Why Do Schools of Thought Fail? Neo-Freudianism as a Case Study in the Sociology of Knowledge." *Journal of the History of the Behavioral Sciences* 34 (2):113–134.

Murphy, Jeffrie G. 1979. *Retribution, Justice, and Therapy.* Dordrecht: Reidel.

Neustadter, Roger. 1991-92. "Szasz, Lasch, and Illich on the Problem of the Thera-peutic State." *Quarterly Journal of Ideology* 15 (3–4):29–49.

Nolan, James L., Jr. 1998a. *The Therapeutic State: Justifying Government at Century's End.* New York: New York University Press.

Nolan, James L., Jr. 1998b. "The Therapeutic State: The Clarence Thomas and Anita Hill Hearings." *Antioch Review* 56 (1):5–25.

Pallone, Nathaniel J. 1997. "Mental Healing Under Managed Care." *Society* 35 (1):8–16.

Parsons, Talcott. 1978. *Action Theory and the Human Condition.* New York: Free Press.

Peele, Stanton. 1990. "Behavior in a Vacuum: Social-Psychological Theories of Ad-diction That Deny the Social and Psychological Meanings of Behavior." *Journal of Mind and Behavior* 11 (3–4):513–530.

Peele, Stanton. 1995. *Diseasing of America: How We Allowed Recovery Zealots and the Treatment Industry to Convince Us We Are Out of Control.* New York: Lexington Books.

Pegnato, Joseph A. 1997. "Is a Citizen a Customer?" *Public Productivity and Manage-ment Review* 20 (4):397–404.

Peyrot, Mark. 1985. "Coerced Voluntarism: The Micropolitics of Drug Treatment." *Urban Life* 13 (4):343–365.

Polsky, Andrew J. 1991. *The Rise of the Therapeutic State.* Princeton, NJ: Princeton University Press.

Putnam, Robert D. 1996. "The Strange Disappearance of Civic America." *The Ameri-can Prospect* 24:34–48.

Redfield, Robert. 1947. "The Folk Society." *American Journal of Sociology* 52:293–308.

Reid, William J. 1997. "Long-Term Trends in Clinical Social Work." *Social Service Review* 71 (2):200–213.

Rieff, Philip. 1966. *The Triumph of the Therapeutic.* New York: Harper & Row.

Rigazio-DiGilio, Sandra A. 1996. "Defining the Mental Health Counseling Profes-sion: Embracing Historical and Contemporary Perspectives at the Interface of

Theory, Practice, Research, and Professional Exchange." *Journal of Mental Health Counseling* 18 (4):291–299.

Rowe, Dorothy. 1994. "Forward." Pp. 7–23 in *Against Therapy*, J. M. Masson. Monroe, ME: Common Courage Press.

Schissel, Bernard. 1997. "Psychiatric Expansionism and Social Control: The Intersection of Community Care and State Policy." *Social Science Research* 26:399–418.

Scott, James C. 1998. *Seeing Like a State: How Certain Schemes to Improve the Human Condition Have Failed.* New Haven, CT: Yale University Press.

Shorter, Edward. 1997. *A History of Psychiatry.* New York: Wiley.

Sibeon, Roger. 1991. *Towards a New Sociology of Social Work.* Aldershot, UK: Avebury.

Silverman, David. 1997. *Discourses of Counseling.* London: Sage.

Specht, Harry and Mark E. Courtney. 1994. *Unfaithful Angels: How Social Work Has Abandoned Its Mission.* New York: Free Press.

Sternberg, Joel. 1977. *Radical Sociology: An Introduction to American Behavioral Science.* Hicksville, NY: Exposition Press.

Stout, Nancy. 1994. "Visiting a Seriously Ill Friend." A pamphlet in the *CareNotes* series. St. Meinrad, IN: Abbey Press.

Sutton, John R. 1991. "The Political Economy of Madness: The Expansion of the Asylum in Progressive America." *American Sociological Review* 56:665-678.

Szasz, Thomas S. 1963. *Law, Liberty, and Psychiatry.* New York: Collier.

Szasz, Thomas S. 1978. *The Myth of Psychotherapy.* Garden City, NY: Doubleday.

Szasz, Thomas S. 1984. *The Therapeutic State.* New York: Prometheus.

Szasz, Thomas S. 1990. "Law and Psychiatry: The Problems That Will Not Go Away." *Journal of Mind and Behavior* 11 (3–4):557–563.

Szasz, Thomas S. 1994. "Psychiatric Diagnosis, Psychiatric Power and Psychiatric Abuse." *Journal of Medical Ethics* 20:135–138.

Sweeney, Thomas J. 1995. "Accreditation, Credentialing, Professionalization: The Role of Specialties." *Journal of Counseling and Development* 74:117–125.

Thomas, Sydney Carroll. 1996. "A Sociological Perspective on Contextualism." *Journal of Counseling and Development* 74:529–536.

Toennies, Ferdinand. 1957. *Community and Society*, translated by C.P. Loomis. East Lansing, MI: Michigan State University Press.

Torpey, John. 1998. "Coming and Going: On the State Monopolization of the Legitimate 'Means of Movement.'" *Sociological Theory* 16 (3):239–259.

Turner, Bryan S. 1992. *Regulating Bodies: Essays in Medical Sociology.* London: Routledge.

Varacalli, Joseph A. 1997. "The Failure of the Therapeutic: Implications for Society and Church." *Faith and Reason* 23 (1):3–22.

Vatz, Richard E. and Lee S. Weinberg. 1990. "The Conceptual Bind in Defining the Volitional Component of Alcoholism: Consequences for Public Policy and Scientific Research." *Journal of Mind and Behavior* 11 (3–4):531–544.

Vaughan, Susan C. 1997. *The Talking Cure: The Science Behind Psychotherapy.* New York: Putnam.

White, Susan. 1998. "Interdiscursivity and Child Welfare: The Ascent and Durability of Psycho-Legalism." *Sociological Review* 46 (2):264–292.

Conceptualizing the State   1

Children and the Civic State: A Covenant Model of Welfare[1]

2

John O'Neill

INTRODUCTION

Children do not do well among us. We treasure them and we trash them. We love them and we beat, starve, and overwork them. We prey upon them while demanding that they trust us. There is no time in human history and no human society in which children have not experienced both good and evil at the hands of adults. We have, of course, imagined our childhood otherwise. We have assigned it to an age of innocence and placed upon it all our hopes for the betterment of our kind. We wish our children health, intelligence, and happiness. We pray that their goodness will be a model of the goodness we hold out to them and to ourselves. We even imagine ourselves living in one great human family whose dealings, thefts, and murders may be lessened by our kinship.

Our children and our families are a puzzle to us. I propose that we cannot grasp the basic issues in family theory unless we start from the *cultural aporia* that we are at once sentimental and cruel toward our own kind, toward workers, toward women, and toward children (O'Neill 1994). The institutionalization of our species-ambivalence is experienced collectively in class, race, and gender relations. Even today, liberal state and liberal moral theorists still have to decide whether children are the passive subjects of political economy, class, and family structures or whether children should be given political rights and moral autonomy. In the meantime, child poverty increases and the injustices to children become structures of both intragenerational and intergenerational injustice.

Children's life chances are still dependent on a "state of nature" concept of social and political life. Here the principal actors are found to be disembodied, defamilialized, and degendered individuals—actually, virgin males—who exit the state of nature into society through a social contract whose intergenerational effects on children are completely ignored (Barker 1948). I should say that I am concerned only with the broad frame of contract theory (Hume, Locke, and Rousseau) in order to contrast it with *covenant theory*, namely, the insistence on the intergenerational and communal bases of life chances. Human reproduction raises as much of a conundrum for liberal

33

individualism as any other altruistic behavior unless one has no conception of the "other responsibilities" in pregnancy and birth. Such denial is possible only if we imagine individuals who copulate outside families. But this is a state of affairs that human society has imagined only as a prehuman state, as one of animality or barbarism prior to the founding of human families whose reproduction enters us into civil history and kinship. Ancient law, as Sir Henry Sumner Maine pointed out, "knows next to nothing of Individuals. It is concerned not with Individuals, but with Families, not with single human beings, but with groups" (Maine 1905:250). Yet, it is the opposite state of affairs that is assumed in the state of nature from which contractarian theory takes its start.

From Hobbes to Rawls (Rawls 1971) it has been assumed that the child is entirely in the power of the male parent. This assumption is further aggravated by the exclusion of the female parent from the public domain:

> The question is less what Hobbes says about men and women, or what Rousseau sees the role of Sophie to be in Emile's education. The point is that in this universe, the experience of the early modern female has no place. Women are simply what men are not. Women are not autonomous, independent, and aggressive but nurturant, not competitive but giving, not public but private. (Benhabib 1987:192)

Contract theory, which Benjamin Barber (1984:40) has described as "zookeeping," operates exclusively in the fraternal order in which males have to fear only one another. Here, "their" women and children are sources of either pride or shame, best experienced in domesticity but to be excluded at all costs from the domain of politics:

> For many reasons children have been the companions of women in the closet of political science. A few short years ago women began to set up such clamor that a few were released. Children remain, with few exceptions, both silent and invisible—relegated to a conceptual space (which is presumed to reflect social reality) that has been declared apolitical. *The political study of childhood remains in its infancy.* (Bethke Elshtain 1982:289; emphasis added)

In effect social contract theorists espouse a virgin myth of the individual citizen as "one" who exits from the state of nature into society through an act of will to contract into a superordinate political authority (Pateman 1988). Thus the political subject of liberal theory is disembodied, dispassionate, defamilialized, and degendered as a precondition for exercising the universal virtues of generalization and impartiality that would otherwise be contaminated by the particularities and affections of an embodied subject whose familial bonds both delimit and enable political conduct. Yet without the very embodied subjects overlooked in liberal ontology, ethical and political choices would be entirely without context or purpose. The *tabula rasa* or clean-slate individual of liberal contract theory constitutes a fiction as great as its counterpart fiction of the many-headed monster state, or Leviathan. *It is especially harmful to the political status of children.*

In a covenant theory of the state and community, it is recognized that gender, age, infirmity, health, intelligence, and strength are the very elements of moral and political life and require of us judicious weighing of the contributions of both *justice* and *care* perspectives in dealing with one another (Gilligan 1982). Nobody enters the world except by means of another body. This intercorporeality is the basis of covenant society (O'Neill 1989). It is only a romantic fiction that marks birth as the appearance of an *individual* rather than as the reappearance of a *family*. What is involved here are two time frames within the lifeworld (Schutz 1973). Thus "birth" marks both an *intragenerational* event within a "marriage" and an *intergenerational* event between "families." Or, we might say that the birth of a child marks the inaugural moment of its "parents," in the first case and of its "grandparents," in the second. In covenant theory, we cannot think of children without thinking of families and communities. But in liberal contract theory we do not think of families and communities because we think only of individual agency. This makes it even harder to think of social institutions, classes, and races except as slight obstacles in the path of the individual. We thereby displace the burden of the past institutions on the futures of our children.

In short, liberal theory operates with a "thin" concept of the necessary institutional framework of individual agency as such, while engaging the fiction that societal activity is merely the sum of a myriad of individual behaviors. On this view, society is encountered only in the marketplace or in the autonomy of the forces of competition and scarcity. In such a society, children are thought of as the happy entrants in its game of opportunity. Here, although each child is as lovely as any other, each one may become more lovely, more healthy, more intelligent, more happy, more housed, more fed, and more amused.

The terms of social contract theory should be recast—not to reinvent its prefamilialized political subject—but to make the subject of politics answerable to the needs of children whose peculiar plight is that they are "spoken for" (what we call *political mutism* later on) by agents who may not be sufficiently aware of the dilemmas this raises in such a case. We propose, therefore, to set out certain regulative principles of political covenant that may serve to benefit the cause of children:

1. The political subject is an intersubject whose intrasubjectivity is social before it is asocial.
2. The political subject is familialized and gendered.

3. The gendered political subject is both intrasubject (with child) and intersubject (with family and community).
4. The spatiotemporal environment of the political subject (1–3) is the intergenerational community into which the child is inscribed before birth and which it enters not simply as a subject of desire but as a subject of care, already indebted, enabled/disabled prior to all other life contracts.

COVENANT VERSUS CONTRACT THEORY OF CHILD RISK

From a covenant perspective, it is children who are the ignored tokens in the move from the presocial state of nature to the state of liberal society. Children are not individuals from the start. They must be apprenticed in their families and schools to the rules of the game of competitive individualism. Thus, in liberal society, children are equal only to the extent that their families are sufficiently equal to apprentice them to a good enough start in the game of inequality (Coleman et al. 1982; Jencks 1972). The evidence of this circumstance is all around us. Yet we still sentimentalize the horror of our practices of rendering our children poor, unhealthy, ignorant, and unloved. We imagine that such injustice can be accounted for only by the absence of an ideal start in life. But the truth is that we believe that an ideal start should prepare children for the unequal outcomes that are, in turn, the starting points of that *intergenerational inequality*, injustice, and ignorance that sets the floor of liberal society.

Just as we like to imagine equality as the initial state of children, so we like to think of freedom as a state of children enjoyed before they assume the burden of institutions in later life (Bellah 1992). But since in liberal society formal freedom of opportunity is more valued than substantive equality of chances, children are doubly subject to the lack of freedom and equality that marks their family position. To save itself from this social contradiction liberal ideology requires the following:

1. Children are not visibly predictable winners/losers in the inequality game.
2. Children are not procedurally equal in any process of talent discrimination.
3. No child is to be in violation of (1) as a result of the cumulative class effects of meritocratic competition.

Fairness to children, then, means that they are not to be "seen" to have been born with an unequal chance in the competition that reproduces liberal inequality. But in reality *children's equality* before the law, before the health system, the education system, and the employment system is determined by *family inequality* in those systems (Glendon 1989). Yet the legitimacy of liberal society is underwritten by the belief among its individual members that their lives began with a childhood whose ideal circumstances afforded their future prospects. The legacy of such a childhood then enters into the next generation's account of its life story. But since it is children who at birth are marked by sex, race, and even family background characteristics that are due to no competitive effort of their own, it must be understood that children are even more condemned to contractarianism than their parents whose individualizing ideology they have not yet acquired. Only by overlooking the child–family bond can we imagine the child as the subject of political equality whereas *the child's equality is a myth to which it is committed to save the inequality within and between families.* Here, therefore, liberal society must allow the state to ensure that the family not constitute an overwhelming impediment to the child's citizenship. The latter notion implies, at the very least, provision for adult socialization and the learning of such rights and duties that currently constitute the civic rite of passage from childhood to adulthood (Blustein 1982). Conversely, the state's interest in the child's education, broadly conceived, will involve it in the prevention of neglect, harm, and abuse to children. Yet, according to strict liberal ideology, the family ought to escape civic governance on the grounds that it constitutes a sphere of privacy or of intimacy without "other-regarding" concerns.

THE RISKY MATRIX

In view of the preceding arguments, it may be advanced on the child policy and research level that what must now be exposed in the liberal contractarian theory of child care is that its patriarchalism is grounded in the "speechlessness" (*infans,* not speaking) of the infant and of its mother. Let us call this the politics of mutism, by which we mean that children's interests are articulated on their behalf by those on whom they depend for achieving the shift to relative independence. Thus a child's experience of justice and care is determined by its unequal relations with adults and elder children, as well as with professional care managers without whom it is unlikely to survive. The life chances of children must also be looked at in terms of the changes in family/household structures and their resourcefulness in commanding employment, education, and health resources. Broadly speaking, the following features are to be observed: an increase in single-person households (surviving elders, divorced singles); a decline in intergenerational households; an increase in female-headed households; an increase of married women in the labor force; and a decline in employment for young people. Single-mother households with growing children have suffered a decline in per capita resources, aggravated by gender, age, and lack of kin networks. In other households, elders without children or with few children will experience dependency either without caretakers or with severely reduced care due to time demands on a working mother/daughter (Connides 1989). Children are caught in the middle, often destined for long periods of unemployment in and out of school, while parents cope with a similar syndrome.

As a result of the preceding trends, a considerable number of children at risk are now children born into another child's poverty, the *single, teenage parent, poverty syndrome*. These children are the new foundlings whose plight renders even more urgent the task of rethinking family and child care. Although we have no intention of simplifying the complex cultural apparatus that currently shapes child–society relations, it is necessary to start from a *structural paradox of child risk*, that is, the recognition that even before a child takes steps for itself:

1. Biorisks are incurred in the uterine environment.
2. Biophysic and sociopsychological risks are incurred in the domestic environment.
3. Socioeconomic risks are incurred in the social class environment of the family.
4. Global risks are incurred by families and communities.

This complex structure of *family risk* will determine, to different degrees, the vulnerability of children born in families *whose class and national comparative (dis)advantage* has until recently required that "risk reduction" be undertaken jointly by the kin/community and professional therapeutic agencies working in the context of welfare society and state endowment. As we shall see shortly, however, the helping professions will come to play an increasingly smaller role in child welfare and in the reduction of family risk as the current therapeutic welfare state gives way to the civic state, the latter of which drawing more on the resources of community and family ("social capital") than on the market and on professional expertise. This reflects, in effect, the transition from a welfare state covenant to a civic covenant.

CHILDREN AND THE WELFARE STATE COVENANT

In view of the current exhaustion of totalizing concepts of well-being and development—while faced with ever expanding risks to which communities, families, and children are exposed—future child policy research must reconceptualize the life chances and social pathways that enable/disable families and children in interaction with community, state, and professional institutions. Thus, we have examined how it is that the child functions as a metaphor for our collective development, progress, and well-being, while simultaneously standing as a metaphor for the failure of society, for its inhumanity, poverty, and ignorance that stunts the lives of so many children (Hamburg 1992). The civic covenant that I have proposed requires us to revise the assumption in liberal anthropology that individuals are exclusively utility driven in favor of the broader civic assumption that individuals seek to develop "essentially human capacities" in ways that are not inimical to each other's ability to do likewise. This redefinition of individual capacity involves a shift from a contractarian to a covenant model of human agency mediated by a positive concept of welfare state agency to reduce the risks to families and communities, as well as to promote social politics that will enhance everyone's life chances.

I have argued that the child has no "theoretical home" (Etzioni 1988:157) in liberal political anthropology:

1. The child is a "missing" link in liberal contract theory, whereas it is the basic social cell in a covenant theory of society and family.
2. The child is at risk both conceptually and morally in a contract society because its worth is determined only by the relative worth of its family vis-à-vis the market.
3. Children are especially at risk when born into families that are socio-economically weak; where the parent(s) is deskilled on both the domestic and the market front; and where individualizing and possessive body ideologies are espoused by young women without sufficient resources to make them workable either for themselves or their children.
4. Any improvement to the life chances of children at risk requires that we preserve the civic covenant between generations that is the fundamental achievement of the welfare state.

All the trends that weaken family and community resources aggravate the niggardliness of liberal individualism and remove us ever further from the civic provision of the resources that sustain an intragenerational and intergenerational covenant. The market reduces the temporal horizon of the family to instant gratifications eked out by credit payments. Moreover, consumerism pits generations against one another. The all-knowing media child is the corporate terminal in families and schools without authority. The result is that their childhood is shortened, while its quality is thinned. Thus, civic society is hollowed out with the uncivil language of the self's obligations toward itself and the market's identification of autism with individual-ism. Because these trends prevail by separating individuals from their past as well as from their future, individuals are all the more bound to an ignorant present without either presence or perspective. These are the parameters of the thin self that characterizes liberal society in the absence of any under-standing of the civic covenant that would sustain the politics of intergenera-tionality and the commonplaces of childhood.

NATIONHOOD: OVERCOMING THE THIN SELF
OF LIBERAL SOCIETY

To understand the complex relation of childhood to other aspects of state and society already discussed, it is important to consider the citizenship status of children—and people in general—as this applies to various con-ceptualizations of nationhood. I now want to move beyond the question of the citizenship status of children per se by suggesting that the thin self of liberal society can be overcome only if national identity is itself grounded in a civic concept of state, economy, family, and community relations. This argument is made by tracing a historical/structural model of the evolution of welfare regimes from (1) a gendered social compact grounded in class, to (2) a genderless market contract grounded in status, to (3) an intergenerational covenant grounded in civic ethos.

The question now before us is whether national states can survive with civic identities (O'Neill 1994). A strategy for civic sustainability must oper-ate on several interlocking levels:

1. state provision of civic income, health, and education;
2. community provision of those civic goods whose enjoyment is ethi-cal only when universal; and
3. pursuit of social justice on two levels of intragenerationality and intergenerationality in order to align class justice and future justice.

A civic society comprises four levels of institutional transfers: (1) national state, (2) national economy, (3) local community, and (4) household. A more complex model for these transfers will be presented shortly. For the moment, given the tendency of the subsystem levels of society to invoke relative autonomy, legitimation crises are to be expected, whether in the form of (post)modern hyperindividualism, corporate and populist tax withdrawals, or intergenerational renunciation. In such cases, the market, the household, or the state may become the focus of crisis of legitimation expressed in fundamen-talism, antistatism, and elitism that are so dangerous for a civic society. Ordinarily, civic society is an achievement of group organizations—churches, schools, professions, media, small business, and community agencies. The functions of the these groups are never fixed because they are both inner and outer directed in their concern with the just and efficient use of their own resources and the state's power to legitimate the overall configuration of social well-being. The barometer of a civic state is set on the political middle, which is reached by the avoidance of elite polarization and minority exclusion.

A national civic identity cannot be sustained apart from a committed political culture in which the centrifugal forces of globalization are molded at a level deeper than the supercultural sphere. Otherwise, responses to globalism such as multiculturalism, pluralism, and localism represent only a weak aestheticism without any serious address of the underlying troubles of dislocation, labor migration, racism, and political refuge. Nor can a national civic identity flourish where the cultural sector promotes life-style issues and ideologies around a political void. The absorption of civic autonomy by market sovereignty and the consequent substitution of a vocabulary of consumer choice in place of moral freedom offer only a fragile culture of lifestyles. This represents the thin self of liberal society. By contrast, the continuance of a national identity demands that we rethink the grounds of a civic ethos of family and community well-being.

The contemporary dominance of market discourse over a civic and national voice threatens once again to reduce political life to the squalid condition of those incapable of the competitive struggle for private affluence. The civic respite afforded by postwar welfare states is now under fiery attack by the forces of antigovernance in the name of private provision and public neglect. We are faced with a renewal of moral solitude in a global world whose compass is greed undeflected by national or civic compassion. Thus in Canada the "social" marketeers now demand (1) that we ignore the social costs of a low wage economy, (2) that we treat the negative consequences of a market society only after the fact, and (3) that we leave the market to do its worst and only then call in the government to try to do its best.

What is extraordinary is that the demands made in the name of a *social* market in fact represent the privatization and commercialization of the basic elements of social welfare (Social Justice 1994). If they were implemented, the economic market would entirely absorb the social market. As a result, we would lose the countervailing structure of welfare and civic state practice.

If the reprivatization of the social market were to be achieved, it would drive Canada toward a polarized society at the very time when policy theorists in Britain, for example, have begun to pursue the direction of a second generation or "intelligent" welfare state. In the United Kingdom public finance is called on to invest in social justice as a complementary factor in stimulating and sustaining economic growth (Gilbert and Gilbert 1989). In the United States a lively debate over the nature of civil society has been launched by the liberal communitarians, led by Amitai Etzioni, Alan Wolfe, and others (Etzioni 1988; Wolfe 1989). The context of these debates is the collapse of the neo-Keynesian pact between government, business, and labor since the late 1970s, accompanied by the extreme polarization of rich and poor—despite gender and minority market entrance. At the same time, public discourse has polarized around an elite celebration of merit and money and an excommunication of incompetence, dependence, and vulnerability.

With the removal of the external threat of communism, capitalism has gone global and greedy while calling for the thinning of every other institution except the market and marketized communication services. The extraterritoriality of global capitalism is the new specter with which national governments are encouraged to haunt themselves. At the same time, the nomadic potential of the global corporation is discovered in the very nature of its "symbolic analysts," i.e., those who command the high value-added enterprises on which depend the lowly paid routine producers and interpersonal servers as they are called by Reich (1991). We are also asked to believe that the new elitism of the global corporate economy is so written into nature that we can finally abandon past political history by realigning social institutions with a biogram known as the Bell Curve (Fraser 1995; Herrnstein and Murray 1995; Kamin 1995). Here the aim is to confirm what neoconservatives have always suspected, to celebrate what neoliberals have always hoped, and to ground both in a science that rejects the left ideology of institutional improvement. The Bell Curve in fact offers a fiscal bonus—it reveals that welfare creates a secondary culture of dependence among the unfit that prevents them from finding their just wage in the free labor market. It does not matter that the science in the Bell Curve thesis is distorted. What matters is that the Curve reinforces restructuring the economy around symbolic manipulation, that it supports cutting back education to information servicing, and that those who benefit most from the new economy can now appeal to quasinatural meritocracy whose cultivation would repay society far more than any public investment in the poor and vulnerable.

The danger for civic society is that the new meritocracy is surreptitiously grounding itself as an aristocracy of intelligence rather than of compassion. The aim is to root a crude plutocracy in biology and at the same time to put the IQ elite beyond the history and politics that swept away earlier aristocracies in the name of democracy. The new Lockeanism of brains over sweat encourages an extraordinary sense of self-possession unmodified by any recognition of indebtedness even toward the educational institutions that foster intelligence. The civic insensitivity of the new economic elite amounts to what Reich calls a "secession"—the abandonment of national identity in favor of a cosmopolitanism that is rootless and as absolutely alienated from the lower orders at home as it is fascinated with its unabashed imperialism. Moreover, the elite colonization of the lifeworld can count on the dominance of life-style ideologies in the family, work, and political spheres to recycle elite possessiveness.

Ruled by cognitivism, consumerism, and individualism, which give it a strong identity with itself, the new global elite is extraordinarily self-loving. It promotes its own health, safety, families, and children with unusual sensitivity. It is devoted to education, law, and order. It is its own haven in a heartless world through which it drives in Volvos, Jeeps, and Land Rovers to protect itself from the outside to which it has become even more alien. A national civic policy must find a path between the neoliberal submission of social institutions to the primacy of the market and neoconservative exemptions of private institutions from state and market rule. The hyperindividual agent of market consumerism now threatens to claim sovereignty over politics, culture, and morality. This claim ignores the objective stratification of subject positions in market society as well as the mismatch between consumer sovereignty and worker dependence. At the same time, the promotion of the hyperindividual is a populist strategy perfectly suited to the elite interest in the abolition of the middle ground of the civic state and society. This is particularly clear in the current promotion of the so-called tax revolt. Here the choice-model promotes the idea that consumers can choose less governance, or less civic security, in favor of having more of some other commodity, such as a walled community in a criminogenic society. Thus the civic withdrawal of the elites is identified with the need of the lesser classes to eke out a living by saving on taxes even though the end result is a further reduction in their quality of life.

As Bellah (1992) has shown, what underlies the liberal contradiction is a particular concept of social institutions—namely, that institutions are but a necessary evil. At the same time, liberal antiinstitutionalism still requires a set of therapeutic institutions to deal with the pathologies of persons who are incompetent with the practices of market society.

What is missing in the liberal concept of institutions is an understanding of the mediating functions of those civic institutions that reduce disparities between persons' physical and moral circumstances. As such, civic institutions are a public legacy flowing from a political center that cannot be subsidiary or residual to the market. The civic center is not to be compared with those corporate centers whose postmodern architects have absorbed the dead symbols of the village clock, the church steeple, and the public square in buildings that are nothing but billboards of corporate arrogance. Nor is the civic center identical with that flight into localism, neighborhoods, and nostalgia that appears to be the last resort for cultural critics like Lasch (1995). These divergent notions of institutions must be brought out in a public policy debate on the nature of the *center* around which our social, economic, and political institutions should turn. The civic center is not defined solely by consensus. However, pluralism without a center soon falls into nihilism and minoritarianism. Indeed, pluralism easily degenerates into a violent perspectivism, aggravated by rhetoric and a forceful exclusion of the incorrect antagonism from the public arena. The result is that the tyranny of a marketized monoculture is left unchallenged and may even coopt the state in order to control those whom the market itself excludes.

In Adam Smith the self-generating capacity of the economy working through the social division of labor is celebrated as the unique source of economic development. Provided the state oversees but does not interfere in its natural workings, the economy should service the wealth of nations. Yet Smith's economics turn on a moral paradox, namely, that the stunting of each worker enhances the wealth of the whole society (Hont and Ignatieff 1983; McNally 1988). The freedom lost by the laborer at work is restored in the enhanced consumption generated by mass production. Here, especially, Smith had to invoke the civil tradition to set moral limits to the new economy of desire released by an autonomous production system. But, as Hegel and Marx argued, the liberal concept of civil society is nothing else than the social form of a capitalist economy and it cannot be invoked to restrict the economy either morally or politically. It is the factory and not the civic republic that is the model of capitalist society. Now that the old factory has shifted into its postfordist shape, global capitalism continues to discipline labor through flexibilization, minimum wages, unemployment, and the contraction of the welfare state along with the overall threat of national capital flight. This means that contrary to Adam Smith's hopes for restrained liberalism, today's neoliberal economy rejects any civic restraint on its structuring of work, family, and community. Yet what liberals reject in principle, they are obliged to take back in practice insofar as they demand better policing of the society whose fabric is weakened by public disinvestment. Paradoxically, latter day liberals become statists on issues of law and order because they have rejected the costs of that civic governance that ensures everyday security and well-being.

Our appeal to the politics of a civic center is not an exercise in backward looking republicanism (Kramnick 1982). Nor is it a utopian call for a future community well beyond our grasp. Rather, we are revisioning civic institutions that are rediscovered from time to time in response to national need (Marshall 1975, 1977; Turner 1986). Thus we may distinguish several historical eruptions of civic claims on market society:

1. eighteenth century republican critique of agrarian capitalism;
2. late nineteenth/early twentieth century critique of industrial capitalism:
   a. Bismark (Germany)
   b. Beveridge (United Kingdom)
   c. Roosevelt (United States)

3. late twentieth century critique of global capitalism:
    a. liberal communitarianism (United States)
    b. social justice: strategies for national renewal (United Kingdom)
    c. civic nation state (Canada).

The welfare system as we have known it was the product of a social compact between the state, business, and labor (Sklar 1988). It provided for softening class inequality and unemployment without challenge to the national expansion of the system of mass production extended through imperialism. The society of mass production required adaptations of family and individual life-styles, as well as moral and consumer sovereignty coupled with political docility. Prior to globalization, national states extended their territorial reach through colonialism and imperialism, improving the condition of their internal proletariat at the expense of international labor. The emergence of globalism threatens not only to deterritorialize the nation state but also to delegitimate its social constitution built on the welfare compact between business elites, labor, and government that has been in effect for the past 50 years.

As the U.K. Borrie Commission on Social Justice insists, what is currently at stake is our civic reinvestment in those institutions and policies that put a premium on collective and long-term interests in the complementarity between economic growth and public investments in social justice, health, and education. For its own purposes, the Commission has bravely abstracted from British political history three rival models of the welfare state—investors, deregulators, and levellers—each with its own strategy for national renewal. *Investors* favor the productive complementarity of social justice and economic growth whereas *deregulators* would favor growth rather than justice but *levellers* would believe that economic growth should be subordinated to social equity. The Commissioners sketch their ideal of an "intelligent" second-generation welfare state in the following portrait.

THE INTELLIGENT WELFARE STATE

An intelligent welfare state works with rather than against the grain of change:

*   Wealth creation and wealth distribution are two sides of the same coin; wealth pays for welfare, but equity is efficient.
*   Social justice cannot be achieved through the social security system alone; employment, education, and housing are at least as important as tax and benefit policy in promoting financial independence.
*   Labor-market and family policy go together; the social revolution in women's life chances demands a reappraisal of the role of men as

workers and fathers as well as that of women as employees and
mothers.

- Paid work for a fair wage is the most secure route out of poverty.
  Welfare must be reformed to make work pay; if 80% tax rates are
  wrong at the top, they are wrong at the bottom too.
- The intelligent welfare state prevents poverty as well as relieving it,
  above all through public services that enable people to learn, earn,
  and care.
- The welfare state must be shaped by the changing nature of people's
  lives, rather than people's lives being shaped to fit in with the welfare
  state; the welfare state must be personalized and flexible, designed to
  promote individual choice and personal autonomy. (Social Justice
  1994)

Of course, the three models contain a considerable clash of political opinion
on the theory and practice of the welfare state. It would be naive to think that
there is any simple choice between the models since each of them is constructed from bits and pieces of English history that have been fought for in
long and bitter struggles.

I propose to extract from a complex and laminated evolution of welfare
state practices *three grammars of welfare* imbedded in complex institutional
configurations that achieve a certain identity but without closure either to
past and future states of welfare so long as we are politically and morally
committed to restraining bare market forces. I shall argue that we are experiencing an historical shift in the political semantics of the welfare state. The
latter has moved from a productivist to a social security rationale that in turn
now needs to be rephrased around a civic income provision. The concept of
civic income (basic income, citizens income) derives from a set of considerations that is moral as well as economic and ultimately ground in claims of
citizenship (Offe 1992; Social Justice 1994). Whatever the nature of social
needs, the groups involved, and the fiscal allocations, all national states
reduce the potential for extreme marginalization and political unrest by the
provision of "social security," i.e., through a class consensus around levels
of insecurity, unemployment, ignorance, and ill-health deemed tolerable in
a political democracy (O'Neill 1995; Ringen 1987). Contemporary withdrawals of legitimation focused on particular policies, recipients, and deficit
levels in the welfare system—withdrawals of universalism, entitlement, and
public care—are part of an antiwelfare semantics of the global economy
and its elite ethic of individual competence without public care. Leftist
criticism (Habermas 1987) also risks throwing out the welfare baby with its
critique of state regulation of the lifeworld. The latter exists, of course. But I
see it as an effect of the implosion of life-style difficulties without any focus
in class politics.

Additionally, the apologists of globalism, while recognizing that the productivist foundations of work, family, and the national state have shifted, nevertheless hark back to family values and the household economy as the missing link in the responsible conduct of minimalist government, on one side, and as the driving force in individual achievement, on the other side. At the same time, liberals and conservatives remain divided over the bottom line of economic reality, efficiency, the fiscal wall, remoralization, policing, minoritarianism, and social exclusion. But the polarization of incomes produced through restructuring for the global economy threatens to melt down the middle income groups whose voice and values have hitherto been loyal to the social security system.

With more than a little desperation, I shall try to take account of the variety of historical, political, and social factors that are at work in our endeavor to constrain the market through welfare state interventions on behalf of a sustainable civic ethos. This cannot be done without considerable abstraction from detail on behalf of an intelligible pattern whose corrigibility nevertheless lies in its accountability to significant detail. I offer, therefore, an ecological model of the institutional relationships through which we grasp the basic elements of consensus and reciprocity presupposed by civic welfare.

Compare Titmuss' three models of social policy based on the degree to which welfare policy is a residual element in market society, an adjunct to industrial achievement and the formation of class loyalties, or an integrated institution serving redistribution (Titmuss 1974; Furniss and Tilton 1977). Esping-Andersen (1990) also describes three welfare state regimes—the liberal welfare state (residual), the corporativist state, and the social democratic state. In the first two regimes the traditional family is essential, while in the third the individual is the principal agency. Mitchell (1991:185) has mapped these typologies with data on transfer programs from the Luxembourg Income Study Project (LIS) (see Table 2.1).

All three of the above models are somewhat deficient in not making explicit the linkages between the therapeutic helping professions and the state, especially as the former have arisen concomitant to late industrialization and the rise of the service sector. The history and politics of the welfare state, then, are best modeled (Figure 2.1) in terms of a selective interpretation of the late nineteenth- and early twentieth-century political economy of the family, state, and church (GSC) and the significant twentieth-century shift toward professional and therapeutic state intervention (GMC). Current attempts to resist the end of the welfare state along the lines of a revised civic state provision of community, family, and intergenerational endowment (ICC) may then be seen to be well grounded in a past and present history rather than to derive from either nostalgia or utopia.

I think we have to treat the welfare state as an evolutionary institution embedded in a set of mutually defining exchanges between family, church, professions, state, and economy that in the first stage may be designated as a

Table 2.1. The Classification of the LIS Countries According to the Three Typologies

	Titmuss		Furniss and Tilton		Esping-Andersen	
Institutional	Social welfare	Sweden Norway Netherlands	Social democratic	Sweden Norway Netherlands		Sweden Norway Netherlands
Industrial achievement	Social security	Germany France Switzerland	Corporativist	Germany France Switzerland		Switzerland Germany France
Residual	Positive	United Kingdom Australia Canada United States	Liberal	United Kingdom Australia Canada United States		United Kingdom Australia Canada United States

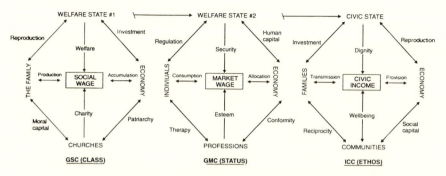

Figure 2.1.   Evolution of welfare regimes.

gendered social compact (GSC) grounded in class. The benefit of an ecological model is that it avoids the current issues of foundation/antifoundationalism because each subsystem in the model is defined through its exchanges with other subsystems. For example, "the family" that lives off a *social wage* in GSC is structured by a different constellation of exchanges with the church, state, and economy than "individuals" who live off a *market wage* in GMC. The difference is due to a large number of socioeconomic and political realignments that in overlaying class and status have altered the family's productive role in the economy to that of a set of individual consumers with corresponding changes in the moral and therapeutic status of family members with respect to church and professional authorities. These shifts are witnessed by changes in the state's attention from a reproductive to a regulative interest that in turn correlates with a shift in the relation between the state and the economy defined by the shift from technical to human capital investment.

The historical shift from GSC to GMC entails the differentiation of the welfare state from a moral-demographic agency to a therapeutic-regulative agency designed to professionally administer the formation and repair of the human capital input to late capitalist economy. In the first stage (GSC), "welfare" is administered by means of state and church supports to the social wage through which families reproduced the labor force demanded by early modern capital accumulation. In the late capitalist phase (GMC), the state and the therapeutic professions secure conformity and the pursuit of a market wage through which genderless individuals reproduce their self-esteem. We may also rephrase the shift from GSC to GMC as a shift from the reproduction of *moral capital* through family, church, and state exchanges in service of the early modern economy, to the reproduction of *human capital* through individual, professional, and state exchanges in service of the late modern economy. Of course, these two states of capitalism are not entirely distinct and are to be understood only relative to one another so that there is no notion of normativity or degeneration involved in their evolution.

The same considerations hold with respect to the potential shift from GMC to ICC in which we think that the reproduction of *social capital* through state, community, and family exchanges is necessary to sustain a *civic income* in the new context of the globalization of production and consumption processes. ICC restructures the exchanges between families, communities, and the state in terms of a set of provisions for community well-being, family transmission, and personal dignity that would sustain the ethos of a national economy with a civic identity. ICC represents an ecological structure of civic attachments (from class to status to ethos) in response to the current restructuring of the nation-state and of the corporate compact. It also underwrites the revision of our structures of moral care and intergenerational reciprocity as citizen investments (King and Waldron 1988; Shugarman 1993).

From the standpoint of the structural evolutionary model through which I am trying to capture shifts in the basic social compact, I believe that the national state must realign around a *nonproductivist civic covenant* in which

1. neither class nor status but ethos is the basis for the civic provision of transfers and services;
2. not work but civic service is the basis for civic income;
3. neither class nor status but ethos should define civic needs;
4. not today's growth but sustainable civic provision should be made with regard to the claims of intragenerational and intergenerational justice.

The effect of 1–4 would be to redefine the relations among income, work, families, and the vulnerable, and to reduce the dependence of social justice on economic growth or wage-determined worth. The basic proposal for a civic income would, of course, require an explicit political consensus on the civic contribution of members of society without a market wage. As I began this chapter by arguing, the civic recognition of children, but also of elders and women, is recognition of innumerable activities that create and reproduce well-being, which should also enhance the narrowly occupational realm of society, affording it unearned benefits. Implicit in these exchanges is, of course, a civic reframing of our current cultural concepts of political space, time, and generation.

To look for an alternative to the global swamping of our national political culture is not a reactionary response to an unavoidable fate. To resist the domination of public life by private capital we must reassert the national priority of civic capital formation in the provision of a democratic society. In the civic state both the liberal and the communitarian dimensions of citizenship are exercised inasmuch as the state affords the individual civic rights and duties while the community provides the context in which citizenship acquires meaningful exercise. Where civic capital is depleted, institutions are weakened by opportunism, free-riding, and fear. Civic capital, as Putnam (1993) has shown, is doubly marked by a virtuous cycle of improvement from use and vicious cycle of degradation from abuse. Each cycle has its own cumulative history. The art of politics is especially challenged when civic institutions have been depleted. Policymakers must find strategies to recombine the moral and physical resources that underwrite civic life. Moreover, it better serves a democracy to have within it a healthy civic realm from which citizens derive their sense of what governance is suited to them while in turn making government itself more practical:

> The harmonies of a choral society illustrate how voluntary collaboration can create value that no individual, no matter how wealthy, no matter how wily, could produce alone. In the civic community associations proliferate, memberships overlap, and participation spills into multiple arenas of community life. The social contract that sustains such collaboration in the civic community is not legal but moral. The sanction for violating it is not penal, but exclusion from the network of solidarity and cooperation. (Putnam 1993:183)

It is in the civic community that liberalism flourishes rather than statism and therapeutocracy because solidarity outweighs anarchy in the calculations of individual lawfulness. By the same token, citizenship flourishes through social, cultural, and political organizations that fulfill public purposes. Statism, by contrast, derives its power from the civic vacuum created by amoral familism and bureaucratized corruption. Whenever the civic tradition is strong, it proves to be a better foundation for future socioeconomic development than are the solely material indicators of economic growth. To the extent that we affirm our national will to sustain a civic middle ground, our everyday lives are less privatized and our institutional lives are less politicized. The civic state we have in mind is neither a local community nor a national community but exists in those practices of civic discovery through which local communities acquire a national claim that is met by the civic effort of the national state to sustain and promote its local institutions (Reich 1988). Civic policy formation involves public deliberation through which the community may come to reformulate its problems and their solutions and enlist volunteers to act on specific remedies. In this process citizens may acquire insights from one another that modify personal beliefs and interests, sifting them in the light of the concept of the public good that has been generated precisely through these mundane steps toward civic discovery. Civic education is not merely an instrument of political life. It is a constitutive good of shared political deliberation and implementation. Civic reflection is not ruled by tradition any more than it is the servant of technochange. It resists the dominance of economic interests that subordinate national life to economic growth. It weighs the costs of displacement, migration, and speculative flights that leave ghost towns along the highway of progress and undermine the public life of the nation.

NOTE

1.   This chapter contains material, in revised form, from O'Neill (1997a, 1997b).

REFERENCES

Barber, B. R. 1984. *Strong Democracy: Participatory Politics for a New Age*. Berkeley: University of California Press.

Barker, E. (ed.) 1948. *Social Contract: Essays by Hume, Locke and Rousseau*. Oxford: Oxford University Press.

Bellah, R. N. 1992. *The Good Society*. New York: Vintage Books.

Benhabib, S. 1987. "The Generalized Other and the Concrete Other: The Kohlberg-Gilligan Controversy and Moral Theory." In *Women and Moral Theory*, edited by E. F. Kittay and D. T. Meyers. Totawa, NJ: Rowman and Littlefield.

Bethke Elshtain, J. 1982. *The Family in Political Thought*. Amherst: University of Massachusetts Press.

Blustein, J. 1982. *Parents and Children: The Ethics of the Family*. New York: Oxford University Press.

Coleman, J. S., T. Hoffer and S. Kilgore. 1982. *High School Achievement: Public, Private and Catholic High Schools Compared*. New York: Basic Books.

Connides, I. A. 1989. *Family Ties and Aging*. Toronto: Butterworths.

Esping-Andersen, G. 1990. *The Three Worlds of Welfare Capitalism*. Cambridge, UK: Polity Press.

Etzioni, A. 1988. *The Moral Dimension: Toward a New Economics*. New York: Free Press.

Fraser, S. (ed.) 1995. *The Bell Curve Wars: Race, Intelligence and the Future of America*. New York: Basic Books.

Furniss, N. and T. Tilton. 1977. *The Case for the Welfare State*. Bloomington: Indiana University Press.

Gilbert, N. and B. Gilbert. 1989. *The Enabling State: Modern Welfare Capitalism in America*. London: Oxford University Press.

Gilligan, C. 1982. *In a Different Voice: Psychological Theory and Women's Development*. Cambridge, MA: Harvard University Press.

Glendon, M. A. 1989. *The Transformation of Family Law: State, Law and the Family in the United States and Western Europe*. Chicago: University of Chicago Press.

Habermas, Jurgen. 1987. *Theory of Communicative Action*, Vol. 2, translated by T. McCarthy. Boston: Beacon Press.

Hamburg, D. 1992. *Today's Children: Creating a Future for a Generation in Crisis*. New York: Random House.

Herrnstein, R. and C. Murray. 1995. *The Bell Curve: Intelligence and Class Structure in America*. New York: Free Press.

Hont, I. and M. Ignatieff (eds.) 1983. *Wealth and Virtue: The Shaping of Political Economy in the Scottish Enlightenment*. Cambridge, UK: Cambridge University Press.

Jencks, C. 1972. *Inequality: A Reassessment of the Effect of Family and Schooling in America*. New York: Harper & Row.

Kamin, L. J. 1995. "Behind the Curve." *Scientific American* (Feb.):99–103.

King, D. S. and J. Waldron. 1988. "Citizenship, Social Citizenship and the Defense of Welfare Provision." *British Journal of Political Science* 18:415–443.

Kramnick, I. 1982. "Republican Revisionism Revisited." *American Historical Review* 87:629–664.

Lasch, C. 1995. *The Revolt of the Elites and the Betrayal of Democracy*. New York: Norton.

Maine, H. S. 1905. *Ancient Law: Its Connection with the Early History of Society and Its Relation to Modern Ideas*. London: Routledge and Sons.

Marshall, T. H. 1975. *Social Policy in the Twentieth Century*. London: Hutchenson.

Marshall, T. H. 1977. *Class, Citizenship and Social Development*. Chicago: University of Chicago Press.

McNally, D. 1988. *Political Economy and the Rise of Capitalism: A Reinterpretation*. Berkeley: University of California Press.

Mitchell, D. 1991. *Income Transfers in Ten Welfare States*. Aldershot: Avebury.

Offe, C. 1992. "A Non-productivist Design for Social Policies." In *Arguing for Basic Income: Ethical Foundations for a Radical Reform*, edited by P. V. Parijs. London: Verso.

O'Neill, J. 1989. *The Communicative Body: Studies in Communicative Philosophy, Politics and Sociology*. Evanstone, IL: Northwestern University Press.

O'Neill, J. 1994. *The Missing Child in Liberal Theory: Towards a Covenant Theory of Family, Community, Welfare and the Civic State*. Toronto: University of Toronto Press.

O'Neill, J. 1995. *The Poverty of Postmodernism*. London: Routledge.

O'Neill, J. 1997a. "The Civic Recovery of Nationhood." *Citizenship Studies* 1 (1):19–31.

O'Neill, J. 1997b. "Is the Child a Political Subject?" *Childhood* 4 (2):241–250.

Pateman, C. 1988. *The Sexual Contract*. Oxford: Blackwell.

Putnam, R. C. 1993. *Making Democracy Work: Civic Traditions in Modern Italy*. Princeton, NJ: Princeton University Press.

Rawls, J. 1971. *A Theory of Justice*. Cambridge, MA: Harvard University Press.

Reich, R. B. (ed.) 1988. *The Power of Public Ideas*. Cambridge, MA: Ballinger.

Reich, R. B. 1991. *The Work of Nations: Preparing Ourselves for Twenty-First Century Capitalism*. New York: Knopf.

Ringen, S. 1987. *The Possibility of Politics: A Study in the Political Economy of Welfare State*. Oxford: Clarendon Press.

Schutz, A. 1973. *The Structures of the Life World.* Evanston, IL: Northwestern University Press.

Shugarman, D. P. 1993. "Citizenship and Civil Society: Redressing Undemocratic Features of the Welfare State." In *A Different Kind of State? Popular Power and Democratic Administration*, edited by G. Albo, D. Langille and L. Panitch. Toronto: Oxford University Press.

Sklar, M. 1988. *The Corporate Reconstruction of American Capitalism, 1890–1916: The Market, the Law, and Politics.* Cambridge, UK: Cambridge University Press.

Social Justice. 1994. *Strategies for National Renewal. Report of the Commission on Social Justice.* London: Vintage.

Titmuss, R. 1974. *Social Policy.* London: Allen and Unwin.

Turner, B. S. 1986. *Citizenship and Capitalism: The Debate over Reformism.* London: Allen and Unwin.

Wolfe, A. 1989. *Whose Keeper? Social Science and Moral Obligation.* Berkeley: University of California Press.

INTRODUCTION

It is intended that this chapter will help identify a number of conceptual and empirical issues relating to themes that recur throughout the book as a whole. In the early part of the chapter, which refers to the importance of rigorous theorizing, critique of theoretical and methodological problems in social science leads to a conceptual framework that is geared to the task of investigating the nature of the state and contemporary governance (this is described more fully in Sibeon 1996, 1997, 1998). Though the theoretical and methodological framework described is sociological, the overall approach is interdisciplinary in so far as, when it comes to analyzing specific policy events or processes, concepts and materials from political science and policy analysis are drawn on; this will become apparent later in the chapter, where there is a focus on conceptual and empirical issues pertaining to the state and the policy process, and to (post)modern as well as "postnational" forms of governance.

A THEORETICAL AND METHODOLOGICAL FRAMEWORK

The theoretical framework described in the early part of the chapter is built on a critique of four illegitimate modes of theoretical reasoning. The first of these is *reductionism*, that is, *the attempt to explain social life in terms of a single unifying principle of explanation* ("capitalism," "patriarchy," "racism," "post-Fordism," "the state," "globalization," or whatever). Lena Dominelli (1997), currently the leading British advocate of radical social work, employs a reductionist form of reasoning. I shall cite her text as an exemplar of the intellectual and practice limitations of radical social work in Britain. Actually, Dominelli's is a *compounded reductionism* in that it conflates more than one reductionist element; that is, one reductionism is compounded by another. Her commitment is to an "anti-racist feminist perspective" (1997:1). A problem here is that her advocacy of "black activism" (1997: 75) in social work rests on a notion that is no less reductionist than her notion of gender: she refers (1997:196) to "the dominant ideology" and believes that the nature and purpose of social work (and of the welfare state more generally) can be explained in terms of a structurally given function, that of oppressing women and black people and securing "the hegemonic position of white middle-class men." That social inequalities exist is beyond question: however, Dominelli's is an effort to synthesize mutually exclusive reductionisms and the end result, inevitably, is a inchoate theoretical cocktail that, as will become clearer later, has no empirical explanatory value nor any practical usefulness for social policy or social work.

Second, *essentialism*, which is often associated with or a product of reductionist theory, *presupposes in aprioristic fashion a structurally necessary unitariness or homogeneity of social phenomena*; the phenomena in question might be culture, or a social institution such as law, or, for example, taxonomic collectivities such as "women," "men," "black people," or "the working class." Against essentialism, it can be argued that where unitariness exists, this is a contingently produced and contingently sustained outcome of social processes—not a "necessary effect" of the social totality. Dominelli's (1997) reductionist and essentialist constructions of "women" and "black people" (and very occasionally, of "the working class") suggests, in one phase of her analysis, that each of these constructed categories, considered separately without attempting to fuse or synthesize them, is an analytical and a programmatic/political prime mover. Herein lies a logical impossibility, for one analytical (or programmatic) prime mover cancels out the other(s).

A still further confusion—a confusion associated, in another phase of her analysis, with a compounded reductionism in which Dominelli attempts to synthesize these mutually exclusive prime movers—is pushed even further when she conflates her essentialized categories. Dominelli's conflation of "men," "black people," "women," etc. in the terms that she defines these categories ultimately leads her to a hopelessly muddled and contradictory attempt to simultaneously construct, in reductionist and essentialist fashion, putative commonalities—of experience, of social situation, of perception, of possibilities for political action, and so on—within *and* across each of her essentialized social categories. Thus each phase of her analysis is flawed by theoretical contradiction. The empirical subtleties of pragmatic affiliations, cross-cutting inequalities, and multiple identities of the kind investigated in nonreductive and nonessentialist terms in, for instance, Bradley (1996) and Woodward (1997), find no place in the work of social work theorists such as Dominelli.

Third, there are good reasons for rejecting not only reductionism and essentialism, but also *reification*; the latter involves *the illegitimate attribution of agency to entities that are not actors or agents*, as in Dominelli's

(1997: 202, 205) supposition that "the state" and "white people" are actors. The problem of reification will be returned to shortly, in connection with the idea of agency.

Finally, *functional teleology* refers to illicit attempts to explain the *causes* of social phenomena in terms of their *effects* (where "effects" refers to outcomes or consequences viewed as performances of "functions"). This relates to a logical problem; an effect succeeds a cause in time, hence the former cannot account for the latter. The point to be made here is that in the absence of intentional planning by actors somewhere, sometime, efforts to explain the causes of social phenomena in terms of their effects are illegitimate insofar as they rest on a teleological fallacy (Betts 1986:51). An instance of functional teleology that incorporates structuralist elements of Althusser's and Foucault's work is Philp's (1979) account of social work discourse in Britain. Philp claims that in Victorian Britain the onset of large-scale unemployment together with the expansion of trade unionism created a schism between the "respectable," unionized working class and an "underclass" who constituted the residuum: the function of social work, a time-frozen function that Philp claims persists to the present day, is that of restoring members of the residuum to responsible citizenhood. Philp's account is reductionist, and it is reified inasmuch as actors' purposes and actions are omitted from his explanatory account of the nature and purposes of social work. Philp's theory, in purporting to explain the structure and function of contemporary social work, also invokes functional teleology. Using a theoretical scheme that accords no explanatory significance to agency, Philp's theory is an illicit functional teleology that imputes a particular form and function to present-day social work, and then "works backwards" in a misplaced effort to show that the "cause" of that form and function is that it fulfills a systemic functional "need," that of rehabilitating members of the residuum.

It was suggested earlier that critique of the above four illegitimate modes of theoretical and methodological reasoning—reductionism, essentialism, reification, and functional teleology—provides a suitable basis on which to build a theoretical framework. Any such framework should, it can be argued, explicitly address the agency-structure debate. An antireductionist and nonreified conception of *agency* is contained in Hindess's (1986:115) definition of an actor (or agent) as "a locus of decision and action where the action is in some sense a consequence of the actor's decisions." In terms of this definition there are *individual human actors* and *social actors*; examples of the latter are small groups, committees, and organizations of various kinds (government departments, private firms, voluntary bodies, professional associations, organized interest groups, and so on). Social actors or "supra-individuals" (Harre 1981:141) exhibit agency, so these are not analytically reified entities; they exhibit emergent properties—in particular, causal powers and forms of agency—that are not reducible to the actions of human individuals (Clegg 1989:187–188). But that *ensemble* that we call "the state" is part of the conditions-of-action, or social structure (see later), and *not* an actor; only individuals, committees and small groups, and organizations (public, private, or voluntary) exhibit agency. Entities that cannot formulate and act upon decisions are not actors. Nor can merely taxonomic collectivities be regarded as actors. Dominelli's (1997) reified conception of agency presumes the category "men" is a social actor (that, it is claimed, oppresses "women"), and that "white people" is also a social actor (one that, says Dominelli, oppresses "black people"). Dominelli, whose work, as I noted earlier, exemplifies the intellectual and practice limitations of radical social work in Britain, is here pursuing an analytically and programmatically self-defeating course. To impute causal responsibility for social conditions— among which are included forms of inequality—to social aggregates ("society," "the state," "the middle class," "men," "white people," and so forth) that do not have the means of formulating and acting on decisions, is to refer to "fictitious actors" (Hindess 1986:116). This has the two unfortunate consequences of obscuring the social processes resulting in those conditions and of obscuring analysis of what can be done to change them (1986:116–117).

The "agency versus structure" debate—or as I prefer to call it, debate of agency *and* structure—is central to social science (Archer 1988:ix–x). In the framework being described here, the concept *structure*—defined in a way that avoids the twin reductionisms of methodological individualism and methodological collectivism—refers to temporally and/or spatially extensive social conditions that to a greater or lesser extent influence actors' forms of thought, decisions, and actions, and which, depending on the circumstances, may facilitate or constrain actors' capacities to achieve their objectives. *Structure* may be regarded as the "conditions-of-action" (Betts 1986:41) or, put more simply, "social conditions." Structure exists at micro- and macrolevels of social process or, always providing the relative autonomy of these levels is acknowledged (Mouzelis 1995), at both levels simultaneously.

The concept "time-space" is relevant here. *Micro*structure consists of two main elements, the first being relatively enduring social conditions that are local ramifications of temporally and spatially extensive ("macro") conditions-of-action (for example, social work activity in a particular local setting is to some extent influenced by wider, transsituational cultural meanings and definitions of the role of "social worker"). Second, microstructure also consists of temporally relatively enduring but spatially local, idiosyncratic conditions of action (such as a particular friendship pattern or power relationship) that are unique to the particular local setting; for the actors involved in the local setting, and for other actors who have dealings with that setting, enduring setting-specific properties of interaction are no less a part of the conditions-of-action ("structure") than those features of the setting that are local ramifications of the macrosocial order.

*Macro*structure in public policy sectors such as education, health, or social work, refers to, for example, political, bureaucratic, and professional discourses; the degree of consensus or conflict within the policy sector; the state of the economy; public opinion and the mass media; international capital flows, and so on. An implication of the earlier theoretical remarks is that the conditions of action/social conditions, whether micro or macro, are not structurally predetermined. They are potentially fluid and shifting; whenever social conditions ("social structure") become stabilized and extensive across time and/or social space, any such stabilization is a contingent outcome of social processes and not a structural or historical "necessity."

It is not enough to talk about agency and structure without also bringing *social chance* (M. Smith 1993) explicitly into the picture. Despite Durkheimian or structuralist reasoning to the contrary, it is, I suggest, mistaken to regard social chance as a residual analytical category. By social chance I mean unplanned *combinations* of agency, chance events, and structure/social conditions, together with the *outcomes* of these unplanned combinations in which such outcomes are neither enduring setting-specific micropatterns of the type mentioned earlier nor outcomes of the kind that are widely disseminated and institutionalized across macroextensions of time-space. In the latter case, involving the diffusion and institutionalization of a political or policy outcome (or, say, an outcome that becomes institutionalized in the form of an established style of welfare practice) across large extensions of time-space, the outcome in question—which in this illustration began its life as a contingent and unplanned result of dialectical linkages between agency, structure, and social chance—is best regarded as no longer an instance of social chance, but rather as having become a part of social structure (the "conditions-of-action").

There is no intention here to embark on elaboration of other elements of the framework referred to above (see Sibeon 1996 for a fuller theoretical and methodological account that relates to governance and policy analysis), though it is appropriate, bearing in mind the various themes addressed by contributors to this volume, to make a brief observation concerning ontological flexibility. The conceptual framework developed in this chapter rests on a presumption that the social and political terrain is relatively indeterminate across time and social space: there are no analytical prime-movers and any instances of the stabilization and institutionalization of politics, policy, and practice across large extensions of time-space are contingent (and in principle, reversible) outcomes of dialectical interactions between agency, structure, and social chance. Agency, structure, and social chance tend to have a mutually shaping influence on each other: but *how* these elements combine and which, if any, of them predominate in any particular situation are questions not for theoretical predetermination but for empirical investigation in each instance (Sibeon 1996).

Put another way, the framework outlined in this chapter is predicated on a flexible ontology that in some respects is "post-postmodern"; however, the ontology, though highly flexible, is realist—there *is* a real, though empirically contingent and potentially highly variable, social world "out there"—and therefore, as should be clear from the earlier remarks on agency and structure, we are speaking here of a framework that does not go as far as endorsement of the relativism and hypercontextualism of postmodern theory. The social world may well be socially constructed, but as Mouzelis (1995) observes, many social constructs become institutionalized and regularly practiced and thereby acquire a material reality that is amenable to social scientific inquiry.

THE STATE AND "BEYOND THE STATE"

Keeping the above theoretical and methodological framework in mind, let us now look more closely at governance and the policy process, beginning with the nature of "the state" and conceptions of its relation to public policy and, implicitly, to practice in social work and other fields. Among conventional social science theories of the state, four have predominated: pluralism, elitism, Marxism, and corporatism.

The basics of these theories are well known and there seems little point in elaborating them here. Briefly stated, *pluralism* supposes that power—defined as a capacity to shape events and secure preferences—tends to be fairly widely spread across society, rather than concentrated in the state or in one or two dominant interest groups.

Elite theory, sometimes referred to as neopluralist theory, rests on a view that power is held by a relatively small number of interest groups, that is, by fewer groups than pluralists suppose: also, elite theorists regard the groups in question as being relatively highly integrated.

Marxist theorists of the state argue that the state is directly or indirectly an instrument of the ruling class; public policy, it is claimed, can be adequately explained in terms of its function, which is said to be that of reproducing the interests of the capitalist class.

Corporatism refers to a society that is jointly ruled by the state and large corporate groups that (usually) represent labor and employer interests, though other organizations (such as professional associations or voluntary bodies) may also be part of corporatist arrangements. Corporatism, it is worth noting, is not the same as elitism. Under elitism, groups may exercise power per se rather than, as happens in a corporatist arrangement, in conjunction with government.

A major difficulty with the above general theories of the state is that they lack ontological flexibility, and each of them is reductionist; each is predicated on a single unifying principle of explanation (pluralism or corporatism, or whatever) that is intended to apply to *the whole of* society, the state, and public policy. In the rest of the chapter it will be argued that conventional theories of the state should be abandoned in favor of a synthetic conception of public policy and welfare practice, a conception that draws on the following: policy network analysis, recent writing on governance, a revised version of post-Foucauldian work on "governmentality," and the idea of postnational governance. It will be argued that although the state "still matters," a great deal of power and social action in the public policy domain are to be found, to use Rose and Miller's (1992) expression, "beyond the state."

Unlike conventional theories of the state, the *policy network* approach—at least in the version described below—makes a priori or reductionist assumptions neither about the state–civil society relation nor about power distributions and policy dynamics in the various policy sectors (such as agriculture, health, education, welfare and social work, and housing). Data produced by political scientists who employ the policy network concept as an investigative tool indicate that in some policy sectors government actors are strong, while in other sectors the government may be a weak actor. And within a policy sector, the power of government actors in relation to nonstate actors may vary over time, or according to the nature of the policy issue and the prevailing circumstances. An ontologically flexible conception of the policy process, and here policy network analysis has a useful part to play, sensitizes empirical researchers to the fact that, in principle, some policy sectors may be corporatist or elitist, and others pluralist; moreover, these configurations may shift over time or they may even vary from the handling of one policy issue to another. Also, although the policy process is not uninfluenced by the nature of national political systems, there is no invariant "national policy style" or macrostructural predetermination of the policy process.

For example, although the American policy process in general—despite the existence of some "iron triangles" (close, institutionalized relationships between executive agencies, congressional committees, and interest groups)—tends, partly for reasons to do with the federal political system, to be "loose," indeterminate, and pluralistic (Hague 1992), some policy networks in the United States, such as health, are notably pluralistic, whereas others, however, such as trade policy in the 1950s and 1960s, have been corporatist.

Put at its simplest, a policy network is an array of state and nonstate actors who jointly participate in policy formulation and implementation; for example, the British health policy network includes the Department of Health, the British Medical Association, The Royal College of Surgeons, and a number of other actors involved in the health field. As this example shows, the policy network approach is a mesolevel of analysis, that is, the approach is interorganizational and hence refers to social ("organizational") actors in the sense that these were defined earlier: this provides an invaluable focus although, as some political scientists recognize (M.J. Smith 1993), there is a need in the future to link policy network analysis more explicitly to analyses concerned with macro- and microlevels of social process. More generally in terms of the theoretical framework outlined earlier, the policy network approach embodies a partly *relational* conception of power, interests, and social action: state and nonstate actors' interests, intentions, and capacities— what they will want to do, what they decide to do, and what they are able to do—are not structurally predetermined, but rather are in part a processual and contingent outcome of interaction and exchange among participants in policy networks.

Networks, though, are not all of the same kind. Marsh and Rhodes's (1992) typology of policy networks suggests an important distinction between two types of network: "policy communities" and "issue networks." In *policy communities* (examples are British health policy and British agriculture) there are relatively few state and nonstate actors, and these have a stable and continuing relationship with each other. Other characteristics of policy communities are that there tends to be a relatively high frequency of interaction among the actors; membership of the network does not fluctuate very much, if at all; there is a fairly high degree of consensus within the network in regard to values, means, and policy goals; and in terms of mutual resource dependencies, each of the major actors in the network has some power insofar as they have valued resources (such as technical or professional knowledge, financial resources, legal power, or political influence) that they are able to "exchange" with other actors in the network.

In contrast, an *issue network* is a much "looser," less integrated type of policy network. Examples are American health policy and also agricultural policy, and British industrial policy and urban renewal policy (M.J. Smith 1993). Issue networks tend to have a relatively large number of participants (that is, more than one state actor, and a large number of nonstate organizations and groups) together with a shifting rather than stable membership; there may be a minimal amount of agreement over values and policy, but there is usually also conflict over numerous issues; and with regard to mutual resource dependencies, there tends to be a number of network participants who, because they have few valued resources to exchange with others, are likely to have only limited power within the network.

It should be noted that this analytical distinction is not a dichotomy but a policy-network continuum with policy communities at one end and issue networks at the other. It should also be observed, in light of the theoretical framework outlined earlier, that empirical investigators ought not assume that these categories are static, or "necessary effects" of the social totality. In principle, an issue network may become a policy community, and vice versa. Nor, in terms of types of policy network, should it be assumed that policy sectors are homogeneous; a loose sectoral issue-network at the national level may contain subsectors that are tightly integrated policy communities. Further, although there undoubtedly is in general a transition away from binary categories (state/society, public/private, plan/market) and hence a blurring of the state–civil society distinction, the extent of state–civil society boundary blurring may shift over time and may also vary from one policy sector or policy network to another.

Among American (Kenis and Schneider 1991) and particularly among European political scientists and public administration academics the policy network approach has become a key analytical tool (Richardson 1996:4), which also has practical application in terms of a growing interest in the management of interorganizational networks (Kickert et al. 1997a). Interorganizational networks, though they have not completely replaced organizational hierarchies and markets (Thompson et al. 1991), are an increasingly important part of "postmodern" public administration (Fox and Miller 1995). The network metaphor is, as Kenis and Schneider (1991:34) observe, "an appropriate metaphor for responding to a number of empirical observations with respect to critical changes in the political governance of modern democracies." Notice that in their statement, Kenis and Schneider refer to "governance"; in what follows the intention is to look at this important concept more closely.

It is mainly to the disciplines of political science and public administration/public policy that we must turn for a theoretically and empirically developed conception of governance (for example, Kooiman 1993; Kickert et al. 1997a; Marin and Mayntz 1991). Rhodes (1996) claims we live in an era of "governance without government." Governance is the management of networks, but more in the sense of a negotiable and interactive process of "steering" than of top-down management control exercised from a central position (Kickert 1993:193). Kickert et al. (1997b:188), in a text grounded more closely in a European rather than American history of the relation of the state to the policy process, describe the movement from government to governance in the following terms.

The illusion prevalent in the heyday of the welfare state, that government would be able to "steer" societal policy processes by means of integral planning methods, and the illusion of the state as the central governing authority in society, have given way to a more realistic view of government as one of many interdependent social actors influencing complex policy processes; i.e., the concept of a policy network . . . the policy network concept . . . [is] . . . the scientific answer to the empirical observation of failing top-down hierarchical government control.

Rhodes (1996:666) refers to what he describes as the "fragmentation" of European public policy systems in the 1980s, associated with decentralized, semiautonomous public administration (in Britain this has taken the form of major reform of the civil service and the creation of semiautonomous executive agencies) together with greatly increased involvement of commercial and voluntary bodies in the planning and provision of services: "The state becomes a collection of interorganizational networks made up of governmental and societal actors with no sovereign actor to steer or regulate."

Government actors' loss of steering capacity is, for Rhodes and various other commentators, a potential threat to political accountability and democratic control of the policy process. Unlike Rhodes, however, Richardson (1994) believes that, by and large, governments exercise a fairly high level of influence over the operation of governance networks. Empirical evidence relating to this matter is not entirely clear-cut. If we look, for example, at British social work education and training, there is some evidence to support Richardson's thesis: despite intense and protracted opposition from academics and professional groups, the government has largely succeeded in its policy objective of making social work training less academic and more "practical" (Jones 1994).

On the other hand, there is some evidence that tends to support Rhodes's thesis. A key actor in the British social work policy-network, the Central Council for Education and Training in Social Work (CCETSW)—the national body that accredits social work training courses—has managed to pursue, largely against the wishes of governments, a "left-wing" feminist and antiracist strategy of the kind supported by, for example, Dominelli (1997). The irony associated with the fact that the CCETSW's "anti-oppressive" training regulations, which "read . . . like a Marxist Manifesto of the 1960s (but without the class analysis!)" (Stevenson 1994:185), successfully dominated the British social work training and practice agenda at a time—the mid-1980s onward—of conservative governments who were unconvinced by, and at times downright hostile toward, the CCETSW's stance, is not lost on Stevenson (1994).

This and many other examples suggest that government actors do not always dominate the policy process (James 1997). Indeed, in general it does seem that, increasingly, power and social action lies "beyond the state." However, it should be noted that this statement refers to an empirical variable and enough has been said earlier in the chapter to indicate that government actors' steering capacity is not structurally predetermined; variations in the outcomes of dialectical linkages between agency, structure, and social chance, quite often mean that government actors' power varies across policy sectors, or sometimes, according to the nature of particular policy problems, issues, and circumstances (Lindblom and Woodhouse 1993).

A rather different and also a more sociological approach—though one that has certain affinities with the political science perspectives on policy networks and governance described above—is to be found in post-Foucauldian sociology of governance, which is quite often referred to as the "governmentality" approach to the study of power and public policy: see, for example, Miller and Rose (1993), Rose and Miller (1992), Rose (1990), and O'Malley et al. (1997).

Foucault (1980a, 1980b, 1982, 1991), and governmentality writers, regard power as a shifting and precariously sustained outcome of networks and alliances and of the operation of discourses; power, for Foucauldians, is not an expression of a monolithic or unitary source of power such as "the sovereign," "the state," or "the government." In Foucault's theoretical scheme, power is largely an effect, not cause, of discursive practices (in politics, administration, law, social work, psychiatry, medicine, criminal justice, and so on). Contained within these discourses are definitions of the objects or "problems" that are to be acted on. In the work of Foucault and governmentality writers, the topics of social policy—general topics such as social needs, rights, or dependency, and more specialized topics such as poverty, homelessness, or child abuse—are not "given" or preconstituted, but rather, are formed by political, professional, and welfare discourses that "construct" their own topics and imbue them with particular meanings.

Family policy, for instance, constructs a sense of what "the family" *is*, just as economic policy formulates a conception of "the economy." Discourses also specify solutions or responses—in the form of therapies, guidance, or controls—to those problems that have been identified and defined by the discourse in question. It may also be noted that discourses are widely disseminated across time-space and Foucault argues that discursive practices, including social work practices (Stenson 1993), are not the intentional effects of the will of any individual actors or of the state; and nor, Foucault insists, should discourses—whether of government, of administration, or professional discourses—be regarded as expressions of *structurally given* ("objective") interests.

The significance of this last point should not be overlooked: as Hindess (1988:110) notes, "Interests have consequences only insofar as they enter actors' deliberations and contribute towards providing them with reasons for action." Self-formulated interests have a legitimate part to play in social scientific explanation of intentional behavior; but reductionist, essentialist, reified, or teleological theories that impute interests to actors who neither recognize nor act on those interests have no empirical explanatory value.

Another theme in the Foucauldian notion of governance is the idea of "self-government" or "action-at-a-distance" (Miller and Rose 1993:83): this relates to discourses that, in terms of what Foucault calls "discipline," promote self-regulation among individuals, families, factories, government organizations, or any other entities that are the subject of governance. It should also be observed that governmentality writers, who reject theories of structural predetermination, subscribe to a fluid and processual conception of the social world. Policy domains are seen as contingent and performative outcomes of interactions between actors, institutions, discourses, procedures, conflicts, unplanned events, and so on. The extent to which discourses come into alignment is a variable factor. That is, in Foucauldian theory there is no single sovereign or integrating source of power; public policy and welfare practice are not unambiguous series of controlled and coordinated responses to commands issued from a "center" such as "government," "the state," or a ruling class or gender or racial elite. Rather, the policy process is an empirically "messy" affair in which power is loose, uncoordinated and "everywhere" (O'Malley et al. 1997).

Foucauldian work on governance can usefully be combined with, and add a particular kind of processual and relational dimension to, the previously described non-Foucauldian political science and public administration approaches to the study of policy networks and governance "beyond the state." This observation, however, requires some qualification in the light of two limitations of Foucauldian analysis.

First, Foucault and governmentality theorists tend to underplay *agency*. Foucault writes as if discourses—linked sets of ideas, knowledge, and practices—were actors or agents (Best and Kellner 1991:60–61, 66). If the theoretical framework described earlier in the chapter is accepted, it can convincingly be argued, against Foucault, that discourses affect (though do not determine) actors, and are part of the conditions-of-action ("social structure"). But discourses, as such, are not actors. Discourses cannot *do* anything; they have no intentional causal power and unless they are invoked or drawn on by actors, they are ineffective. Hence, particularly in light of the theoretical arguments developed earlier in the chapter, one aspect of Foucauldian and governmentality writers' work that we should not wish to employ is their reified view of agency.

Second, Foucault's view of *power* requires modification. Almost entirely missing from his work is the idea of power *storage* and power *distributions*. For Foucauldians, including governmentality writers, power is not something that can be "possessed"; it is a contingent effect or *outcome*, not *cause*, of interactions and discourses. Power, to put the matter another way, is not a structurally predetermined "fixed-capacity" inherent in any particular actors; it is relational, emergent, and strategic (Clegg 1989:32–33).

In this relational as distinct from systemic conception, power is not already (pre)constituted ("stored") in social systems or networks: rather, it is an *effect* of the operation of discourses (medical, aesthetic, legal, occupational and professional, political discourses, and so on) and the product or "outcome" of social relations. However, Foucauldian theory of governance has largely ignored the commonplace observation that not only do agents possess power but that some agents "possess" more power than others (Best and Kellner 1991:70).

A literal reading of Foucault prevents us from speaking of *distributions* of power. A problem here, as Law (1991:170) has noted, is that, for example, everyone knows that the American President has "more power" than a junior White House official: at the same time we also know that Presidents' positions are sometimes only precariously sustained (or not sustained at all). The point to be made here is that we need not embrace an either/or position in regard to power. Foucault's work can be combined synthetically with a version of systems-oriented sociology. Power is almost always partly relational, strategic, emergent, and contingent—and Foucault helps us glimpse this emergent, relational, and processual face of power. As Latour (1991:118) put it, in emphasizing the idea that power is a relational *effect* of social relations and not a capacity: "Nothing becomes real to the point of not needing a network to upkeep its existence."

Latour is adamant that power cannot be stored. But we have just seen that power also has another face, for the analysis of which we have to go beyond Foucault and Latour: there are aspects of power that, as in the example of the political power of the President in relation to that of a junior official, can be "stored" in social institutions, in rules and roles/positions, and in networks of social relations, even if not always securely. What is required is a way of combining Foucauldian/relational and systemic conceptions of power as a basis for investigating governance and the policy process.

Here, the earlier theoretical framework is relevant. An antireductionist and nonreified, nonteleological systemic extension of, and simultaneously a revision of, Foucauldian scholarship is achievable through the making of an analytical distinction between a *social integration* approach (the study of agency/actors and of social relations—whether cooperative or conflictual—between actors) and a *system integration* approach (the study of relations, which may or may not involve incompatibilities, between rules, roles/positions, and social institutions). This analytical distinction is important. Society or any other unit of analysis such as a family, a committee, an organization, or a profession such as social work, has at least two "faces"—one relational or figurational, the other systemic and institutional—each of which requires investigation in its own right and also in terms of its relation to the other (Mouzelis 1995).

Finally, there is another sense, additional to those already discussed, in which politics, power, governance, and welfare practice operate partly "beyond" the sphere of the nation-state and national government. In Europe, the increasing importance of the European Union (EU) has prompted the emergence of the concept *postnational governance* (Sibeon 1996, 1997, 1998). This concept, as used here, refers to multiple levels of governance (the supranational, transnational, national, and subnational) viewed in terms of this chapter's ontologically flexible theoretical and methodological framework: it is not assumed on a priori grounds that one level determines the others or predominates in every situation (which level has the greater relative significance in any particular instance is a matter for empirical inquiry).

Relatedly, it is assumed levels of social process are relatively autonomous and that if any empirically significant linkages between them develop, this is a contingent outcome of dialectical interactions between agency, social structure, and social chance. By *transnational* is meant cross-national relations among national governments, subnational governments, or nonstate actors, or, as often happens in the case of transnational European policy networks, cross-national relations among actors from each of these categories; herein lies one source of complexity in patterns of contemporary European governance. The *supranational* dimension of governance occurs when a number of nation states set up a supranational organization (such as the European Union) and transfer certain national sovereign rights to it and are bound by decisions made by that body. *National* governance refers, of course, to the nation-state, to national governments and national nonstate actors. *Subnational* governance includes the activities of regional and local government actors.

In Europe, in terms of these levels of the policy process, governance has become a highly complex mixture of vertically related "tiers" of governance, which, however, interact with laterally related "spheres" of governance, with the end result that the European policy process is, so to speak, more like a marble cake than a layer cake; this analogy illustrates why, empirically speaking, it has become increasingly difficult to disaggregate "levels" of governance and also difficult to distinguish "levels" from "spheres" of governance (Meny et al. 1996). Moreover, patterns of postnational politics and policy in Europe tend to be fluid and sometimes vary from one policy sector or policy issue to another, which is sometimes referred to as the "variable geometry" of (post)modern European governance. In any event, it is clear that traditional state-centric notions of government no longer hold sway.

Notice, too, that there are at least three parallels between American and contemporary European governance. First, European governance, in regard to the early stage of the policy process involving actors placing issues on the political and policy agenda ("agenda-setting" in the language of political science), is becoming more like the United States in so far as there are now, in Europe, multiple and multilevel points of access to the policy process. Second, the United States, of course, has in public policy terms a long history of social regulation as distinct from European-style "welfare state" provision; it is noteworthy that EU social policy is primarily based on regulation and not EU-funded programs. And third, the pluralism, contingency, and fluidity of the American and European policy process has converged to such an extent that now there is what Richardson (1996:17) refers to as an "uncanny resemblance" between European and American styles of governance.

CONCLUSION

I suggested in this chapter, initially with reference to the crudity of recent "radical social work" writing in Britain, that analysis of the structure and forms of contemporary governance has much to gain from a theoretical and methodological framework that is ontologically flexible and that avoids "modernist" conceptual pitfalls associated with reductionism, essentialism, reification, and functional teleology, but without, however, embracing the relativism of postmodern theory. One such framework, centered on the concepts *agency*, *structure*, and *social chance*, was outlined in the first part of the chapter. In terms of substantive issues and themes relevant to the concerns of this book, the chapter's theoretical framework offers a basis for investigating a changing scenario of governance, one in which, while the nation-state "still matters," older and state-centric assumptions concerning politics, policy, and welfare practice, have long since had their day. It was shown, in particular, that the policy process, as well as becoming more fluid and indeterminate, is increasingly located in domains of governance that to a significant—though variable—extent, operate "beyond the state."

REFERENCES

Archer, M. 1988. *Culture and Agency: The Place of Culture in Social Theory.* Cambridge: Cambridge University Press

Best, S. and D. Kellner. 1991. *Postmodern Theory: Critical Interrogations.* London: Macmillan.

Betts, K. 1986. "The Conditions of Action, Power and the Problem of Interests." *The Sociological Review* 34 (1):39–64.

Bradley, H. 1996. *Fractured Identities: Changing Patterns of Inequality.* Cambridge: Polity.

Clegg, S. 1989. *Frameworks of Power.* London: Sage.

Dominelli, L. 1997. *Sociology for Social Work.* London: Macmillan.

Foucault, M. 1980a. *Power/Knowledge.* New York: Pantheon.

Foucault, M. 1980b. *The History of Sexuality.* New York: Vintage Books.

Foucault, M. 1982. "The Subject and Power." In *Beyond Structuralism and Hermeneutics*, with an Afterward by Michel Foucault, edited by H. L. Dreyfus and P. Rabinow. Brighton: Harvester Wheatsheaf.

Foucault, M. 1991. "Governmentality." In *The Foucault Effect: Studies in Governmentality*, edited by G. Burchall, C. Gordon and P. Miller. Hemel Hempstead: Harvester Wheatsheaf.

Fox, C. J. and H. T. Miller. 1995. *Postmodern Public Administration: Towards Discourse.* London: Sage.

Hague, R. 1992. "The United States." In *Power and Policy in Liberal Democracies,* edited by M. Harrop. Cambridge: Cambridge University Press.

Harre, R. 1981. "Philosophical Aspects of the Macro-Micro Problem." In *Advances in Social Theory and Methodology,* edited by K. Knorr-Cetina and A. V. Cicourel. Boston: Routledge.

Hindess, B. 1986. "Actors and Social Relations." In *Sociological Theory in Transition,* edited by M. L. Wardell and S. P. Turner. London: Allen and Unwin.

Hindess, B. 1988. *Choice, Rationality and Social Theory.* London: Unwin Hyman.

James, S. 1997. *British Government: A Reader in Policy Making.* London: Routledge.

Jones, C. 1994. "Dangerous Times for British Social Work Education." Paper presented to the International Association of Schools of Social Work 27th Congress, Amsterdam, 11–15 July.

Kenis, P. and V. Schneider. 1991. "Policy Networks and Policy Analysis: Scrutinizing a New Analytical Toolbox." In *Policy Networks: Empirical Evidence and Theoretical Considerations,* edited by B. Marin and R. Mayntz. Boulder, CO: Westview Press.

Kickert, W. 1993. "Complexity, Governance and Dynamics: Conceptual Explorations of Public Network Management." In *Modern Governance: New Government - Society Interactions,* edited by J. Kooiman. London: Sage.

Kickert, W., E. H. Klijn and J. F. M. Koppenjan (eds.) 1997a. *Managing Complex Networks: Strategies for the Public Sector.* London: Sage.

Kickert, W., E. H. Klijn and J. F. M. Koppenjan. 1997b. "Managing Networks in the Public Sector: Findings and Reflections." In *Managing Complex Networks: Strategies for the Public Sector,* edited by W. Kickert, E. H. Klijn and J. F. M. Koppenjan. London: Sage.

Kooiman, J. (ed.) 1993. *Modern Governance: New Government–Society Interactions.* London: Sage.

Latour, B. 1991. "Technology Is Science Made Durable." In *A Sociology of Monsters: Essays on Power, Technology and Domination,* edited by J. Law. London: Routledge.

Law, J. 1991. "Power, Discretion and Strategy," In *A Sociology of Monsters: Essays on Power, Technology and Domination,* edited by J. Law. London: Routledge.

Lindblom, C. and E. J. Woodhouse. 1993. *The Policy-Making Process.* Englewood Cliffs, NJ: Prentice-Hall.

Marin, B. and R. Mayntz (eds.) 1991. *Policy Networks: Empirical Evidence and Theoretical Considerations.* Boulder, CO: Westview Press.

Marsh, D. and R. A. W. Rhodes. 1992. "Policy Communities and Issue Networks: Beyond Typology." In *Policy Networks in British Government,* edited by D. Marsh and R. A. W. Rhodes. Oxford: Oxford University Press.

Meny, Y., P. Muller and P. Quermonne (eds.) 1996. *Adjusting to Europe: The Impact of the European Union on National Institutions and Policies.* London: Routledge.

Miller, P. and N. Rose. 1993. "Governing Economic Life." In *Foucault's New Domains,* edited by M. Gane and T. Johnson. London: Routledge.

Mouzelis, N. 1995. *Sociological Theory: What Went Wrong?* London: Routledge.

O'Malley, P., L. Weir and C. Shearing. 1997. "Governmentality, Criticism, Politics." *Economy and Society* 26 (4):501–517.

Philp, M. 1979. "Notes on the Form of Knowledge in Social Work." *The Sociological Review* 27 (1):83–111.

Rhodes, R.A.W. 1996. "The New Governance: Governing Without Government." *Political Studies* 44 (4):652–667.

Richardson, J. 1994. "Doing Less By Doing More: British Government 1979-93." *West European Politics* 17 (3):178–197.

Richardson, J. 1996. "Policy-Making in the EU: Interests, Ideas, and Garbage Cans of Primeval Soup." In *European Union: Power and Policy-Making*, edited by J. Richardson. London: Routledge.

Rose, N. 1990. *Governing the Soul: The Shaping of the Private Self.* London: Routledge.

Rose, N. and P. Miller. 1992. "Political Power Beyond the State: Problematics of Government." *British Journal of Sociology* 43 (2):173–205.

Sibeon, R. 1996. *Contemporary Sociology and Policy Analysis: The New Sociology of Public Policy.* London: Kogan Page and Tudor.

Sibeon, R. 1997. "Anti-Reductionist Sociology and the Study of Postnational Governance." Paper presented to the Third Conference of the European Sociological Association, University of Essex, UK (September).

Sibeon, R. 1998. "Governance and the Postnational Policy Process." In *Future Worlds: Migrations and Globalization*, edited by M. Mac an Ghaill. London: Macmillan.

Smith, M. 1993. "Changing Sociological Perspectives on Chance." *Sociology* 27 (3):513–531.

Smith, M. J. 1993. *Pressure, Power and Policy: State Autonomy and Policy Networks in Britain and the United States.* London: Harvester Wheatsheaf.

Stenson, K. 1993. "Social Work Discourse and the Social Work Interview." *Economy and Society 22 (1):42–76*

Stevenson, O. 1994. "Social Work in the 1990s: Empowerment—Fact or Fiction?" In Social Policy Review, Vol. 6, edited by R. Page and J. Baldock. University of Kent at Canterbury: Social Policy Association.

Thompson, G., J. Frances, R. Levacic and J. Mitchell (eds.) 1991. *Markets, Hierarchies and Networks: The Co-ordination of Social Life.* London: Sage.

Woodward, K. (ed.) 1997. *Identity and Difference.* London: Sage.

Therapy, Organizations, and the State: A Blackian Perspective

4

James Tucker

INTRODUCTION

Therapy directed at the human mind is often social control—a means of defining and responding to deviant behavior. Unlike social control that punishes people for violating prohibitions, therapy treats individuals as victims who need help returning to normal (Black 1976:4–6; 1984b:8–12). Although therapy is usually associated with specialists such as psychiatrists and other mental health professionals, it also occurs informally among family, friends, and even co-workers during the course of everyday life. Moreover, therapy is not confined to the modern western world. It is found in one form or another in most societies past and present (Frank 1973; Horwitz 1984). Even so, therapy is attracted to some social environments more so than others.

Donald Black's (1976, 1984b, 1990, 1993, 1995) general theory of social control provides a powerful framework within which to examine the "social structure" of therapy. Blackian theory predicts that therapy in its purest, least authoritative forms should occur across close distances in "social space," where people are equal, intimate, and homogeneous. It should become less common, although more authoritative, as social space expands. In this chapter I present evidence that supports these predictions. Much of the evidence comes from research on social control in organizations, including my own study of therapy in corporations (Tucker 1999). As predicted, therapy thrives in decentralized communal settings such as worker collectives, utopian communities, and modern corporations with "postbureaucratic" structures. By comparison, violent punishment is the most common form of social control on slave plantations, colonial work camps, serf estates, and in other settings with high levels of inequality and social distance (Black 1993:151–152).

The findings presented in this chapter have implications beyond the workplace. Among other things, they suggest that the broader expansion of therapy in contemporary society is a by-product of changing social structures, in particular, the shrinking of social space. As hierarchy has weakened in families and schools, for example, therapy has increased and punishment decreased. The traditional authority of the state is also declining and, as we would predict, a growing number of counseling programs have emerged in prisons and other government institutions (see Nolan 1998). Yet therapy does not occur everywhere. Punishment and other forms of social control still appear when the social conditions are right. Workers may be verbally berated by their bosses, children spanked by their parents, students reprimanded by their teachers, and citizens killed by the state. As Blackian theory predicts, it all depends on the direction and location of social control in social space: How much status does the social control agent have in relation to the recipient? How intimate are the parties? How similar are they culturally? These matters are crucial in predicting whether someone will be counseled, punished, or subject to some other form of social control.

THERAPY AS SOCIAL CONTROL

Black (1995:835–836) provides an explanation of therapy as part of his theory of "moralism" (see also, Black 1976:4–6, 29–30, 47, 78–79, 98–99, 103, 106, 119). Moralism is a tendency to act authoritatively, "to treat people as enemies" (Black 1993:144). It varies along four dimensions: formalism, decisiveness, coerciveness, and punitiveness (Black 1993:145– 149; 1995:834–835, note 34). Strong moralism applies explicit standards of right and wrong, is inflexible, backs its decisions with force, and punishes offenders. Criminal law is strongly moralistic, but so are other authoritative forms of social control such as violence (Black 1984a). Weak moralism is nonauthoritative, characterized by informality, compromise, voluntariness, and helpfulness (Black 1995:836). Negotiation and mediation are weak forms of moralism. Parties work out their differences together through dialogue. Therapy is also a weak form of moralism, much like negotiation and mediation, but instead of addressing conflict between parties, it handles conflict with the self (Black 1995:835). In its pure form, an individual with a self-conflict—a problem defined as existing inside the mind (Horwitz 1984:214)—solicits help from another party. The helper then works with the afflicted individual to improve his or her condition (Black 1976:4-5). Like other forms of weak moralism, a key feature of the therapeutic process is talk: "Words, rather than force, are the major mechanism of social control" (Horwitz 1984:216). In this sense, anyone who listens and gives advice to troubled individuals engages in therapy.

But therapy is not always pure. It may attempt to convince people they need help (Black 1976:5). In modern America, for example, a large mental health industry uses the marketplace to sell its therapeutic services. Television and print advertisements encourage people to seek professional help for various psychological ailments, including alcoholism, drug addiction, and depression. Both organizations (such as private drug treatment centers and mental health facilities) and individual therapists generate business in this manner, while insurance companies frequently participate in the therapeutic marketplace by paying for the costs of treatment. Market therapy in general is more authoritative than therapy offered voluntarily by family, friends, and others. Professional therapists speak with the authority of the mental health establishment and are likely to use formal psychiatric categories to define and respond to internal conflicts.

Therapy can take on even more authoritative forms. In socialist societies such as Maoist China and the Soviet Union, for example, people were pressured by fellow citizens to seek therapeutic treatment. This often included coercive efforts to "reeducate" individuals so that their thoughts conformed to Communist ideology. Therapy in these settings was also standardized, with little variation across cases. Unique characteristics of individuals were ignored (Horwitz 1984:228–231). More extreme forms might entail forced biochemical and physical treatments used in conjunction with counseling. Such treatments, which include psychoactive drug and electric-shock therapies, were especially common in Soviet "psychoprisons" (Fireside 1979).

Regardless of who initiates it or how pure it is, therapy everywhere follows a similar pattern. The process normally commences with a diagnostic phase, in which the therapist along with the troubled individual attempt to discover the nature of the alleged problem. The therapist will often ask the individual a question or series of questions. When done informally this might involve a family member or friend saying simply: "I've noticed you have been down lately. Is anything wrong?" Professional therapists are apt to perform a formal "assessment," often with a preestablished list of questions that reflects a particular therapeutic tradition. Many administer written "personality inventories," and a few still use the Rorschach (or inkblot) test to determine an individual's psychological makeup. Freudian therapists often have people describe their dreams on the assumption that the source of mental illness lies somewhere deep in the subconscious and can be identified only through extensive investigation of the psyche.

A therapeutic diagnosis may also explore possible supernatural sources of internal conflict. In tribal settings, healers in the supernatural arts trace mental problems to various conditions, the most frequent of which are soul loss, breach of taboo, and spirit intrusion (Clements 1932). Priests, ministers, and rabbis, who regularly counsel members of their churches and synagogues, are also likely to view psychological problems in supernatural terms. Similarly, a growing number of so-called "New Age" practitioners in

modern America, many of whom can be properly called "cosmic psychotherapists" (Brown 1997:37), consider the supernatural to be an important
factor in causing mental difficulties. For these practitioners, psychological
well-being is linked to psychic energies, ancestral spirits, extraterrestrial
beings, or other supernatural entities (Brown 1997; Tucker 1998).

After the diagnosis is complete, therapy moves to another phase, in which
people are encouraged to acknowledge their problems and talk about them.
Again, this can occur informally. An individual may console a troubled
friend: "Why don't you tell me what's going on? I think talking about it will
help." Yet it can follow a standardized procedure. Consider, for example,
Alcoholics Anonymous. At AA meetings, people are permitted to address the
group only if they first utter the following phrase: "Hi, my name is _____
and I am an alcoholic." In fact, confession before a group is a fundamental
part of the therapeutic process in all communal groups (Horwitz 1984:225).
Psychiatrists also assume that healing is possible only when patients recognize the source of their troubles. Thus, a key focus of modern psychiatry is
"self-awareness" (Horwitz 1984:235–238).

Therapists employ various strategies to get people to open up. Group
pressure is common in traditional settings, in which the therapeutic process
takes place among kin and fellow tribesmen (Horwitz 1984:223–228). In
modern one-on-one therapeutic relationships, other strategies are used to
encourage talk. Many psychoanalysts believe that patients will be most at
ease, and thus apt to talk about themselves, if lying down on a couch. A
more active strategy is hypnosis, which can break down inhibitions and
cause people to discuss matters they might normally find uncomfortable or
even impossible to talk about. "Gestalt" or "expressive" therapists prefer
more unconventional techniques such as dramatic exercises, painting, and
"primal screaming" to help people recognize their problems and disclose
their feelings (Hunt 1993).

Psychoactive drugs may also be introduced in the therapeutic process to
enhance talk. Alcohol, a popular mind-altering drug, is a frequent component of informal therapy among friends: Drinking loosens people up. It plays
the same role at social gatherings in some work settings (see Rohlen 1974:109;
van Maanen 1992:39). In Japanese corporations, for example, "office parties
with dinner and drinks permit the subordinate to adopt the guise of mild
inebriation" and express themselves more freely than when on the job (Ouchi
1981:45). Drugs are often introduced during therapeutic ceremonies in traditional societies. Among the Plains Indians of North America, for instance,
disturbed individuals would ingest peyote before confessing and discussing
their problems before a group of intimates (Kiev 1972:112). A wide variety
of psychiatric drugs, including Prozac and other antidepressants, are prescribed to patients of modern psychotherapists. While some of these drugs

are designed to work as a substitute for talk therapy, many are prescribed because they are thought to enhance the therapeutic process by making people more expressive (Kramer 1993).

Supernatural forces are also called on to help people open up. Among the traditional people of St. Lawrence Island (Alaska), for example, shamans would invoke spirits during collective therapeutic rituals such as seances (Murphy 1964). In modern America, New Age healers, like shamans, help people with their mental problems by calling on the assistance of spirits (Brown 1997; Tucker 1998). Many of these healers assume that individuals with psychological difficulties can summon their "spirit guides" to help alleviate suffering and act to protect people from future trouble. It is also widely believed among New Age healers that souls of the dead, including family members and well-known historical figures, can be contacted and can give people insight into their current difficulties (Tucker 1998).

Even the most authoritative forms of therapy include an acknowledgment and discussion of problems. In totalitarian settings, for example, people are beaten, deprived of food and sleep, and coerced in other ways in an attempt to get them to admit to having treasonous or politically incorrect thoughts. Talk is a fundamental feature of the reeducation process, which forces people to take on new selves. Consider the following account provided by a physician who had been confined for several years to a Chinese prison, or "reeducation center," in the early 1950s: "In the cell, twelve hours a day, you talk and talk—you have to take part—you must discuss yourself, criticize, inspect yourself, denounce yourself. Little by little you start to admit to something" (quoted in Lifton 1961:27). In this case, as in others in Maoist China, individuals "admit" to being "bourgeois" and "imperialist" and in need of treatment for their "sickness" (Lifton 1961).

Therapists often just sit and listen to people, assuming that talk in and of itself is therapeutic. Yet they may also take further action and advise people on how to overcome their troubles. This can be an informal suggestion from a friend: "Perhaps you should take a vacation. You might have a better perspective on life after you return." Professional therapists give advice based on a formal therapeutic discipline. "Cognitive" therapists, for example, provide patients with specific strategies for changing how they think and how they react emotionally to circumstances that affect their lives. By contrast, "behavioral" therapists have people modify their living patterns, including their diets, friendships, hobbies, and other personal activities (Hunt 1993). Authoritative therapies such as those found in totalitarian societies not only advise people to think differently or change their behavior, they force them to do so.

To summarize, in its pure form, therapy is a form of social control that appears in many different settings. It assumes people experience inner conflicts that can be discovered and cured through talk and, in some instances, other more active measures. Next we examine why, according to Blackian theory, therapy appears in some settings and not others.

THE SOCIAL STRUCTURE OF THERAPY

Under what conditions are people helped rather than punished? Blackian theory states that "moralism is a direct function of social remoteness and superiority" (Black 1993:144). Thus the most authoritative forms of social control are directed at socially remote inferiors such as slaves and serfs (Black 1995:151–152). Moralism weakens as people become closer and more equal. Therapy should accordingly appear at the smallest distances in social space. And it does. For example, therapy occurs in its purest forms only when therapists and those subject to therapy share a symbolic universe and are part of an ongoing relationship (Horwitz 1984:216–217). In traditional societies, therapy normally "occurs in the presence of family and community members" during the "collective activities of the group, such as feasts and dancing" (Horwitz 1984:226). In the modern psychiatric relationship, closeness emerges during the therapeutic process itself, which requires patients to meet with therapists over long periods of time and discuss the most private aspects of their lives, such as their sexual practices and fantasies (Black 1995:836, note 40).

Blackian theory can explain other variation in the behavior of therapy. It explains, for instance, why psychotherapy in modern societies is popular among the middle and upper classes, who are closer in status and cultural orientation to professional therapists (Horwitz 1990:84–86). Moreover, it explains why members of Chinese and Hispanic ethnic groups often resist attempts by mostly white mental health professionals to provide therapeutic help (Garrison 1977; Lin et al. 1978, both cited in Horwitz 1990:85).

Therapy in organizations and elsewhere follows the same principles as therapy in the offices of psychiatrists and the wards of mental hospitals: It occurs in its purest forms under conditions of equality and social closeness. One setting in which these conditions are prevalent is the utopian commune, where people publicly express concerns about themselves and ask others to help them return to normal (Kanter 1972:106). For example, public pleas of forgiveness were common in the Oneida community of nineteenth-century New England, where members shared property and successfully operated a furniture manufacturing enterprise. Individuals who violated informal standards of conduct would voluntarily come forward and acknowledge their shortcomings before a group of well-respected members (Kephart 1976:68–72). Similarly, in the Bruderhof commune in early twentieth-century America, people would willingly admit to inner conflict: "The Bruderhof socialization process is designed to make it a torment to withhold information about oneself on any matter" (Zablocki 1971:225). As a result, members regularly sought out others and made "unsolicited confessions." The Bruderhof were compelled to confess even their innermost negative thoughts, including sexual fantasies expressed in dreams (Zablocki 1971:193).

People living on communes are also likely to provide and receive counseling. This often takes the form of "criticism." In the Oneida community: "One version of criticism [was] called historical criticism . . . [which] has a surprising flavor of Freud and more recent psychiatric thinking" (Robertson 1970:131). Individuals subject to this kind of social control would meet with a committee of esteemed members, who encouraged the discussion of problems that, according to the founder of the Oneida community "in the past had been laid secret, perhaps half forgotten, but are necessarily darkening and poisonous to present experience" (Robertson 1970:131). Similarly, senior members of the Bruderhof commune, "who are skilled diagnosticians of attitudinal failings" (Zablocki 1971:226), counseled individuals on a regular basis. Counseling was geared toward identifying the "deeper disturbances" thought to be causing members to think and act in inappropriate ways. Deviance was said to be caused by something over which individuals had little control but that can be cured when people discover the sources of their internal problems and talk about them.

A THERAPEUTIC CORPORATION

Although it may seem surprising, the social conditions conducive to therapy also appear in a growing number of American companies. I conducted research in one such firm in the early 1990s. This firm—which we will give the name HelpCo—is located on the east coast of the United States and employs about 200 people. It is a worker-owned manufacturing company with a streamlined hierarchy and democratic committee system that allows broad participation in decision making. Social ties among employees are especially strong due to the presence of small employee "teams" and numerous company-sponsored extracurricular activities such as parties and sporting events. As I will show in some detail, the kinds of social control traditionally found in the workplace are uncommon at HelpCo (see also Tucker 1999). Moralism is rare and the degree of authoritativeness is low. Individual circumstances rather than rules guide the social control process, while condemnation and coercion are discouraged. Punishment is applied only to those lower ranking production workers who continually offend others. According to Blackian theory, this is not surprising. Relations at the

firm are relatively equal and close, conditions that are associated with therapy wherever it occurs.

Consider first how social control is initiated at HelpCo. More often than
not, recipients instigate the therapeutic process. The following comments
come from a HelpCo accounting manager who noted that several members
of his team have solicited his help over the years:

> I've had a number of people [on my team] come to me when they've had
> outside problems and tell me things like "I've been making a lot of mistakes the
> last couple of days and I'm not talking to people because of what's going on in
> my life." It's not as if they are making excuses. Sometimes I don't even know
> their performance is hurting. And whatever the issue is, it usually gets better
> when they come talk to me, although I may say very little.

Even when parties other than the recipient initiate therapy, the process is
strikingly nonauthoritative. A manager will normally pull an employee aside
in a private office and discuss the perceived problem at length. The following case, where a production worker was counseled for a general "attitude
problem," is typical. According to his supervisor, the worker "bad mouthed
virtually every decision that was made in this company." He also attracted
"poor performers, who would cry on his shoulders, and he would make
them feel better by telling them the company was unfair and that everyone
had it out for them." His supervisor and another manager eventually determined it would be useful to talk with the worker about his problems. As his
supervisor explained:

> We [the supervisor and other manager] told him what we thought was going
> on. . . . He evidently didn't know how we felt about him. Then just he and I
> talked. We discussed how he carries everyone else's problems around with
> him, which makes him feel important and some of the other workers feel good,
> but in the long run brings him down and hurts him. We met again a week later
> and he said he couldn't push away those people [who like to cry on his
> shoulder]. So he asked if he could be transferred to another group, which I
> arranged. Now he is doing better though I still think he likes getting attention in
> unhealthy ways, like stirring up trouble for the sake of it.

Supervisors at HelpCo may offer advice, but they rarely criticize people
or demand that they change. Consider the case of a young production
worker, who received counseling for continually "getting on the nerves" of
others. His supervisor understood the worker's problem as follows:

> He was one of those people who tried to be everybody's friend. He tried so
> hard he would fabricate stories. Someone would say I went fishing this week-
> end and caught five big bass, and he would say he went fishing and caught ten.
> After a while I knew he was lying, but he was trying so hard to be accepted. I

sat down with him, and this was kind of an emotional thing, I told him, "You've got to understand that if someone is going to be your friend, then they'll be your friend, but you can't make people be a friend. You can't buy a friend or lie about yourself to be accepted." He understood where I was coming from and although it took some time he's better now.

HelpCo's director of human relations often plays a role in the therapeutic process, counseling employees who are thought to need help. He has a private office that has the look and feel of a psychiatrist's office. A large couch fills much of the office and the walls are lined with bookshelves with selections by Freud, Rogers, and other well-known twentieth-century psychologists. When meeting with employees in his office, the human relations (HR) director often employs a modern psychotherapeutic technique known as "transactional analysis." This technique, which was most popular in America during the 1970s, is consensual, ultimately relying on offenders to discover their own problems and solutions. As the HR director states: "Once they verbalize the problem they are more than halfway home in terms of addressing what's bothering them." In one illustrative case, the HR director counseled an accountant, who was said to be "moody." According to the accountant's supervisor:

> You never knew from day-to-day whether he would be cooperative or nasty. Sometimes he would just give everybody the silent treatment. It drove me and everybody else crazy trying to figure out when he would be okay to talk to.

The supervisor eventually sought the HR director's assistance. After initially rejecting the idea, the accountant met with the HR director for about an hour one day late in the afternoon. He "opened up" and confessed that he was very insecure in his job. He felt like others knew more than he did and thus "sometimes got stressed out to the point where he didn't want to deal with anybody." According to the HR director, the accountant "felt better" simply by expressing his "feelings."

As the following case illustrates, however, therapy does not always resolve intrapersonal conflict. In this case, the HR director counseled a production worker who was having trouble communicating with his co-workers in the repair department. Again, the hope was that a solution would emerge if the parties could talk through the problem. Yet here the troubled employee was prone to silence. As the worker's supervisor explained:

> I couldn't figure out what was wrong with this guy. I would have to talk with him every day about something, anything to make him feel he was important. If I didn't, he would start stacking bricks up, start building this wall. So [then] I have to go talk to him and knock it down. But one time I neglected him for a while and the wall got so high he wouldn't even acknowledge me. He was completely turned off.

At this point the supervisor solicited the assistance of the HR director, who met briefly with the production worker during lunch time. The worker was not especially receptive, although he did agree to end his silence with his supervisor. According to his supervisor, the worker's future at HelpCo is in doubt: "I still have to be careful with him. It's funny, he's a good technician, he's smart, but his personality may end up ruining his career with us."

If the HelpCo HR director is unsuccessful addressing employee troubles, he may recommend professional therapeutic services. For example, shortly after her promotion to team leader, a young accounting manager allegedly started acting "bossy" and alienating her co-workers. She sought assistance from the HR director. During their first meeting she broke into tears, claiming that domestic troubles were negatively influencing her demeanor on the job. After several meetings, the HR director suggested a local psychiatrist, with whom the accountant has since met several times. She now "feels better" and refers to the time before she sought help as "back when I was acting all funny." A senior marketing employee was referred to professional help after being demoted from a management position and becoming, in his words, "extremely depressed." First, he met five times, for over an hour each meeting, with the HR director. After these counseling sessions, the HR director concluded that the employee's troubles were deeper and referred him to a psychologist. Although the demotion occurred 4 years before the research, the employee claims he is still getting over the effects of the event, which he says was a "personally devastating experience to go through." Nonetheless, he claims that because of professional help and "a lot of soul searching" he has experienced an "important psychological change" that allows him to function without many "leftover negative feelings." On another occasion, the HR director advised a female employee whose marital problems were determined to be affecting her work in the marketing department to attend a local support group where people with similar difficulties met weekly to console each other. And an accountant with an admitted drinking problem was directed to Alcoholics Anonymous.

Therapy appears in diverse companies other than HelpCo as well. Many larger American firms, for example, provide formal counseling services for their employees. The Employee Assistance Program, or EAP as it is commonly called, is especially popular. EAPs are typically administered by an organization's human resources department, whose members distribute information and offer therapy to employees thought to be experiencing "substance abuse" problems related to alcohol and illegal drugs (Trice and Sonnenstuhl 1990). The assumption is that alcoholism and drug abuse are diseases, and that people who are so afflicted are helped somewhat when they talk to others about their condition.

It is worth noting too that many corporations, including HelpCo, hire management consultants to address personnel problems. These consultants, some of whom are academics (Kunda 1992:78, note 16), usually have advanced training in psychology or a field known as "organizational behavior." When they intervene in corporate life, they operate much like therapists. They conduct employee surveys to determine how people feel about their jobs and co-workers, hold seminars on how to handle workplace stress, organize weekend retreats for employees to get to know each other outside the work setting, and counsel individual employees.

Private enterprises are increasingly compelled by the state to provide therapeutic services for its members. Most large corporations, for example, are legally required to make accommodations, and under some circumstances offer professional counseling, to employees officially diagnosed as mentally ill (Olson 1997). With the range of behavior classified as mental illness rapidly expanding (Davis 1997), some companies hire attorneys whose whole responsibility is ensuring compliance with the numerous mental health employment laws (Olson 1997). But therapy sponsored by the state is more authoritative than therapy provided voluntarily by organizations. Organizations often have little choice but to comply with demands of the new therapeutic laws. In fact, as the next section demonstrates, the state has a significant effect on therapy wherever it occurs. It influences both the likelihood of therapy and its degree of authoritativeness.

THERAPY AND THE STATE

Therapy in its purest, least authoritative form occurs beyond the reaches of the state, among socially close equals. The involvement of the government in the social control process introduces inequality and social distance, features conducive to punishment rather than therapy. Nonetheless, state therapy does occur. Consistent with Blackian theory, it is more authoritative than when it appears without the government. Governments put people in institutions and asylums, restrict their freedom, and subject them to coercive therapies, often physical (see Goffman 1961; Szasz 1961). Because centralized governments are the most superior and socially distant from citizens (Black 1995:151), they have the most state-run mental hospitals and the harshest treatments (see Fireside 1979). Therapy is also more formalistic when the government is involved in the therapeutic process. Mental disorders are named, psychiatric categories created, and patients classified and labeled (see Scheff 1966).

Because the superiority of the state is declining, especially in democratic societies, the most authoritative forms of therapy are less common today.

Asylums, for example, are disappearing, as are lobotomies and electric-shock treatments. At the same time, less authoritative forms of state therapy are becoming more commonplace. For instance, most western governments have large bureaucracies run by professionals who have the authority to intervene in the mental lives of citizens. In the United States, "human service" agencies—including child welfare departments, vocational rehabilitation centers, homeless shelters, public assistance departments, and drug rehabilitation centers—treat millions of people a year who are thought to be experiencing mental difficulties (Polsky 1991; Nolan 1998).

According to Blackian theory, inequality and distance not only increase the authoritativeness of social control, but also increase the likelihood that it will be applied according to the logic of "collective liability" (Black 1984a:12, note 12; Senechal de la Roche 1996:116). Collective liability occurs when members of a group or social category are held accountable for the actions of others (Black 1984a:3). Thus, distant parties, including states, sometimes apply social control to anyone or everyone who is a member of a racial, religious, or other group. Whereas modern American criminal law always follows the logic of individual liability, therapy is sometimes applied collectively by the state. In the aftermath of a several widely publicized school shootings in the late 1990s, for example, the government took a series of actions that operated on the assumption that all school children in the country—not just those who shoot their classmates—are suffering from stress and related mental conditions. Counseling programs were implemented, task forces created, and research centers established to study the "pressures" facing children in today's world. Similarly, a series of racial incidents during the 1990s resulted in the government sponsoring a "President's Initiative on Race." In this case, the state determined that all Americans (especially whites), whether they knew it or not, had racist attitudes and thoughts. The cure was to have people admit to their racial prejudices and then talk with others about how to overcome their racism. A "national dialogue on race" was initiated and "town meetings" were held across the country for this purpose.

Blackian theory also predicts that state therapy varies across cases within a society. According to the theory, those who are closest to the government (in terms of wealth, social distance, and so on) should be the most likely recipients of state therapy. Evidence is supportive. For example, law directed at wealthy people is more likely to be therapeutic than law directed at those of lower status (Black 1976:29–30; Horwitz 1990:84–86). Likewise, members of dominant cultural groups are more frequently subject to state therapy than are cultural minorities (Horwitz 1990:82–83). The socially disadvantaged, including lower class minorities, are vulnerable to punishment. If they subject to therapy, it is apt to be authoritative. Thus, American mental hospitals became more custodial (like prisons) over the course of the nineteenth century with the increase in the proportion of foreign-born patients—who were socially remote and mostly poor (Grob 1973). Moreover, in contemporary America, lower status mental patients are more likely than higher status patients to be committed involuntarily to mental hospitals (Linsky 1970).

The fact that young people are more likely to be subject to state therapy (Horwitz 1990:90–94) would seem to contradict the pattern just described—that higher status people tend to attract more state therapy. But the kind of therapy applied to juveniles is often quite authoritative. Juveniles are unwillingly placed in rehabilitation centers that combine therapy and punishment. Moreover, the pattern identified above holds among juveniles: Lower class juveniles are treated more authoritatively by the state than middle and upper class juveniles (Reiman 1997:Ch. 3).

CONCLUSION

Although modern American government is sometimes called a "therapeutic state" (Polsky 1991; Nolan 1998), it is strongly moralistic under certain circumstances. For example, foreign states and citizens are never treated therapeutically. This is because the social structure of intergovernmental relations is not conducive to therapy. States often have ties to each other, but their relationships are usually characterized by a certain degree of distance, which produces moralism. Unilateral measures such as trade embargoes, deportations, and violent attacks are likely when the distances between states are greatest. We might therefore conclude that it is inappropriate to speak of the therapeutic state. As Blackian theory demonstrates, we must look beyond the characteristics of the party initiating social control (such as the state) in order to predict the degree of moralism. This means that moralism is not a characteristic of persons, organizations, states, or any single actor of any kind. It depends on the social structure of each case—the amount of inequality and social distance between the parties (Black 1995:852–858). The same applies to therapy: No person or group is therapeutic all the time. In this sense, the therapeutic state, as a reified concept, does not exist.

ACKNOWLEDGMENTS

I would like to thank Donald Black, Mark Cooney, Roberta Senchal de la Roche, and James Chriss for helpful comments on a previous draft.

REFERENCES

Black, Donald. 1976. *The Behavior of Law*. New York: Academic Press.

Black, Donald. 1984a. "Crime as Social Control." Pp. 1–27 in *Toward a General Theory of Social Control*, Vol. 2: *Selected Problems*, edited by D. Black. Orlando: Academic Press.

Black, Donald. 1984b. "Social Control as a Dependent Variable." Pp. 1–35 in *Toward a General Theory of Social Control*, Vol. 1: *Fundamentals*, edited by D. Black. Orlando: Academic Press.

Black, Donald. 1990. "The Elementary Forms of Conflict Management." Pp. 43–69 in *New Directions in the Study of Justice, Law, and Social Control*, prepared by the School of Justice Studies, Arizona State University. New York: Plenum Press.

Black, Donald. 1993. *The Social Structure of Right and Wrong*. San Diego: Academic Press.

Black, Donald. 1995. "The Epistemology of Pure Sociology." *Law and Social Inquiry* 20:829–870.

Brown, Michael F. 1997. *The Channeling Zone: American Spirituality in an Anxious Age*. Cambridge, MA: Harvard University Press.

Clements, Forrest E. 1932. "Primitive Concepts of Disease." *University of California Publications in American Archeology and Ethnology* 32:185–252.

Davis, L. J. 1997. "The Encyclopedia of Insanity: A Psychiatric Handbook Lists a Madness for Everyone." *Harper's Magazine* Febuary:61–66.

Fireside, Harvey. 1979. *Soviet Psychoprisons*. New York: Norton.

Frank, Jerome D. 1973. *Persuasion and Healing*, 2nd ed. Baltimore: John Hopkins University Press.

Garrison, V. 1977. "Doctor, Espiritista, or Psychiatrists? Health Seeking Behavior in a Puerto Rico Neighborhood of New York City." *Medical Anthropology* 1 (entire issue).

Goffman, Erving. 1961. *Asylums: Essays on the Social Situation of Mental Patients and Other Inmates*. Garden City, NY: Anchor Books.

Grob, Gerald N. 1973. *Mental Institutions in America: Social Policy to 1875*. New York: Free Press.

Horwitz, Allan V. 1984. "Therapy and Social Solidarity." Pp. 211–250 in *Toward a General Theory of Social Control*, Vol. 1: *Fundamentals*, edited by D. Black. Orlando: Academic Press.

Horwitz, Allan V. 1990. *The Logic of Social Control*. New York: Plenum Press.

Hunt, Morton. 1993. *The Story of Psychology*. New York: Doubleday.

Kanter, Rosabeth Moss. 1972. *Commitment and Community*. Cambridge: Cambridge University Press.

Kephart, William M. 1976. *Extraordinary Groups: The Sociology of Unconventional Life-Styles*. New York: St. Martin's Press.

Kiev, Ari (ed.) 1972. *Transcultural Psychiatry*. New York: Free Press.

Kramer, Peter D. 1993. *Listening to Prozac: A Psychiatrist Explores Psychiatric Drugs and the Remaking of the Self*. New York: Viking.

Kunda, Gideon. 1992. *Engineering Culture: Control and Commitment in a High-Tech Corporation*. Philadelphia: Temple University Press.

Lifton, Robert Jay. 1961. *Thought Reform and the Psychology of Totalism.* New York: Norton.

Lin, T., K. Tardiff, G. Donetz and W. Goresky. 1978. "Ethnicity and Patterns of Help Seeking." *Culture, Medicine, and Psychiatry* 2:3–14.

Linsky, Arnold S. 1970. "Who Shall Be Excluded?: The Influence of Personal Attributes in Community Reaction to the Mentally Ill." *Social Psychiatry* 5:166–171.

Murphy, Jane M. 1964. "Psychotherapeutic Aspects of Shamanism on St. Lawrence, Alaska." Pp. 53-83 in *Magic, Faith, and Healing,* edited by A. Kiev. Glencoe: Free Press.

Nolan, James L., Jr. 1998. *The Therapeutic State: Justifying Government at Century's End.* New York: New York University Press.

Olson, Walter K. 1997. *The Excuse Factory: How Employment Law Is Paralyzing the American Workplace.* New York: Martin Kessler.

Ouchi, William. 1981. *Theory Z: How American Business Can Meet the Japanese Challenge.* New York: Addison-Wesley.

Polsky, Andrew J. 1991. *The Rise of the Therapeutic State.* Princeton: Princeton University Press.

Reiman, Jeffrey H. 1997. *The Rich Get Richer and The Poor Get Prison: Ideology, Class, and Criminal Justice,* 5th ed. New York: Allyn and Bacon.

Robertson, Constance Noyes (ed.) 1970. *Oneida Community: An Autobiography, 1851-1876.* Syracuse: Syracuse University Press.

Rohlen, Thomas P. 1974. *For Harmony and Strength: Japanese White-Collar Organization in Anthropological Perspective.* Berkeley: University of California Press.

Scheff, Thomas. 1966. *Becoming Mentally Ill.* Hawthorne, NY: Aldine de Gruyter.

Senechal de la Roche, Roberta. 1996. "Collective Violence as Social Control." *Sociological Forum* 11:97–128.

Szasz, Thomas S. 1961. *The Myth of Mental Illness: The Foundations of a Theory of Personal Conduct.* New York: Harper.

Trice, Harrison M. and William J. Sonnenstuhl. 1990. "Alcohol and Mental Health Programs in the Workplace." *Research in Community and Mental Health* 6:351–378.

Tucker, James. 1998. "Therapy and the Supernatural." Unpublished paper, Department of Sociology, University of New Hampshire, Durham, New Hampshire.

Tucker, James. 1999. *The Therapeutic Corporation.* New York: Oxford University Press.

van Maanen, John. 1992. "Drinking Our Troubles Away: Managing Conflict in a British Police Agency." Pp. 32–62 in *Hidden Conflict in Organizations: Uncovering Behind-the-Scenes Disputes,* edited by D. M. Kolb and J. M. Bartunek. Newbury Park: Sage.

Zablocki, Benjamin. 1971. *The Joyful Community.* Baltimore: Penguin.

The Institutionalization and Deinstitutionalization of the Mentally Ill: Lessons from Goffman   5

Philip Manning

INTRODUCTION

The aim of this chapter is to clarify several strands of Goffman's thinking concerning mental illness, the total institution, and deinstitutionalization. To do so, I will have to retrace an argument through his work, restoring complexity to it. Once Goffman's position has been clarified, I will consider its role in his overall work, particularly with regard to his analysis of what he called the "interaction order" (Goffman 1983b).

Erving Goffman is widely recognized as one of the most influential critics of the institutional treatment of the mentally ill. Based in part on his observations of St. Elizabeth's hospital in Washington, D.C. during 1955–1956, Goffman's *Asylums* (1961) documented the oppressive and threatening conditions of one mental hospital, and by extension, of all closed organizations, which he referred to as *total institutions* (see also Davis 1989; Delaney 1977). Everett Hughes had first proposed this suggestive phrase in lectures at the University of Chicago (Burns 1992:142).

Goffman recognized the comparative power of this idea, although it is doubtful that he understood how pervasive it would become; indeed it is now a central concept in the vocabulary of twentieth-century social science. The success of *Asylums* crossed academic disciplines and national borders. It is assigned reading for many university courses and has been widely translated. The second chapter of *Asylums*, which was initially published in *Psychiatry*, has since been reprinted 33 times, ironically, more than any other paper in the history of that journal. Goffman's arguments have also been used as evidence in legal proceedings (Weinstein 1994:349).

The wide audience for *Asylums* has led some commentators to suggest that it had some definite impact on the plight of the institutionalized mentally ill. Specifically, it has been suggested that his work helped initiate the program of deinstitutionalization that reduced the inmate population of American mental hospitals from a high of 559,000 in 1955 to their present levels of around 110,000 (Mechanic and Rochefort 1990:301).

However, to attribute a direct connection between Goffman's *Asylums* and the social policy of deinstitutionalization is, as has been forcefully argued elsewhere, far too strong a claim (Gronfein 1992; Mechanic and Rochefort 1990; Scull 1984, 1989; Weinstein 1994). As has been demonstrated statistically, the process of deinstitutionalization began at about the same time as Goffman first started his research, and hence he could not be held responsible for a chain of events that had already begun. As Mechanic (1989:148) put it, "Goffman's work had only a subsidiary role in the massive changes in mental health policy," although he immediately added that *Asylums* was "as influential as any theoretical statement or study can hope to be."

It is also important to consider that there were powerful groups whose interests were well served by the deinstitutionalization of the mentally ill, and for them Goffman was simply ammunition in a battle that had already begun (Scull 1984, 1989). Scull (1989:265) has argued forcefully that the driving force behind deinstitutionalization was fiscal constraint:

> For the mentally ill, at least, states have been only too willing to grant the negative right to be left alone, to be free from the obvious coercion that involuntary hospitalization represents. Neglect, after all, is cheaper than care.

According to Scull's account, Goffman's ideas did not bring about a social policy of deinstitutionalization; rather they were used to justify and defend such a policy. Used in this way, Goffman's significance was not as an innovative thinker but as a quasimember of the "antipsychiatry" school, and his ideas were thought to be in line with those of Laing, Szasz, and Foucault, among others (see also Sedgwick 1982 and Weinstein 1994:349). As Mechanic and Rochefort (1990:304) put it, Goffman was seen as an advocate of community health and as such a defender of federal policy. Clearly, when seen as just a representative of a school, the singularity of Goffman's thought is lost.

GOFFMAN'S ACCOUNT OF MENTAL ILLNESS

In assessing Goffman's account of mental illness, it is important to recognize that his work primarily addressed four interwoven issues. These were an account of the nature of mental illness, criticisms of psychiatry, criticisms of the institutional treatment of the mentally ill, and an assessment of the merits of deinstitutionalization. In addition, he offered reflections on the career trajectories of psychiatrists and a more sustained investigation of the psychiatrist–client relationship. With the exception of the last of these issues, Goffman rarely treated them as discrete topics of inquiry, with the result that the apparent lightness of his prose often disguised a dense thicket of observations, reflections, analyses, and complaints with several intended targets.

There are other reasons for being cautious in assessing Goffman's account of mental illness. Part of the difficulty in clarifying his views is that mental illness was of recurring interest to him, with the result that he wrote about various aspects of it throughout his career. The result of this is that any attempt to reconstruct his "general understanding" of the problem requires disparate materials written at different points in his career to be integrated into a single account, and this can violate the content or probable intent of particular texts. Second, as mentioned above, Goffman often conflated ideas that would have been clearer if allowed to stand separately. Thus, many important passages contain references to, among other things, his understanding of the nature of mental illness, criticisms of psychiatry, ironic commentary about psychiatrists, and hints at his overall sociological intentions. The result is that the relevant passages in Goffman's work successfully convey a tone of dissatisfaction but they rarely provide a concise, discrete, reasoned position. This has allowed a plethora of commentators to respond to Goffman in quite different ways. Finally, despite Goffman's general willingness to footnote every twist and turn of his sociological arguments (in fact his references make fascinating reading by themselves, and offer a glimpse of his *modus operandi*), Goffman rarely footnoted key claims concerning his understanding of psychiatry and mental illness. As a result, it can be difficult to substantiate or clarify some of the positions that he presented elliptically.

Nevertheless, a coherent position regarding mental illness does emerge from his work. Goffman stated quite clearly that he believed that some specific mental illnesses were caused by biological problems (1961:313–316; 1963:235–236; 1971:335–336). He routinely referred to these as "organic" mental illnesses, and he believed them to be the proper domain of medicine. After having determined that a particular episode involved organic mental illness, he rarely if ever continued to discuss it. It is as if he considered these cases to be protected from sociological commentary (for example, see Goffman 1961:316). His willingness to provide such protection has been the subject of critical commentary by Sedgwick (1982).

It is also clear that Goffman thought the majority of cases seen by psychiatrists—perhaps the overwhelming majority of cases—did not involve a diagnosis of organic mental illness. Instead, he believed that they involved "functional" mental illness, and his use of the term in context indicated that he believed that he was following an established, although unreferenced, psychiatric vocabulary. Functional mental illness was not diagnosed by medical test but by the disclosure of inappropriate behavior. Early in his career Goffman began referring to different types of inappropriate behavior as *situational improprieties* (1963:23–24; 1967:142). It is not clear whether Goffman thought that some kinds of situational impropriety might be symptoms of an underlying organic disease, or whether the situational impropriety was the problem itself.

Whether or not a class of situational improprieties betrays an underlying disease, Goffman did acknowledge that there was a distinction, albeit a conceptually difficult one, between "symptomatic situational improprieties" and "non-symptomatic situational improprieties." The latter is easier to identify than the former. Clearly, there are various kinds of situational improprieties that do not suggest that the person performing them is mentally ill. Rather, there is an available public explanation for the delict: perhaps the person does not understand what he or she is expected to do, is tired, drunk, joking, arrogant, selfish, or so on. In each case the situational impropriety can be recognized as inappropriate behavior without an accompanying attribution of mental illness. By contrast, a person exhibiting a symptomatic situational impropriety both acts in an inappropriate way and does so such that other observers, both lay and professional, cannot supply an accompanying explanation that condemns the misconduct but affirms the sanity of the norm-violator. Goffman (1961:145) made this point in *Asylums* with regard to the construction of medical case histories:

> The events recorded in the case history are, then, just the sort that a layman would consider scandalous, defamatory, and discrediting. I think it is fair to say that all levels of mental hospital staff fail, in general, to deal with this material with the moral neutrality claimed for medical statements and psychiatric diagnosis, but instead participate, by intonation and gesture if by no other means, in the lay reaction to these acts.

Goffman tried at different times to explain the strangeness of behavior through the metaphor of language, suggesting that everyday behavior has a "grammar" and a "syntax," whereas the behavior of the mentally ill is "ungrammatical." Symptomatic situational improprieties defeat all efforts at interpretation until designated as symptoms of mental illness. For example, in *Asylums* he noted that "self-insulation [from the symbolic implications of the hospital setting] may be so difficult that patients have to employ devices for this which staff [presumably falsely] interpret as psychotic symptoms" (Goffman 1961:139, footnote 30).

In one of his last papers, Goffman (1983a) returned to this issue, invoking the work of the Oxford philosopher John Austin to suggest that the actions of the mentally ill fail to meet "Felicity's Condition." The connection Goffman made here to ordinary language philosophy ties into his earlier ideas about the grammaticality of behavior, as Austin's (1961) work on speech acts used the notion of the felicitous condition to explain how people make sense of what other people say. Related to this, Felicity's Condition describes those circumstances in which no sense can be made of a person's actions. Thus, anyone who does not demonstrate Felicity's Condition does not demonstrate his or her sanity.

These ideas framed Goffman's understanding of the legitimacy of psychiatry. Goffman suggested that if psychiatry is to have a scientific understanding of functional mental illness, psychiatrists must explain how they are able to distinguish symptomatic and nonsymptomatic situational improprieties. He believed that, as of the mid-1960s, psychiatrists were not even close to being able to do this. Instead, Goffman (1961:322) suggested, psychiatrists appealed to their clinical experience, and by so doing merely invoked lay standards of mental illness:

> while psychiatric knowledge often cannot place the psychiatrist in a position to predict the patient's conduct correctly, the same nescience provides the psychiatrist with interpretive leeway: by adding posthoc qualifications and adumbrations of his analyses, the psychiatrist can provide a picture of what has been happening with the patient that can no more be disproved than proved. . . . To this authority that cannot be discredited, the psychiatrist can add a force derived from tradition, "clinical experience." Through this magical quality, the formally qualified person of longest experience with the type of case in question is accorded the final word when there is doubt or ambiguity, this person also being apt to be the ranking practitioner present.

Goffman is not conciliatory here: psychiatry is a "nescience" that lacks a biological understanding of mental illness, is unable to predict the behavior of patients, and hides behind vague formulations that cannot be disproved. These sins of omission are themselves wrapped in the language of clinical experience that has a "magical quality" rather than a scientific content. Another example, also from *Asylums*, is instructive:

> there is a still more fundamental issue, which hinges on the applicability of the concept of "pathology." Ordinarily the pathology which first draws attention to the patient's condition is conduct that is "inappropriate to the situation." But the decision as to whether a given act is appropriate or inappropriate must often necessarily be a lay decision, simply because we have no technical mapping of the various behavioral subcultures in our society, let alone the standards of conduct prevailing in each of them. Diagnostic decisions, except for extreme symptoms, can become ethnocentric, the server judging from his own culture's point of view individuals' conduct that can really be judged only from the perspective of the group from which they derive (Goffman 1961:316–317).

It is interesting to note that much of Goffman's own work about "unremarkable" conduct in public settings was an attempt to provide part of this "technical mapping." It is only by understanding the constraints operating in the "interaction order," that is, in the ordinary circumstances of face-to-face interaction, that the behavior of the mentally ill can be properly understood to be inappropriate. Goffman (1963:232) pointed to this in *Behavior in Public Places*:

> the sociologist might find cause to nibble at the psychiatric hand that feeds him data. For while psychiatry forcibly directs our attention to situational improprieties, there appears to be ways in which psychiatry embodies and rationalizes lay attitudes toward this aspect of conduct, instead of carrying us beyond these conceptions.

On several occasions, often in the context of a discussion of Garfinkel's ideas, Goffman mentioned that one of the goals of research in this area should be to learn to "program insanity" (for example, Goffman 1974:5). Without this knowledge, psychiatric knowledge about the symptoms of mental illness and lay opinions about mental illness are too closely connected.

This observation relates to one of the controversial arguments underlying Goffman's ethnographic study of St. Elizabeth's, namely, that most of the situational improprieties exhibited by mental patients in the hospital were nonsymptomatic. For the most part, Goffman claimed, the apparently strange actions of patients were understandable "secondary adjustments" to an oppressive and threatening environment. Goffman (1961:172) defined a secondary adjustment as anything people learn to do to get around what the institution thinks they should do and hence what they should be. If patients were making secondary adjustments, their behavior made sense and hence was not symptomatic of mental illness. And, as Goffman argued in the first essay of *Asylums*, many examples of these secondary adjustments could be found in other kinds of total institutions as well. In the third essay, Goffman (1961:303) was quite explicit about this, arguing that it is "presumptuous" to assume either that the mentally ill are "ill" or that they are even at one end of a continuum of normal behavior. Rather, he suggested, "a community is a community" and the actions of patients are simply examples of "human association." As will be discussed shortly, Goffman implicitly claimed in these passages to have a better understanding of mental illness than that of psychiatrists. This claim places a special burden on ethnographic observation to prove that its understanding of mental illness is superior to that of psychiatry.

In addition, and just as controversially, Goffman claimed that nearly all the behavior exhibited by patients at St. Elizabeth's (except that on the "back wards") could also be observed in other total institutions, such as military barracks, prisons, monasteries, and boarding schools. In settings other than the mental hospital, inmate behavior is rarely interpreted—that is, diagnosed—

as mental illness. This theme recurs throughout Goffman's (1961:269) work on total institutions:

> Acts of hostility against the institution have to rely on limited, ill-designed devices, such as banging a chair against the floor or striking a sheet of newspaper sharply so as to make an annoying explosive sound. And the more inadequate this equipment is to convey rejection of the hospital, the more the act appears as a psychotic symptom, and the more likely management feels justified in assigning the patient to a bad ward.

And as Goffman (1961:269) went on to say:

> When a patient finds himself in seclusion, naked and without visible means of expression, he may have to rely on tearing up his mattress, if he can, or writing with faeces on the wall—actions management takes to be in keeping with the kind of person who warrants seclusion.

The same line of inquiry is pursued in the third essay of *Asylums*. Goffman (1961:186) summarized this point nicely:

> From the point of view of psychiatric doctrine, apparently, there are no secondary adjustments possible for inmates: everything a patient is caused to do can be described as a part of his treatment or of custodial management; everything a patient does on his own can be defined as symptomatic of his disorder or of his convalescence . . . a patient who settles down in the hospital, making a good thing of it, may be felt not to be abusing a place of treatment but to be really ill since he elects this adaptation.

What is easily recognized as a tone of dissatisfaction in Goffman's writings can now emerge as a reasoned and poignant critique of the work of psychiatrists: Goffman's argument is that with the exception of organic mental illness, psychiatrists primarily diagnose functional mental illness, that is, they identify situational improprieties. Since it is patently false that all situational improprieties indicate mental illness, psychiatrists must claim to have a way of knowing which improprieties are symptomatic and which are not. This requires a "technical mapping" of the kind mentioned by Goffman above. In the absence of a technical mapping, or in the absence of a protocol for distinguishing symptomatic and nonsymptomatic situational improprieties, psychiatrists are often doing little more than applying a technical vocabulary to lay ideas and opinions. As Goffman (1967:138) put it in *Interaction Ritual*, "Psychiatrists have failed to provide us with a systematic framework for identifying and describing the type of delict represented by psychotic behavior." Goffman (1963:232) also made this point in *Behavior in Public Places*:

At present, the psychiatrist who carries an appreciable load of diagnostic and commitment work in an office tends to give weight to his own spontaneous response to the conduct of the individual to whom he is giving a diagnostic interview, and it is largely in terms of this response that the psychiatrist decides whether the behavior of the subject is appropriate or inappropriate in the situation. If the behavior is inappropriate, he decides whether it is to be placed in one of the nonsymptomatic classes of situational impropriety, or whether it betokens mental illness. In this, of course, he is acting somewhat like a layman, however expert his analysis of the psychodynamic implications of a particular impropriety, because while everyone in the society also makes these distinctions, there is no great consensus, especially in regard to the milder offenses, as to how the distinction should be applied.

The inadequacy of psychiatric diagnosis—even the perception of inadequacy—threatens psychiatry's disciplinary legitimacy. Perhaps it is not by chance that its knowledge claims are more often debated in courtroom proceedings than in scientific settings. Goffman argued that there was a gaping discrepancy between what psychiatrists and other mental health professionals said about what they did in mental hospitals and what they actually did in mental hospitals. In fact, the existence of discrepancies between accounts and actions is the best and basic justification for all ethnographic research.

According to Goffman, the absence of a formal way of distinguishing symptomatic and nonsymptomatic situational improprieties produced three problems: the conflation of custodial and therapeutic roles, the invisibility of secondary adjustments, and the decontextualization of the meaning of the patients' actions. Goffman described the conflation of custodial roles by drawing a distinction between "people-work" and "object-work." In *Asylums* Goffman (1961:73) wrote:

> Many total institutions, most of the time, seem to function merely as storage dumps for inmates, but . . . they usually present themselves to the public as rational organizations designed unconsciously, through and through, as effective machines for producing a few officially avowed and officially approved ends.

Writing a decade later, Goffman (1971:336) reaffirmed this thought, suggesting in "The Insanity of Place" (an essay from *Relations in Public*) that the mental patient's "deal" was "grotesque," an adjective that he earlier used in *Asylums* (1961:321) when analyzing the psychiatrist-patient relationship.

The first essay of *Asylums* contains a tone of moral outrage that is masked by the studied neutrality of its prose. For example, in discussing the impossibility of presenting solitary confinement as a medical treatment, Goffman noted that psychiatrists had renamed this punishment, designating it instead "constructive meditation" (1961:82). He also noted that in the interests of administrative efficiency, some mental hospitals "have found it useful to extract the teeth of 'biters', give hysterectomies to promiscuous female pa-tients, and perform lobotomies on chronic fighters" (1961:77). Goffman's outrage is controlled, and his observations of the mistreatment of patients are presented in a flat tone and often as an aside. Cumulatively, they support his description of total institutions as "forcing houses for changing persons; each is a natural experiment on what can be done to the self" (1961:22). The experiment reveals what can be done "to the self," as a form of control, and not "for the self," as a form of treatment.

Goffman claimed that psychiatrists had little more than a lay understand-ing of the difference between symptomatic and nonsymptomatic situational improprieties. As a result, any effort by a patient to make a secondary adjustment to St. Elizabeth's was likely to be understood symptomatically. As Goffman noted, from "the point of view of psychiatric doctrine, appar-ently, there are no secondary adjustments possible for inmates . . . every-thing a patient does on his own can be defined as symptomatic of his disorder" (1961:186). From Goffman's sociological point of view, all sec-ondary adjustments are nonsymptomatic situational improprieties, since they can be understood as rational attempts to protect oneself from a threat-ening and humiliating environment, and hence they are not properly the concern of the psychiatrist.

However, Goffman's willingness to interpret patients' actions non-symptomatically sometimes led him either to stretch credibility or to claim special access to a patient's intentions. For example, in *Asylums* Goffman (1961:121) made the very general claim that "the craziness or 'sick behav-ior' claimed for the mental patient is by and large a product of the claimant's social distance from the situation that the patient is in, and is not primarily a product of mental illness." It is reasonable to ask how Goffman knows that this behavior is *not* the product of mental illness, unless he has the kind of knowledge that elsewhere he suggested that psychiatrists lack and need. Similarly, in *Behavior in Public Places*, Goffman (1963:224–225) noted:

> At Central Hospital I have observed an otherwise well-demeaned (albeit mute) youth walking down the ward halls with a reasonably thoughtful look on his face and two pipes in his mouth . . . another with a ball of paper screwed into his right eye as a monocle. . . . As already suggested, this situational self-sabotage often seems to represent one statement in an equation of defense. It seems that the patient sometimes feels that life on the ward is so degrading, so unjust, and so inhuman that the only self-respecting response is to treat ward life as if it were contemptibly beyond reality and beyond seriousness. . . . In short, the patient may pointedly act crazy in the hospital to make clear to all decent people that he is obviously sane.

And also (Goffman 1963:225):

The aim, then, of some of these bizarre acts is, no doubt, to demonstrate some kind of distance and insulation from the setting, and behind this, alienation from the establishment.

In fact, Goffman has no way to justify the claim that he knows what these various actions mean without claiming to possess the kind of knowledge that elsewhere he claimed no one has. This means that his inclusion of the phrase "no doubt" above was either ironic self-criticism or misplaced emphasis for an unwarranted claim. It is possible that Goffman's use of irony was not simply a way of portraying his detachment; rather, it allowed him to hint that he possessed a special and superior understanding of mental illness (although for another view of Goffman's use of irony, see Fine and Martin 1990:106–109). There is a subtext to much of Goffman's work on mental illness that implicitly suggests that ethnography-based sociology is, to play on one of Wittgenstein's ideas (1958, para. 97), a "super-psychiatry" whose understanding of mental illness is far superior to its poor relation and predecessor, psychiatry. And ironically, the justification for Goffman's claim to understand what motivates mental patients when they perform "bizarre acts" is comparable to the justification used by psychiatrists, namely, observation and experience. Goffman is therefore guilty of what Woolgar and Pawluch (1985) refer to as "ontological gerrymandering." At various points, Goffman claimed—albeit implicitly—to speak from a privileged space from which he could see the "truth" about mental illness. But at no point did he, or could he, justify this claim.

This issue is related to Goffman's frequent complaint that psychiatrists decontextualize their patients' behavior. This is because Goffman's implicit claim to possess a superpsychiatry was based on his ability to recontextualize patients' behavior, an action that he thought transformed our understanding of it: once symptoms have been recontextualized, most hospital-based improprieties can be properly understood as defensive measures, that is, as nonsymptomatic actions. However, Goffman (1961:316) also acknowledged that to recontextualize a patient's behavior fully, it would be necessary to consider all aspects of his or her life outside the hospital:

First, we must see that the discreteness of the entity in which the disorder exists is questionable. True, in cases that are organic in character, the patient encloses within himself the world in which the damage is felt and the world in which repairs, if possible, can be made. This is not so in instances of functional psychosis. In so far as the patient's symptomatic behavior is an integral part of his interpersonal situation, the server would have to import this whole situation into the hospital in order to observe the patient's difficulty and to treat it.

However, the psychiatrist is influenced by a medical model of mental illness that is itself based on the decontextualization of symptoms. That is, insofar as psychiatrists are first and foremost physicians, it is reasonable to expect them to adhere to a view of symptoms that is common among the broad medical profession. To do otherwise would only accentuate the already pronounced difference between psychiatry and other medical specialties. As Goffman (1961:321) put it:

> The limited applicability of the medical model to mental hospitals brings together a doctor who cannot easily afford to construe his activity in other than medical terms and a patient who may well feel he must fight and hate his keepers if any sense is to be made of the hardship he is undergoing. Mental hospitals institutionalize a kind of grotesque of the service relationship.

It would be easy to interpret the cumulative effect of Goffman's arguments as indicating support for deinstitutionalization. If mental hospitals were or perhaps still are as bad as he made them out to be, how could a "community" alternative be any worse? At the beginning of "The Insanity of Place" Goffman (1971:336) appeared to subscribe to this point of view: "Given the life still enforced in most mental hospitals and the stigma still placed on mental illness, the philosophy of community containment seems the only desirable one." Nevertheless, even this endorsement was tempered by his use of the word "seems." It also raises questions about who benefits from deinstitutionalization, what are the kinds of available benefit and what kinds of "community" and "containment" are waiting for ex-patients on their release.

Goffman had earlier argued that mental hospitals exist mainly to ease everyday life for ordinary citizens who would rather not be bothered by the unpredictable outbursts of the mentally ill, and to assist the various personnel who administer to and process those who disrupt the social order. At the end of *Asylums* Goffman (1961:334) made exactly this observation:

> Nor in citing the limitations of the service model do I mean to claim that I can suggest some better way of handling persons called mental patients. Mental hospitals are not found in our society because supervisors, psychiatrists, and attendants want jobs; mental hospitals are found because there is a market for them. If all the mental hospitals in a given region were emptied and closed down today, tomorrow relatives, police, and judges would raise a clamour for new ones; and these true clients of the mental hospital would demand an institution to satisfy their needs.

To which he added: "Mental patients find themselves crushed by the weight of a service ideal that eases life for the rest of us" (1961:336).

In *Behavior in Public Places* Goffman continued this thought, suggesting that one goal of psychiatry is to "protect the sanctity of the social occasion and the sentiments of the participants" (1963:235). In fact this book ended with a similar comment, an often quoted remark that asylums exist primarily to protect our gatherings and occasions (1963:248). If, then, the "true client" of the mental hospital is not the patient but just about everybody else, then community treatment is unlikely to be successful.

Goffman only hinted at the difficulty of implementing community treatment. Research since Goffman's death has presented a fuller picture of the dismal circumstances facing ex-mental patients, both in the United States and elsewhere. Indeed, in a poignant reversal of fortune, the new social movements advocating hospitalization had often been initiated by patients themselves (see Barham 1992).

Goffman's "The Insanity of Place" is a long essay devoted to an investigation of social interaction in families in which one person is mentally ill. It is now clear (see Winkin 1988, 1999, forthcoming) that this essay contains reflections about tensions in his own family. Given the extraordinary detachment of much of his prose, "The Insanity of Place" is striking for its poignant personal insights into these day-to-day familial difficulties. However, as a statement of the general predicament of the ex-patient, it is of only limited interest, because it concerns the situation of an affluent patient returning to a caring family, and clearly most ex-patients are not so fortunate.

THE ROLE OF GOFFMAN'S ANALYSIS OF MENTAL ILLNESS IN HIS OVERALL SOCIOLOGY

Although Goffman's concerns were primarily sociological, it has been possible to reconstruct his account of mental illness because of his stubbornness: Goffman often failed to heed John Clausen's initial advice to avoid "junior psychiatry" and stick to sociology (see the preface to *Asylums*, p. 8). Goffman's main concerns were thoroughly sociological, but these were at times obscured by his wide-ranging arguments. It is necessary, then, to fell some trees in order to see the forest.

Undoubtedly, his experiences at St. Elizabeth's fueled his suspicions about the inadequate treatment of the mentally ill, and this is responsible for the almost pervasive, if subtle, tone of the text, which varies from moral indignation to outright condemnation. As Fine and Martin (1990:110) put it:

> We read *Asylums* as a political tract, aimed, in part, at unmasking the "fraud" of mental hospitals and psychiatric practice. It does not aim to demean individuals, but it does take on this system and those elements of the outside world that are being convenienced by the existence of the system.

I want to suggest that Goffman's account of mental illness should be understood to exist at the intersection of two distinct ideas and projects. The first project is the realization of an empirical, comparative program of research based on Hughes' invention of the term "total institution." Hughes had initially discussed total institutions in the context of nunneries (see Burns 1992:142). It is instructive to keep this in mind, as it clearly separates Goffman's later study from its immediate physical setting at St. Elizabeth's, and indeed from the general question of the appropriate characterization of mental illness.

To realize Hughes' embryonic research program, Goffman had to construct a new genre of ethnographic research (see Goffman 1989). It required him to replace the traditional idea of ethnography as case study with a new model in which there are ethnographies of concepts rather than ethnographies of places (see Manning 1992). In a sense, Goffman was an important precursor to grounded theory, as I have suggested elsewhere (Manning 1999).

A major part of the study of total institutions is (1) an attempt to uncover their underlying structure; (2) the clarification of the typical experiences of a broad array of inmates; and (3) the delineation of a predictable sequence of social psychological hurdles for patients to manage. It is interesting to note that David Rothman saw this comparative analysis of total institutions as Goffman's most enduring contribution, arguing that "historians have confirmed the validity of Erving Goffman's concept of 'total institutions', which minimizes the differences in formal mission to establish a unity of design and structure" (Rothman 1990:xxv).

The study of total institutions is also directed to an analysis of the structural elements of power, surveillance, and discipline, a formulation that highlights the similarity between the research programs of Goffman and Foucault, as Giddens (1984), among others, has recognized. As was noted earlier, Goffman saw total institutions as forcing houses for changing persons, as natural experiments on what can be done to the self. Clearly, the theme here is generalized institutional power, not the diagnostic capabilities of psychiatrists or the peculiarities of the organization of mental hospitals.

Reading *Asylums* with a focus on generalized institutional power allows us to make sense of its rather fragmented account of mental illness. Studying the nature of mental illness was not a dead end for him but rather a detour from his investigation of the interaction order. Goffman could not always resist this detour, especially in the latter parts of *Asylums* and in later essays.

Goffman's second sociological project was to investigate ordinary, unremarkable behavior in public places. He was particularly interested in the management of interaction among the unacquainted. To live in an urban environment is to live in proximity to a large number of other people, about whom we are likely to know only what we can glean from their various presentations of self. Under these circumstances, social life becomes a delicate game in which people must try to show respect for the rights of others while remaining vigilant and aware of possible public dangers. Goffman saw himself as a student of the norms governing human traffic, as a student of the web of practices used in mass society to facilitate and monitor interaction among the unacquainted.

Goffman's analysis of the interaction order permeates all his work, but is clearly set out in *Behavior in Public Places* (1963) and *Relations in Public* (1971). Extended secondary discussions of his account of the interaction order can be found elsewhere (Ditton 1980; Drew and Wootton 1988; Burns 1992; Manning 1992). What is germane to this discussion is that although Goffman's focus was sociological, the behavior of the mentally ill was significant for him because it revealed by default the unremarkable behavior of ordinary people conducting unremarkable transactions in their daily lives. The mentally ill were interesting to Goffman because, as a group, they bungled the performance of these transactions and hence unintentionally demonstrated the norms and constraints that constitute the interaction order.

In principle, Goffman's project did not require him to have any view about the nature of mental illness. As I have tried to demonstrate, the view that he actually had but did not need, was a dubious one, in that it was based on ontological gerrymandering. Goffman exploited an ironic distancing to suggest that he somehow had a superior knowledge of mental illness—a super psychiatry—that superseded conventional psychiatry. But of course Goffman's earlier criticisms of psychiatric knowledge had already cut off the branch that he later wanted to sit on.

Once Goffman's interests are properly located in the sociological investigation of the interaction order, his views about deinstitutionalization can be clarified. Whether in families, as he poignantly analyzed in "The Insanity of Place," or in anonymous social settings, the disruptive and "ungrammatical" behavior of the mentally ill undermines our general capacity to carry on with our day-to-day concerns. It makes the traffic signs of human interaction unreliable; perhaps at its worst it makes us wonder whether there is even a road. Our solution to this problem has not been to broaden understanding of human association; instead, at least until recently, it has been to sequester these "offenders" in closed hospitals. As Goffman pointed out, psychiatrists, social workers, police officers, and judges are the "true clients" of the asylum, and through them, all of us. Sequestration is therefore a way of preserving the "grammar" of the interaction order. The policy of deinstitutionalization, of restoring the mentally ill to the "community," was therefore doomed from the beginning, since it was the community, broadly understood, that first sought institutionalization of the mentally ill. The grim reports by Scull (1984, 1989) and others about the "malign neglect" of the deinstitutionalized mentally ill are depressing but predictable, given Goffman's argument.

Goffman was a moralist and a critic. His detached tone reminded Marx (1984) of a figure from a Raymond Chandler novel. In some ways this is true. However, Goffman was not so detached as to be indifferent to what he saw as the hypocrisy of institutional psychiatry. He believed that the mental patient was on the wrong end of a "grotesque deal" that required a public rhetoric about the legitimacy of psychiatry and that made life easier for everyone else. Goffman hoped that *Asylums* would illustrate the gap between what psychiatrists said about what they do and what they actually do. He wanted to air the truth as he saw it from the vantage point as a knowledgeable and unaffiliated insider. However, he was not naïve enough to think that any manifestation of community care would ease the plight of mentally ill men and women who have the sad distinction of belonging to the most unwanted of social groups.

REFERENCES

Austin, J. L. 1961. *How To Do Things with Words*. Oxford: Oxford University Press.

Barham, P. 1992. *Closing the Asylum: The Mental Patient in Modern Society*. London: Penguin.

Burns, T. 1992. *Erving Goffman*. London: Routledge.

Davis, C. 1989. "Goffman's Concept of the Total Institution: Criticism and Revisions." *Human Studies* 12 (1-2):77-95.

Delaney, W. P. 1977. "The Uses of the Total Institution: A Buddhist Monastic Example." In *Exploring Total Institutions*, edited by R. Gordon and B. Williams. Champaign, IL: Stipes.

Ditton, J. (ed.) 1980. *The View from Goffman*. London: Macmillan.

Drew, P. and A. Wootton (eds.) 1988. *Erving Goffman: Exploring the Interaction Order*. Cambridge: Polity.

Fine, G. and D. Martin. 1990. "A Partisan View: Sarcasm, Satire and Irony as Voices in Erving Goffman's *Asylums*." *Journal of Contemporary Ethnography* 19 (1):89–115.

Giddens, A. 1984. *The Constitution of Society*. Cambridge: Polity.

Goffman, E. 1961. *Asylums*. Harmondsworth: Penguin.

Goffman, E. 1963. *Behavior in Public Places*. New York: Free Press.

Goffman, E. 1967. *Interaction Ritual*. New York: Anchor/Doubleday.

Goffman, E. 1971. *Relations in Public*. New York: Basic Books.

Goffman, E. 1974. *Frame Analysis*. New York: Harper & Row.

Goffman, E. 1983a. "Felicity's Condition." *American Journal of Sociology* 89 (1): 1–53.

Goffman, E. 1983b. "The Interaction Order." *American Sociological Review* 48: 1–17.

Goffman, E. 1989. "On Fieldwork." *Journal of Contemporary Ethnography* (18) 2:123–132.

Gronfein, W. 1992. "Goffman's *Asylums* and the Social Control of the Mentally Ill." *Perspectives on Social Problems* 4:129–153.

Manning, P. 1992. *Erving Goffman and Modern Sociology*. Stanford: Stanford University Press.

Manning, P. 1999. "Ethnographic Coats and Tents." In *Goffman and Social Organisation*, edited by G. W. H. Smith. London: Routledge.

Marx, G. 1984. "Role Models and Role Distance: A Remembrance of Erving Goffman." *Theory and Society* 13 (5):649–662.

Mechanic, D. 1989. *Mental Health and Social Policy*. Englewood Cliffs, NJ: Prentice Hall.

Mechanic, D. and D. A. Rochefort. 1990. "Deinstitutionalization: An Appraisal of Reform." *Annual Review of Sociology* 16:301–327.

Rothman, D. 1990. *The Discovery of the Asylum: Social Order and Disorder in the New Republic*. Boston: Little Brown.

Scull, A. 1984. *Decarceration. Community Treatment and the Deviant: A Radical View*. Cambridge: Polity Press.

Scull, A. 1989. *Social Order/Mental Disorder: Anglo-American Psychiatry in Historical Perspective*. Berkeley: University of California Press.

Sedgwick, P. 1982. *Psycho Politics*. London: Pluto Press.

Weinstein, R. 1994. "Goffman's *Asylums* and the Total Institution Model of Mental Hospitals." *Psychiatry* 57:348–367.

Winkin, Y. 1988. *Erving Goffman: Les Moments et Leurs Hommes*. Paris: Minuit.

Winkin, Y. 1999. "What's in a Life Anyway?" In *Goffman and Social Organisation*, edited by G. W. H. Smith. London: Routledge.

Winkin, Y. Forthcoming. *Erving Goffman: A Biography*. London: Macmillan.

Wittgenstein, L. 1958. *Philosophical Investigations*. Oxford: Blackwell.

Woolgar, S. and D. Pawluch. 1985. "Ontological Gerrymandering." *Social Problems* 32:214–227.

Counseling and Therapy in
Institutional Settings

II

Acquiescence or Consensus?: Consenting to Therapeutic Pedagogy

6

James L. Nolan, Jr.

INTRODUCTION

In the late 1960s Philip Rieff first argued that a therapeutic orientation had triumphed in American culture. Following Rieff others have assessed the continued expansion of the therapeutic sensibility in American culture and its subsequent infusion into America's major institutions (Herman 1995; Lasch 1979; Nolan 1998; Polsky 1991). America's education system is among the institutional spheres most deeply influenced by the therapeutic culture. In full evidence in the schools is the expanding authority of what Rieff identified as the "new priests" of the therapeutic age, namely school counselors and psychologists. State regulations now mandate not only a certain number of counselors per number of students in the schools but also that counselors have a greater presence in the classroom and more substantively contribute to curricular development.

These regulations and related practices—some of which will be highlighted in this chapter—raise questions about the potentially coercive nature of authority vested in the new priestly class, and the concomitant usurpation of parental authority that may result. Although therapeutically legitimated coercion by school counselors may be an important development, I will argue that therapeutic practices and ideas have actually penetrated the education system more deeply and widely than is revealed through the actions of school counselors. Teachers in particular and the defining character of the educational enterprise in general have also been profoundly influenced by the therapeutic culture. Thus, the expanding role of school counselors is only one part of a much larger story.[1]

The nature of instruction in America's education schools and the kind of themes emphasized in the most popular and widely used classroom curricula reveal the ubiquitous quality of the therapeutic orientation in America's schools. The actions of therapeutically trained school counselors in such a context, then, corresponds with the codes of moral understanding that inform American culture and its educational institutions. Given this cultural and educational climate, the exercising of authority by school counselors, teachers, or administrators will generally not be experienced as coercive.

107

In this chapter I will argue that the influence of the therapeutic ethos on America's schools is evident not just in the "coercive" acts of counselors, but in the very content and style of instruction in the classrooms. School counselors, to be sure, have played a part in this transformation, but to focus only on their role is to miss a wider and more profound development, namely, the essential transformation of education into a conspicuously therapeutic enterprise. Put in this broader context we understand that the ideals and practices of school counselors are basically commensurate with the dominant tendencies of American culture and its education system. Because therapeutic instruction and counseling in the schools mirror the sensibilities of the broader culture, it is most often not resisted, though as we will see, there are important exceptions. Generally speaking, consent to therapeutic pedagogy is better characterized by consensus than acquiescence.

SCHOOL COUNSELORS

Nevertheless, the expanding role of school counselors is an important part of the story, and provides a useful starting point for examining the larger process by which therapeutic sensibilities have become central to American pedagogy. The substance of state regulations makes clear that the role of the school counselor has become a very important part of the education system. Many state boards of education mandate not only that schools have a certain number of counselors per number of students, but that a specified percentage of a school counselor's time be devoted to direct individual and group counseling exercises and even involvement in curricular development. The states also provide some guidelines for what counselors should discuss when meeting with students. Not surprisingly, the content of the counseling intervention, as required by the different states, bears the recognizable traits of the therapeutic orientation.

By this I mean such defining features of the therapeutic culture as the emergence of the self as a new standard of cultural judgment (Rieff 1966:5; Bell 1976:xxi); the greater emphasis on emotions over reason, logic, and classical understandings of virtue for making sense of oneself and one's place in the social world (Elshtain 1986:92); and the reinterpretation of an increasing number of human behaviors and actions according to pathological rather than moral categories (Lasch 1977:98; Peele 1989).[2] One would, of course, expect therapeutic practitioners to pass along the ideals and values central to the therapeutic paradigm. A brief review of state guidelines directing the actions of school counselors, however, makes clear that these themes not only are central to the school counselor's job, but they have become fully codified as state regulations.

For example, a preoccupation with the self and with emotions is in full evidence in a Montana state regulation that holds that school counselors should assist the student in developing "a positive self-image, personal initiative, and physical independence," and should assist the student in his or her ability to "identify and express feelings." Likewise, in Massachusetts, according to state standards, the counselor is to help "students and others in such a way as to encourage self-exploration, self-understanding, and self confidence." And in Texas the school counselor is to "provide appropriate counseling and guidance for the changing social, emotional, psychological, and academic needs of students," and "support the efforts of teachers and parents in promoting the student's self-esteem, academic readiness, social and interpersonal sensitivity and skills," among other things.

Helping students to develop high self-esteem and emotional well-being is not limited to the counseling office. In many states, counselors are now required to integrate the substance of developmental counseling exercises into the content of classroom instruction. Often, this is to happen through regular classroom visits as well as through input into the development and selection of curricula. In Missouri, for example, school counselors are to spend 35–45% of their time "within the curriculum delivery component (structured, developmental experiences presented systematically through classroom and group activities)." Likewise, in Pennsylvania, school counselors are to be in "consultation and follow-up with the school staff and administration on the application of psychological principles and knowledge to the curriculum and to classroom instruction." The South Carolina Department of Education requires that its public school counselors do the following:

> Conduct classroom guidance activities in each teacher's class and/or systematically conduct developmental counseling groups for each grade level throughout the year; consult with and/or provide resources to teachers to facilitate their instruction of counseling content and to infuse counseling content into the regular education curriculum.

Listed in Table 6.1 are state regulations concerning counselor/student ratios as well as selected examples of the content of counseling services as regulated by state departments of education.[3]

In addition to building self-esteem and encouraging emotional development (themes that are evident in Table 6.1), counselors take part in ascertaining the presence of certain pathologies among students. Arguably, it is a kind of reinterpretation that justifies the counselor's expanding authority in the schools. As Christopher Lasch observes of the helping professions in education, "In order to justify the expansion of therapeutic authority over . . . the school . . . they ma[k]e extravagant claims for their expertise. They

Table 6.1. Counselor Regulations in State Public Schools*

State	Counselor:Student Ratio	Selected Task Descriptions
Alabama	1:400 (K–12)	Sixty percent of time to be spent in direct counseling services (i.e., conducting large group guidance sessions on topics such as self-esteem study skills, career information, financial aid, etc.).
Georgia	1:221–690 (9–12)	Conducts and evaluates classroom guidance activities related to . . . the developmental level of the students, i.e., motivation, self-esteem, test-taking, interpersonal relations, problem solving, etc.
Hawaii	—	Personal guidance and counseling may include, but need not be limited to, sex education, drugs amd narcotics, moral and spiritual education and values, mental health and behavior.
Idaho	1:400	
Indiana	—	The services shall seek to promote the development of human potential and shall assist the individual in developing confidence and a growing sense of responsibility for his own decisions and self-direction.
Louisiana	1:450	
Massachusetts		The effective school psychologist knows: developmental psychology, psychology of learning, and principles of behavior. . . . The effective school psychologist . . . counsels students and others in such a way as to encourage self-exporation, self-understanding, and self-confidence.
Missouri	1:401–500 (minimum standard) 1:301–375 (desirable standard)	The guidance curriculum adequately addresses identified student needs/competencies in career planning/exploration, knowledge of self and others and educational and vocational development. . . . Elementary school counselors spend 35%–45% of time within the curriculum delivery component (structured, developmental experiences presented systematically through classroom and group activities).

(*continued*)

Table 6.1. (Continued)

State	Counselor:Student Ratio	Selected Task Descriptions
Montana	1:400 (K–12)	Guidance: Learner Goals (1) By the end of the primary level, the student shall have had the opportunity to: (a) Develop a positive self-image, personal initiative, and physical independence; (b) Experience security in his/her school environment; and (c) Be able to identify and express feelings.
New Hampshire	1:500 (elementary) 1:300 (middle and high school)	
North Carolina	—	Uses appropriate counseling processes and techniques for individual and group sessions to meet developmental, preventive, and remedial needs of students
North Dakota	1:450 (secondary) 1:500 (elementary)	
Oklahoma	1:450	Counseling services shall be provided to students, in group or individual settings, that facilitate understanding of self and environment. The counseling services shall provide a planned sequential program of group guidance activities that enhance student self-esteem and promote the development of student competence in tha academic, personal/social, and career/vocational areas.
Pennsylvania	—	Consultation and follow-up with the school staff and administration on the application of psychological principles and knowledge to the curriculum and to classroom instruction.
South Carolina	—	Conduct classroom guidance activities in each teacher's class and/or systematically conduct developmental counseling groups for each grade level throughout the year; consult with and/or provide resources to teachers to facilitate their instruction of counseling content and to infuse counseling content in the regular education curriculum.

(continued)

Table 6.1.   (Continued)

State	Counselor:Student Ratio	Selected Task Descriptions
Tennessee	1:350 (secondary) 1:500 (elementary)	Aid children in academic development through the use and interpretation of test scores, improved self-concept, and early identification and attention to problems that are deterrents to learning and development.
Texas	1:500	The counselor shall: 1) provide appropriate counseling and guidance for the changing social, emotional, psychological, and academic needs of students . . . 3) support the efforts of teachers and parents in promoting the student's self-esteem, academic readiness, social and interpersonal sensitivity and skills.
Vermont	1:300 (secondary) 1:400 (elementary)	
Virginia	1:500	
West Virginia	1:350 (high school) 1:400 (secondary) 1:500 (elementary)	The school counselor shall work with individual pupils and groups of pupils in providing developmental, preventive and remedial guidance and counseling programs to meet academic, social, emotional and physical needs.
Wyoming	—	Services include . . . staff-development for building . . . district staff to help them understand student behavior and to learn intervention strategies which will assist student to practice self-fulfilling behavior.

*From Nolan (1998, pp. 154–55).

set themselves up as doctors not only to sick patients but to a sick society" (Lasch 1995:207). Behaviors once interpreted through the lens of older codes of moral understanding, i.e., religiously defined interpretations of behavior as good/bad, right/wrong, or moral/immoral have been replaced with therapeutic interpretations of behavior in terms of pathologies, disorders, dysfunctions, psychological disabilities, and addictions (Lasch 1992). With the DSM (*Diagnostic and Statistical Manual of Disorders*) in hand, counselors can classify any number of behaviors as some kind of learning disorder.[4]

For example, "Developmental Arithmetic Disorder" can be detected when one's "[a]rithmetic skills, as measured by a standardized, individually administered test, are markedly below the expected level, given the person's schooling and intellectual capacity." Similarly, "Developmental Expressive Writing Disorder" is detectable when one's writing skills are below par. The DSM also includes the "Developmental Reading Disorder," the "Developmental Expressive Language Disorder," and the "Developmental Receptive Language Disorder" (DSM III-R 1987:42–43). At the college level these classifications can result in legally mandated requirements for students to receive extra time on exams and assistance with, if not provision of, lecture notes.

Perhaps the most popular DSM disorder at the primary and secondary school levels, however, is attention deficit disorder (ADD) or attention deficit hyperactivity disorder (ADHD), which refers to what used to be called hyperactivity or even rowdiness. It generally applies to children who have a hard time focusing on their work, though adults are also now included among those suffering from ADD. "Experts" claim that as many as 3.5 million young Americans suffer from ADD. Adopting the "expert" view that 5% of the overall population of children have ADD, school counselors look for a corresponding number of students who should evidence ADD symptoms, and offer interesting explanations for the recent rise in the number of ADD cases.[5] Students diagnosed with this "illness" are prescribed regular doses of ritalin, in some cases even against the objections of parents (Divoky 1989).

In other cases students have been required by school counselors to take psychological surveys and participate in "behavior modification" and others counseling programs without parental consent. In East Stroudsburg, Pennsylvania parents reportedly became incensed when 59 sixth-grade girls from Lambert Intermediate School were given genital examinations by a school sponsored doctor allegedly without parental approval. A couple in Toccoa, Georgia protested the actions of a public school counselor who, without consulting them, assisted their two daughters with pregnancy tests and contraceptives. In an East Lansing, Michigan case, the parents of a third-grade boy sued the school district after their son, Jason, was sent to a counselor even after the father had refused permission for such visits.[6] In the latter case, the court ruled in the school's favor.

Thus, the role of the counselor in America's schools is growing, both in the classroom and in curricular development. Given their ascending status in the schools, counselors do not respond warmly when their authority is challenged.

EVIDENCE OF RESISTANCE

A number of state legislatures have attempted to pass "parental rights" bills aimed at restricting and requiring parental approval for certain counseling practices, though none to date has passed one of these bills. In Pennsylvania, legislative efforts to secure "parental rights" was initially generated, in part, by the protests of parents from the Pittsburgh area, whose children were enrolled, without their consent, in a program called Pittsburgh School-Wide Intervention Model (PSWIM), a "behavior modification" program developed by Western Psychiatric Institute and Clinic at the University of Pittsburgh. Also fueling the effort was the reaction of alarmed parents to the unapproved physical examinations of the Lambert Intermediate school sixth graders mentioned above. The legislation would require parental consent for child involvement in school counseling and other health care services.

School counselor associations have been among the most strident critics of such bills, and the Pennsylvania case was no exception. Consider the reaction of Robert B. Cormany, the Executive Director of Pennsylvania School Counselors Association, to the legislative effort in Pennsylvania. In response to parental concerns that increased authority vested in school counselors represented the further intrusion of the government into private family life, Cormany argued in a letter sent to Pennsylvania legislators that "counselors, teachers and administrators are not the government." The "government" according to Cormany, "is an elected body." This, of course, is a problematic conceptualization, and not just for theorists of the modern state. Such a narrow classification of what constitutes "government" excludes not only educators and school counselors, but military officers, Congressional staff, civil servants, not to mention the Secretary of State, the Secretary of Transportation, the Director of the FBI, and the Attorney General of the United States, all of whom are not part of an elected body.

Instead, according to Cormany, "counselors . . . are merely professionals who are able to take the needs of our students into account in a somewhat more objective manner than can parents." Based on this "objective" expertise, Cormany believes "the idea that parents know what is best for their children is a flawed concept at best." The perceived hubris of this statement fueled political and parental debate over the bill. Cormany's rationale, however, was spelled out further in the same letter: "A parent is much too close to the child and has seen them [sic] in far too different a set of circumstances to always be objective as to their needs." Cormany continues, "A parent does not know better than a doctor what needs to be done medically to preserve their child's health. A parent does not know better than an attorney what to do when a child is in legal trouble. Nor does a parent know better than a professional educator what may be appropriate to the child's educational needs."[7]

As illustrated in the logic of Cormany's assertions, the prospect that public school counselors can act in a coercive, heavy handed way, even against the objections of parents, is quite conceivable. The fact that parental protests led to state legislative initiatives suggests that consenting to the authority of school counselors and counseling programs is not always a harmonious or unconscious surrender. Worth noting, however, is the substance of parental protests. Few of the East Stroudsburg sixth graders reportedly came forth with formal complaints. The father of one who did was reported to have made the following claim regarding his daughter's physical examination: "My daughter was in pain for several days . . . emotional as well as physical." The basis of the protest here is that the girl suffered from the examination, not that the examination was in principle problematic—though the father may certainly have believed that it was. Consider also the actions taken by the parents of Jason, the East Lansing, Michigan third grader discussed above. The grounds for the parents' objections in this case are very telling. Jason's parents allege in the suit, *Newkirk v. Fink*, that "Jason suffered panic attacks and separation-anxiety disorder as a result of psychological tests used in the counseling" (Walsh 1996).

Notice that the objections are based on the same therapeutic categories that define the scope of the counselor's role. So pervasive is the therapeutic sensibility that the most permissible way to object to therapeutically incited violations of individual liberty or parental authority is to make the victimized claim to have been psychologically or emotionally injured. Both the victimizer and the victimized, in these cases, are speaking the same language. They are appealing to the same code of moral understanding. The same basic cultural sensibility has also fully infiltrated the central pedagogical processes of the schools. That is, the same ideals and practices that legitimate and direct the actions of (and reactions against) school counselors have influenced the classroom and are deeply embedded in educational curricula, even in curricular materials used in private and home schooling.[8] Thus although school counselors have gained and work hard to maintain an expanded level of authority, more insidious has been the infiltration of therapeutic themes into the central processes of contemporary pedagogy.

A useful comparison of a very similar process can be found in the criminal justice system. Beginning in 1972, the justice system began "diverting" many offenders to agencies such as Treatment Alternatives to Street Crime (TASC) for counseling. The counseling or intervention was performed by trained counselors, therapists, and psychologists. When treatment was completed the offender would then return to the court for some kind of disposition. The court itself did not do the treatment. With new programs such as the drug court, community courts, and domestic violence courts, however, this has begun to change. In these rapidly expanding new forms of adjudication treatment is performed in and by the court itself, with judges often acting like therapists or social workers and lawyers like Alcoholics Anonymous (AA) sponsors. The judges are certainly given advice by trained therapists, and much of the counseling exercises still take place outside of the courtroom. Thus the special "expertise" of the "new priests" is still a very important feature in these courts. Of greater significance, however, is the very transformation of the traditional adjudicative process and of the traditional actors in the courtroom drama. The court itself becomes a therapeutic enterprise. As such therapy's infusion into the criminal justice process is even more complete than is represented by the presence, practice, and authority of therapeutically trained practitioners.

A parallel process has taken place in the schools. As noted above counselors play an increasingly prominent role in the pedagogical process, but again what is of greater importance is the manner in which the traditional players in the educational process—the teachers and administrators—like the judge and lawyers in the therapeutically oriented courts, have themselves become therapists. Like the new forms of adjudication, teaching in the schools becomes a form of therapy. Certainly the counselors in the schools, like the treatment providers in the courts, play an important role in this new form of education, but the triumph of the therapeutic in the schools has been even more complete than these developments represent. The educational process itself increasingly reflects a decidedly therapeutic disposition. We turn now to a broader analysis of developments in contemporary primary and secondary education to assess the extent of this infusion.

THERAPEUTIC EDUCATION

The substance of instruction in America's schools of education provides a good place to begin documenting the broader suffusion of the therapeutic orientation in America's schools. This, after all, is where teachers first learn how to conduct themselves in the classroom. Rita Kramer, having visited education schools around the country, found a pronounced emphasis on helping prospective teachers become, in essence, classroom therapists.

> Wherever I went . . . I found a striking degree of conformity about what is considered to be the business of schools and the job of teachers. Everywhere I visited . . . I heard the same things over and over again. And failed to hear others. Everywhere, I found idealistic people eager to do good. And everywhere, I found them being told that the way to do good was to prepare themselves to cure a sick society. To become therapists, as it were, specializing in the pathology of education. (Kramer 1991:209)

Consistent with one defining feature of the therapeutic culture, the main means by which teachers are to "cure" their students is through the promotion of self-esteem. Kramer discusses the dominant presence of this concept in educational training:

> What matters is not to teach any particular subject or skill, not to preserve past accomplishments or stimulate future achievements, but to give to all that stamp of approval that will make them "feel good about themselves." Self-esteem has replaced understanding as the goal of education. (Kramer 1991:210)

Along with self-esteem Kramer found emotions to be a central concept passed on to those preparing for the teaching profession. As she explains, "Many if not most of these teachers talk about things like feeling, warmth, empathy more than they do about skills, training and discipline" (Kramer 1991:25).

Therefore, the same ideals emphasized by counselors in their individual dealings with students are also stressed in the process whereby teachers are trained to teach. Moving from the schools of education to the classroom we again find the same basic themes. As with the state regulations guiding the practices of counselors, state directives encourage the inculcation of these themes in the classroom, and the most pronounced of them, once again, is a concern with the building of self-esteem.

John Vasconcellos, the former chairman of the House Ways and Means Committee in the California legislature and champion of the national self-esteem movement, celebrates the expansion of self-esteem in his California's school systems:

> Self-esteem is seeping its way into the culture, and into the schools, schools especially. There was a survey done here a year or so ago. About three-quarters of the schools in California have some self-esteem component: goals, staff-development, parental involvement, parental self-esteem, students, or whatever else. . . . Now, it is kind of in the mainstream, so it kind of seeps around.[9]

A look at state laws in all 50 states reveals that Vasconcellos's assessment of self-esteem's widespread acceptance and institutionalization is on the mark. By the middle of 1994 some 30 states had enacted a total of over 170 statutes that in some fashion sought to either promote, protect, or enhance the self-esteem of Americans. The largest percentage of these (around 75) are, not surprisingly, in the area of education.

Utah, for example, appropriated $60,000 "to increase the self-esteem and physical, intellectual, and life skills of students with disabilities through a holistic integrated arts program." Florida's Department of Education was mandated by state code to "revise curriculum frameworks, as appropriate, to include building self-esteem." Among the educational standards specified in a Georgia statute was the "promotion of high self-esteem." An Illinois law requires its State Board of Education to distribute to "all school districts" a curriculum that emphasizes "life coping skills, self-esteem, and parenting skills of adolescents and teenagers." According to a 1993 Iowa statute: "Each school board [in the state of Iowa] shall provide instruction in human growth and development including instruction regarding human sexuality, self-esteem, stress management, interpersonal relationships, domestic abuse, and AIDS." The stated intent of a 1994 Massachusetts law is to "ensure . . . that each public school classroom provides the conditions for all pupils to engage fully in learning as an inherently meaningful and enjoyable activity without threats to their sense of self-esteem." Louisiana makes provision for "any public elementary or secondary school in Louisiana to offer instruction in . . . self-esteem." And a Wisconsin statute directs schools to provide "instruction to pupils in communication . . . stress reduction, self-improvement and self-esteem."[10]

Therefore, the same emphasis on self-esteem found in state regulations for school counselors is also evident in state directives for classroom instruction. This becomes even more apparent in the content of state curricular guidelines. The Commission on Values-Centered Goals for the District of Columbia Public Schools, for example, issued a report identifying the five most important values it believed the D.C. schools should seek to inculcate into its students. The first of these was "self-esteem." Educators in D.C.'s public schools were thus encouraged to "emphasize building students' self-esteem as a central ingredient of the curriculum at all instruction levels and in all subject matter areas where applicable" (*Commission on Value-Centered Goals* 1988:iv). Likewise, one of the central goals of the *Virginia Family Life Curriculum* is to help students "develop a positive self-concept," and one of the criteria for evaluating the curriculum's success is whether the child "is aware [of] and understands self" (*Family Life Education* 1983:1). This is also the main point of the 1990 California Department of Education report titled *Toward a State of Esteem: The Final Report of the California Task Force to Promote Self-esteem and Personal and Social Responsibility*, a report that served as the basis for the introduction of values curricula in California and other state schools. The California Task Force sees self-esteem as so imperative to moral education that it believes "course work in self-esteem should be required for credentials and a part of ongoing in-service training for all educators" (*Toward a State of Esteem* 1990:6).

SELF-ESTEEM IN THE CLASSROOM

Consistent with these state guidelines, the most popular educational curricula used in today's public schools place a great deal of emphasis on the role of self-esteem. This is certainly the case in the *Character Education Curriculum* (1991), a curriculum put out by the Character Education Institute (CEI) and used in over 45,000 American classrooms and more than 430 cities. In a pamphlet titled "Character Education and the Teacher," CEI asserts that "self-concept" is "the most significant factor in a student's personality." Similarly, according to American Guidance Service (AGS), an organization that claims a clientele of over 150,000 educators, its Developing Understanding of Self and Others (DUSO) program "is first and foremost an educational program, recognizing the relationship between self-esteem and achievement." Its goal is to "help children see themselves as capable and worthwhile people" (Dinkmeyer and Dinkmeyer 1991:2).

The Washington, D.C.-based Community of Caring group, whose *Growing Up Caring* curriculum is used in 49 states and in more than five countries outside the United States, likewise sells its programs on the basis that they help students "experience heightened self-esteem and self-awareness."[11] The third of four stated principles guiding the philosophy of the *Being Healthy* program, a curriculum put out by Harcourt Brace Jovanovich and used in all 50 states, is "to emphasize positive self-concept and high self-esteem." As the teacher's guide to the curriculum states, "*Being Healthy* promotes the idea that the healthier a person becomes, the better the person will feel about himself or herself" (Olson et al. 1990:13). The stated mission of the Pasadena-based Thomas Jefferson Center—an organization whose programs have been used in 2000 U.S. schools, serving approximately 34,000 classrooms and reaching over 1,000,000 students—is to "write, promote and disseminate curriculum and training programs for schools and families to teach . . . self-esteem" ("Thomas Jefferson Center Annual Report" 1989:i). Christine Baroque, a spokeswoman for the Center, states, "The program provides the instruction for a strong self-concept which is essential to a truly successful life" (*San Diego Union*, 11 June 1987:1).

Given these overarching curricular directives, it is not surprising that instructions in the most widely used textbooks consistently encourage children to think highly of themselves. McGraw-Hill's *Health Focus on You*, a curriculum used in all 50 states, devotes the first section of its first-grade health curriculum to mental health. The instructions in the "Feeling Good About Yourself" section are as follows: "You can feel good about yourself. You can like yourself. Always do your best. Do not worry when you make mistakes. Be kind to yourself. Know that you are important" (Meeks and Heit 1990:10–11). Similarly, the first part of Scott/Foresman's *Health for Life* curriculum is entitled, "How Can You Improve the Way You See Yourself?" In this section children are told, "You are special. Realizing that you are a unique human being can help you feel good about yourself. Feeling good about yourself is important" (Richmond et al. 1992:18). The same emphasis is repeated in curriculum after curriculum. The first of DUSO's three main sections is entitled, "Developing Understanding of Self." The first main section in *Me, My World, My Future*, a curriculum put out by Spokane-based Teen Aid and used in all 50 states by more than 100,000 parents and teens, is on "Valuing Self."

Toward the end of raising students' self-esteem a number of interesting activities are employed. The *Growing Up Caring* curriculum, for example, encourages students to write a letter to themselves telling themselves how special they are. Consider the following instructions for this particular self-esteem exercise: "Imagine that you need to be convinced of your worth as a person. Write a letter to yourself. Tell why you are special. Include all your good points. Think of the talents you have that could be developed. Mention your values. End the letter. 'Love,' and sign your name" (Bolin 1990:123). The CEI's *Curriculum News* reports on what is called "The Me Activity." Employing this activity, sixth- and seventh-grade children reportedly raise their self-esteem by cutting out magazine pictures that symbolize their own individual character traits and paste these on construction paper cut to form the word ME. The activity is celebrated as one that gives students a "better understanding of themselves" (*Character Education Curriculum* 1991:1).

Similarly, the *Me, My World, My Future* curriculum encourages students who are feeling down to talk to themselves in order to build themselves up. "When you talk to yourself, say positive things that help you believe you can succeed. 'Negative messages' will only result in self-doubt and a lack of confidence. Positive 'self-messages' could be, 'I know I can do this . . . I did well on that exam . . . I have what it takes to succeed" (Roans and Benn 1989:19). Elsewhere in the same curriculum students with low self-esteem are encouraged to seek affirmation from those around them. If this does not work they are told to give themselves "positive feedback." In this regard students are told, "Concentrate more on building yourself up—or sending yourself frequent positive messages and noting the many good things that you do. Maybe set a weekly goal for yourself and when you achieve that goal 'pat yourself on the back' with a snack, extra TV time, or a phone call to a friend" (1989:21).

EMOTIVISM IN THE CLASSROOM

State reports and curriculum guidelines also place a great deal of emphasis on the place of emotions. This is spelled out most conspicuously in the California Department of Education report. The basic premise offered in the report is that "all feelings are honorable . . . [b]y themselves, feelings are neither good nor bad. They are clues to our most crucial concerns, our deepest commitments, our needs, and our wants" (*Toward a State of Esteem* 1990:26). Similarly, the criteria for successful instruction, according to Virginia's *Family Life Curriculum*, is based in part on whether the student "has a feeling of belonging" and "talks about feelings and emotions and understands positive ways of dealing with them" (*Family Life Education* 1983:9). Major parts of Virginia's guidelines are devoted to understanding emotions.

Students, for example, are taken through sections that consider such matters as "Dealing with emotions . . . Forces that affect emotions . . . Characteristics of emotional maturity." In one exercise teachers have students view "a film on feelings and emotions" and discuss "how the class members have dealt with these feelings and emotions" (1983:19–20).

Consistent with these state curriculum guidelines, emotions are an important part of the popular values educational curricula. It is remarkable how often the various curricula instruct students to arrive at understandings of themselves and of their relations with others through an analysis of their own feelings. A CEI teacher's instructional manual, for example, states that "[l]earning to express themselves freely yet being careful to consider the feelings of others, too, may well be the most important social skill developed in students" (*Family Life Education* 1983:2).

Students are repeatedly told that their feelings are an important aspect of their being. Moreover, they are actually guided through various exercises designed to help them better understand, categorize, express, and act on their feelings. The DUSO program contains an entire unit devoted to "Understanding and Expressing Feelings." In it are sections entitled, "To be conscious of feelings . . . To clearly express one's feelings . . . To act on one's feelings with courage" (Dinkmeyer and Dinkmeyer 1982:9). Another unit is devoted simply to "Understanding Feelings," which includes the following sections: "To see how feelings influence choices . . . To discriminate between real and imagined fears . . . To select appropriate ways to express feelings" (1982:10). Among DUSO's "Feeling Word" activities is a game in which students view a dialogue between two characters (puppets) and identify and discuss how one of the characters feels. In the curriculum there are a total of 41 such feeling word activities (1982:9).

Similarly, Quest International, an organization that has implemented curricula in more than 20,000 schools in 22 countries and whose *Skills for Adolescence* (1988:III-11)curriculum has been used in over 11,000 schools in the United States, claims that "we can understand ourselves only when we know how we're really feeling." Based on this premise it states the following goals for Unit Three of its *Skills for Adolescence* curriculum:

1. To understand that young adolescents experience a wide range of common feelings and that these feelings are normal.
2. To explore appropriate ways to communicate feelings.
3. To examine the range of emotions and learn positive responses to outside influences.
4. To learn how to perceive troubling emotions such as anger and frustration as positive challenges.
5. To learn how positive emotions promote feelings about oneself and others (1988:III-3).

In a later section of the same curriculum students are helped to develop a "feelings vocabulary." In another they are asked to make a "rainbow of feelings" display to illustrate the range of emotions that are experienced by individuals (*Skills for Adolescence* 1988:III-4, 8). In still another they are asked to assign their current emotional state to a "Feelings Continuum." Consider the following instructions from the latter, in which the teacher is to ask students, "How are you feeling? Think about it for a moment. What's been happening to you today that might affect how you feel? I'd like a few volunteers to come up to the Feelings Continuum and write your initials on the line closest to the way you're feeling right now" (1988:III-9). In the *Skills for Adolescence* curriculum students are also told to fill out an "Emotion Clock" worksheet where they are to "remember the day's feelings as well as they can" (1988:III-11, 12). In another section they are asked to make a "Scrapbook of Emotions." For this exercise they are given five sheets of paper. Choosing at least five emotions from the "Feelings Rainbow," they are to begin each paper with sentences like, "I feel delighted when . . ." or "I feel excited when . . ." etc. (1988:III-18).

A first-grade health textbook put out by McGraw-Hill tells students that "You can show your feelings. Your face can show your feelings. Your body can show your feelings." Based on these statements, students are asked, "How do you show your feelings?" They are instructed further that "Sharing your feelings help you be healthy. You can share feelings in different ways. Some ways are better than others. One good way is to talk about them." In this section teachers are instructed to test comprehension by telling students to "make faces" and "use their bodies to demonstrate being afraid, happy, sad, and angry" (Meeks and Heit 1990:14–15).

Educators justify the importance of emotions, in part, because of its integral relatedness to "self-esteem." As stated in *Me, My World, My Future*, "Coming to a better understanding and appreciation of ourselves should include a look at our emotions or feelings." Likewise, "identifying feelings, dealing with them and acting appropriately is very helpful in building self-awareness" (Roans and Benn 1989:11). The California report similarly states that "by expressing our authentic feelings, we also gain more awareness of our deeper selves" (*Toward a State of Esteem* 1990:26). Similarly, the *Growing Up Caring* textbook tells students that the way they handle their emotions has a direct effect on their sense of self-worth. "If you don't express emotions or if you dump them on others, you feel guilty or down on yourself" (Bolin 1990:116).

Therefore, the self esteem and emotional well-being of students, as demonstrated in these popular educational curricula, have become major pedagogical preoccupations. The evidence here suggests that the kind of themes emphasized by school counselors, stressed in America's schools of education, and mandated in state curricular guidelines have also found their way into the classroom. If the curricula are any indication, teachers have indeed, as Rita Kramer asserts, "become therapists . . . specializing in the pathology of education."

THE NATURE OF CONSENT

Because the same therapeutic themes emphasized by school counselors are also found in the central currents of the educational process, critiquing the growing authority of school counselors scratches only the surface. Education in the United States has become a therapeutic enterprise. It is an orientation, moreover, that is commensurate with the therapeutic sensibility that has triumphed in American culture. Consider what Americans think about self-esteem. A 1992 Gallup Poll asked Americans what factors they think are important in motivating a person to work hard and succeed. Of those polled, 89% said that self-esteem (the way people feel about themselves) was a "very important" factor, whereas only 49% thought responsibility to a community was a "very important" motivational factor. The same survey found that 63% of Americans believe that the time and effort being spent on promoting self-esteem is worthwhile (Adler 1992:50).

These findings raise serious questions about the ostensibly coercive qualities of therapeutically trained counselors in America's schools. To be sure, school officials and other state authorities invoke the language of the therapeutic perspective to socially control American citizens in the contemporary context. To send someone to counseling, to treatment, or to a sensitivity training seminar; to talk about self-esteem and one's emotional well-being; to appeal to the expert knowledge of psychologists are all acceptable because they are consistent with pervasive cultural impulses. For this reason, apparently coercive measures are most often accepted by American citizens, and are not really experienced as coercive. As Lois McNay (1994:95) explains,

> Individuals are controlled through the power of the norm and this power is effective because it is relatively invisible. In modern society, the behavior of individuals is regulated not through overt repression but through a set of standards and values associated with normality which are set into play by a network of ostensibly beneficent and scientific forms of knowledge.

In other words, the ideals of a "scientifically based" therapeutic understanding of the world are so embedded in American culture that overt coercion is rarely necessary. Instead, most citizens naturally comply with the programs and policies based on therapeutic rationales because they are so "obviously" plausible. The application of a therapeutic form of coercion represents an extension of psychologically based governmental power in the way, for example, in which Michel Foucault understands it in his work. Foucault (1979, 1984) traces the changes in the penal system from state concern with the behavior of citizens to state concern with the internal workings of citizens, with their intentions, motives, with their souls. He also observes that psychology provided the knowledge base for the new form of state authority.

Evident in America's schools, however, is a more widespread use of this basis of knowledge-power. With Foucault, the power of psychological knowledge was exercised in the enclosed walls of the prison. Here we find that the universal acceptance of and access to therapeutic knowledge justifies a broader and more diffuse application of its premises for the purposes of state authority. No longer is the expert authority of the therapeutic practitioner confined to the enclosed walls of isolated correctional institutions. Instead, the popular acceptance of a therapeutic worldview allows this basis of knowledge-power to be exercised more diffusely, not just in the counselor's office, but in the classroom.

The need for precluding public exposure to the (sometimes egregious) exercise of power based on this knowledge system is less necessary because of the cultural capital ascribed to it. In some instances the exercise of authority based on therapeutic justifications is still hidden from larger public observation. When an ADD-diagnosed child is encouraged to go into counseling, do parents know what is discussed in these sessions? Do they understand the criteria on which such a diagnosis is based? Indeed, the medically and legally sanctioned principle of client confidentiality often protects counselors and the programs they run from public scrutiny. And the defensive efforts by counselors in the Pennsylvania example suggests that challenges to this authority will be forcefully resisted.

The therapeutic experts, then, still maintain a certain monopoly on the exercise of power because of their credentials and ostensible qualifications to interpret and understand human behavior based on this source of knowledge. And the therapeutic ideals of confidentiality and anonymity often make it difficult to raise to the level of public scrutiny the nature of instruction that transpires within the various counseling situations. Though there is still some sense in which the expertise of therapeutic practitioners is exercised within the proverbial black box, this is less the case today than is depicted in Foucault's assessment of the institutional application of psychologically based knowledge-power. In the contemporary American context the popular therapeutic ethos is more diffusely understood and employed.

Irrespective of its substantive qualities, the therapeutic cultural orientation is what presently exists at the cultural level. It rests in the institutionalized background of the collective consciousness. Limited criticism notwithstanding, culturally pervasive therapeutic symbols provide the moral reference points to which individuals increasingly appeal in order to navigate their way through social life. This may help to explain why "parental rights" efforts have so far been unsuccessful, and why some objections to the authority of school counselors have themselves been based on a therapeutic worldview.

Jürgen Habermas (1973, 1988) argues that state authority will be consented to only inasmuch as the state makes reference to common societal values. That is, the exercising of state authority will succeed, over the long term, only if the state makes reference to "authorities which, for their part, must be recognized" by society (1973:101). Habermas (1973:101) explains further:

> If binding decisions are legitimate, that is, if they can be made independently of the concrete exercise of force and of the manifest threat of sanctions, and can be regularly implemented even against the interests of those affected, then they must be considered as the fulfillment of recognized norms. This unconstrained normative validity is based on the supposition that the norm could, if necessary, be justified and defended against critique. And this supposition is itself not automatic. It is the consequence of an interpretation which admits of consensus and which has a justificatory function, in other words, of a worldview which legitimizes authority.

For the most part, it seems that Americans are willing to consent to state authority that is based on therapeutic legitimations. The question remains, however, whether Americans will continue to consent to therapeutically justified state power. John Schaar's (1984:109) conceptual distinction between *acquiescence* and *consensus* is useful for addressing this question. As Schaar conceives it, acquiescence can occur without there really being consensus. One may acquiesce to the state's authority not because one believes the state to be legitimate based on a strongly agreed-on code of moral understanding, but out of "interest or necessity." Consensus, on the other hand, refers to the binding and generally accepted influence of a moral order that possesses "unconstrained normative validity," in the way Habermas refers to it. The latter elicits consent on a much deeper and more widespread level. Which best characterizes the therapeutic basis of authority in the American schools: acquiescence or consensus?

The pervasiveness of the therapeutic sensibility in America's schools and in American culture suggests that consent is presently more appropriately characterized by consensus than acquiescence. That is, most often Americans consent to state authority that is based on a therapeutic basis of knowledge-power not because they feel they must, but because it corresponds with the same basic worldview within which they operate. There are, of course, exceptions to such an unquestioned acceptance of therapeutically justified state authority as illustrated in examples considered above. Recall, however, that in these cases the objections themselves were also based on the therapeutic perspective. If disapproval of the exercise of authority by school counselors can be advanced only in accordance with therapeutic categories, resistance will be very limited. By objecting through reference to therapeutic categories, protesters are implicitly deferring to the very system these "experts" represent. Inasmuch as therapeutic norms are appealed to, the exercising of state authority according to the same norms will be successfully "justified and defended against critique," as Habermas puts it.

In sum, school counselors do exercise a growing level of authority in today's schools, an authority which is legitimated by a therapeutic basis of expertise. The same worldview that justifies this expertise, however, has fully suffused the educational process more generally. Moreover, it is a pedagogical disposition that is fully commensurate with the dominant sensibilities of American culture. For this reason, resistance to the growing authority of school counselors will remain limited. Consenting to the authority of therapeutic experts in the schools, in other words, is best characterized by consensus than acquiescence. Any successful critique of such authority necessitates a broader recognition of the fundamentally therapeutic state of our society as a whole. As long as America remains a decidedly therapeutic culture, consenting to therapeutic experts will generally not be experienced as coercive.

Were the dominant values of American culture to shift away from the therapeutic ethos then the nature of consent might become one of acquiescence rather than consensus. This does not mean, however, that individuals would not have to, for a time anyway, still consent to state authority based on therapeutic ideals. But it would establish the conditions whereby the ostensible expertise of school counselors could more persuasively be called into question.

NOTES

1.   A lengthier discussion of the suffusion of America's schools by the therapeutic ethos is made in Chapter 5 of Nolan, *The Therapeutic State: Justifying Government at Century's End* (New York: New York University Press, 1998), from which sections of this chapter are partially derived.

2.   For an expanded discussion of the various features of the therapeutic culture, see Nolan (1998:1–21).

3.   These data are based on the responses I received after contacting through letter all 50 state boards of education. In the letter I asked them to provide me information regarding state regulations for public school counselors. All "Selected Task Descriptions" listed in Table 6.1 are from the wording of these regulations.

4.   The DSM is "widely accepted in the United States as the common language of mental health clinicians and researchers." *Diagnostic and Statistical Manual of Mental Disorders, Third Edition, Revised* (DSM III-R) (Washington, D.C., American Psychiatric Association, 1987), p. xviii.

5.   In a memo sent to parents of students at an elementary school in central Virginia, for example, the school's counselor explains that one reason for the recent rise is that "we are getting better at diagnosing ADD so we are keeping a number of undiagnosed children from slipping through the cracks." Another reason for the large number of cases among American children is that "our founding fathers (and mothers!) were impulsive enough to leave their homelands to come to a land where they knew not the consequences of their choice. We strongly suspect ADD to be largely transmitted genetically form parent to child. In fact, it is rare that practitioners treat a child who does not have a parent who subsequent to the child's evaluation will say, 'He's just like me!' We do seem to be seeing about 5% of our population with what appears to be true ADD and we strongly suspect a genetic link in most families affected." Memo title: "Attention Deficit Disorder," sent to parents in December 1994, from Lucy Riddick, School Counselor, Meriwhether Lewis Elementary School.

6.   For news accounts of these various cases see Peter J. Shelly and Eleanor Chute, "Does Parental Control Stop at School House Door?" *Pittsburgh Post Gazette*, 10 February 1998; Walter F. Naedele, "Spin on Girls' Physicals Stirs National Tumult," *Philadelphia Inquirer*, 15 May 1996, p. B1; Arnold F. Fege, "Parental Rights: Yes! Parental Rights Legislation: No!" *Educational Leadership*, November 1997, p. 79; and Mark Walsh, "Parent-Rights Cases Against Schools Fail to Make Inroads," *Education Week*, 10 April 1996, p. 11.

7.   The letter, dated 4 December 1997 and on Pennsylvania School Counselors Association stationary, was addressed to Pennsylvania House Representative Samuel E. Rohrer and sent (cc) to "House Education Members." Parts of the letter have since been excerpted in various media accounts of the Pennsylvania "Parents Rights" debate.

8.   Melinda Wagner's (1990) study of private Christian schools in Virginia illustrates this claim. She found the self-esteem theme to be just as prevalent in the schools that she observed as it is in public schools. Relatedly, Alan Ehrenhalt observes that school choice policy ultimately presents "families with the essentially empty freedom of choosing between competing schools that scarcely differ among themselves." See Alan Ehrenhalt, "Making the Curriculum Count," *Washington Post*, 6 August 1995, Education Review, p. 5.

9.   From author's interview with Assemblyman John Vasconcellos, Sacramento, CA, 10 February 1995.

10.   For a more comprehensive list of state self-esteem legislation see Nolan (1998:319–323). The state codes identified above listed in the order presented in the text are the following: Utah Ann Code 53A-15-204 (1994); Fla. Stat. 228.501 (1993); 105 ILCS 5/27-32.2 (1993); IC 279.50 (1993); MAL ch. 69:1 (1994); La.ALS 47 (1994); and Wis. Stat. 115.362 (1993).

11.   "What is the Community of Caring?" Paper issued by Community of Caring, Washington, D.C., p. 1.

REFERENCES

Adler, Jerry. 1992. "Hey, I'm Terrific." *Newsweek* 17 February:48–50.

Bell, Daniel. 1976. *The Cultural Contradictions of Capitalism.* New York: Basic Books.

Bolin, Frances Schoonmaker. 1990. *Growing Up Caring: Exploring Values and Decision Making.* Lake Forest, IL: Macmillan/McGraw-Hill.

Character Education Curriculum News. 1991. San Antonio, TX: Character Education Institute. (February) 3:1.

Commission on Values-Centered Goals for the District of Columbia: Final Report. 1988.

District of Columbia Board of Education. Daniel H Eaton, chair.

Dinkmeyer, Don and Don Dinkmeyer, Jr. 1982. *DUSO-1: Developing Understanding of Self and Others, Revised, Teachers Guide.* Circle Pines, MN: American Guidance Service.

Dinkmeyer, Don and Don Dinkmeyer, Jr. 1991. "Tell Me About DUSO . . ." Circle Pines, MN: American Guidance Service.

Divoky, Diane. 1989. "Ritalin: Education's Fix-It Drug." *Phi Delta Kappan* 70 (8):599-605.

Elshtain, Jean Bethke. 1986. *Meditations on Modern Political Thought.* New York: Praeger.

Family Life Education: Curriculum Guidelines. 1983. Richmond, VA: Virginia Department of Education.

Foucault, Michel. 1979. *Discipline and Punish: The Birth of the Prison.* New York: Vintage Books.

Foucault, Michel. 1984. *The Foucault Reader.* New York: Pantheon Books.

Habermas, Jürgen. 1973. *Legitimation Crisis.* Boston: Beacon Press.

Habermas, Jürgen. 1988. "How Is Legitimacy Possible on the Basis of Legality?" *Tanner Lectures on Human Values VIII*, delivered at Harvard University, October 1 and 2, 1986. Cambridge: Cambridge University Press.

Herman, Ellen. 1995. *The Romance of American Psychology: Political Culture in the Age of Experts.* Berkeley: University of California Press.

Kramer, Rita. 1991. *Ed School Follies.* New York: Free Press.

Lasch, Christopher. 1977. *Haven in a Heartless World.* New York: Basic Books.

Lasch, Christopher. 1979. *The Culture of Narcissism.* New York: Norton.

Lasch, Christopher. 1992. "For Shame: Why Americans Should be Wary of Self-Esteem." *The New Republic* August 10:29-34.

Lasch, Christopher. 1995. *The Revolt of the Elite.* New York: Norton.

McNay, Lois. 1994. *Foucault: A Critical Foundation.* Oxford: Polity Press.

Meeks, Linda and Philip Heit. 1990. *Health Focus on You.* Columbus, OH: Merrill.

Nolan, James L., Jr. 1998. *The Therapeutic State: Justifying Government at Century's End.* New York: New York University Press.

Olson, Larry K., Richard W. St. Pierre and Jan M. Ozias. 1990. *Being Healthy: Teachers Edition.* Orlando, FL: Harcourt Brace Jovanovich.

Peele, Stanton. 1989. *Diseasing of America: Addiction Treatment Out of Control.* Toronto: Lexington Books.

Polsky, Andrew J. 1991. *The Rise of the Therapeutic State*. Princeton: Princeton University Press.

Richmond, Julius B., Elenore T. Pounds and Charles B. Corbin. 1992. *Health for Life*. Glenview, IL: Scott, Foresman and Co.

Rieff, Philip. 1966. *The Triumph of the Therapeutic*. Chicago: University of Chicago Press.

Roans, Nancy and LeAnna Benn. 1989. *Me, My World, My Future*. Spokane, WA: Teen-Aide, Inc.

Schaar, John H. 1984. "Legitimacy in the Modern State." In *Legitimacy and the State*, edited by W. Connolly. Oxford: Blackwell.

Skills for Adolescence: Middle and Junior High Schools, Revised and Expanded. 1988. Granville, OH: Quest International.

"Thomas Jefferson Center Annual Report." 1989. Pasadena, CA: Thomas Jefferson Center.

Toward a State of Esteem: The Final Report of the California Task Force to Promote Self-Esteem and Personal and Social Responsibility. 1990. Sacramento, CA: The California Department of Education.

Wagner, Melinda. 1990. *God's Schools: Choice and Compromise in American Society*. New Brunswick, NJ: Rutgers University Press.

Walsh, Mark. 1996. "Parent-Rights Cases Against Schools Fail to Make Inroads." *Education Week* 10 April:11.

The Emergence of Recovered Memory as a Social Problem

7

Roger Neustadter

INTRODUCTION

The social constructionist study of social problems focuses on the emergence and genesis of social problems (Best 1989; Holstein and Miller 1993; Spector and Kitsuse 1977). Instead of trying to study the social conditions that lead to the identification of a social problem, constructionists examine the concerns that lead to the identification and definition of social problems. Social problems are defined by constructionists such as Spector and Kitsuse (1977:75) as "the activities of individuals or groups making assertions of grievances and claims with respect to some putative conditions."

The social constructionist tradition directs attention away from the features of a particular condition and toward the rhetoric of "claimsmaking." Constructionists examine how particular conditions and behaviors are brought to people's attention and become recognized as social problems (Best 1990:11). Constructivist analysis of social problems focuses on the discourse of "claimsmakers." They see claimsmakers as seeking to convince others that some condition is a social problem, that it has undesirable consequences that must be recognized and addressed. In this view it is the process of claims making that turns conditions or circumstances—which previously may have gone unnoticed—into the focus of concern. Thus, a social problem is perceived and examined as a social construct. Its "creation" requires not only that a number of individuals feel a conflict of value over what is and what ought to be, but also that individuals discursively promote a position, mobilize to change a condition, and achieve at least a modicum of recognition for their efforts from a wider public.

Significantly, much constructionist analysis of social problems has been motivated by concerns about children (Best 1990, 1994). Constructionists have written about the social construction of delinquency (Platt 1969), missing children (Best 1990), hyperkinesis (Conrad and Schneider 1975), and child abuse (Pfohl 1977). Since the "discovery" of child abuse and "the battered child syndrome," American society has experienced waves of concern about various threats to children such as kidnapping, murder, abuse, neglect, and incest (Best 1994).

131

Since the issue first generated public and academic concern, the nature of social discourse on child abuse has undergone several significant transformations. In the early period following the discovery of child abuse discussions of the issue emphasized the deviant nature of those who beat and abused their children. Sexual abuse victims told stories about abuse in the proximal or distant past. Victims told stories held in the form of retrievable memory. As adult victims began to articulate their experiences of early molestation, public concern about the sexual abuse of children intensified.

However, as the boundaries of such threats to children expanded, controversy has emerged over the claims of some of the alleged victims of child abuse who have claimed to have "recovered memories" of abuse (Prozan 1997). This examination is concerned with the rhetorical dimensions and claimsmaking activities of critics of some child abuse allegations, particularly those that are based on the recovered memories of childhood experiences of adults and the delayed memories of abuse of children. It examines published and broadcast narratives on child abuse, focusing on claimsmaking in the emergence of recovered memory as a social problem in the late 1980s. This examination applies constructionist social problems theory put forth by Best (1987) and Holstein and Miller (1993) to the emergence of recovered memory as a social problem.

A review of recent newspaper and magazine articles, books, journals, and recent broadcast stories on recovered memory reveals an increasingly critical and skeptical perspective on such claims. This examination divides the claimsmakers into three groups—(1) the "backlash" composed primarily of victims and defenders of such victims; (2) critical scholarly research; and (3) media coverage—and analyzes how these claimsmakers seek to persuade and convince others that recovered memory is indeed a social problem that needs to be addressed through new social policies.

THE "BACKLASH": CLAIMS AS POLITICAL RHETORIC

As public concern about child abuse heightened, denial of the extent of the problem and strong criticism of some allegations emerged in some quarters. In *The Battle and the Backlash: The Child Sexual Abuse War*, Hechler (1988:3) describes the conflict between those who see child sexual abuse as a social problem and the backlash against this recognition:

> One thing is clear; there is a war. There are those who feel that the country is suffering from an epidemic of child sexual abuse and those who feel that there is an epidemic all right, but not of sex abuse—"sex accuse," as some have

disparagingly called it. The pendulum has swung too far, they say, and what we see now is a blizzard of false accusations.

Hechler describes the growing signs of what has been called a "child abuse backlash." A group of public figures has arisen who openly question some of the assumptions and practices of child abuse advocates. The voices of the backlash include victims, defenders of victims, and victim organizations.

These public figures have made persuasive arguments that some accusations of abuse are irresponsible, problematic, and dangerous, using political rhetoric to state their claims. The arguments of these claimants are aimed to convince others that their concerns about recovered memories deserve attention. Several essentially political themes dominate the claims of the "backlash." These claims focus on such political issues as the use of authority, legitimacy, and political rights and protections.

One common theme in the backlash literature is that the child protection system is dangerously out of control, that institutional power is dramatically being misused. As Richard Wexler (1990:175) writes in *Wounded Innocents: The Real Victims of the War Against Child Abuse*:

> We have turned almost everyone who deals with children in the course of his or her work into an informer, required to report any suspicion of any form of child maltreatment, and we have encouraged the general public to do the same. We have allowed such reports to be made anonymously, making the system a potent tool for harassment.

Wexler's book is only one of many describing the nightmare of false accusations and a system that is on an irresponsible rampage. In *The Abuse of Innocence,* Eberle and Eberle (1993:408) hold that "The child abuse industry has spun out of control and become a voracious monster, hungry for human sacrifice, devouring everything in its path."

This position finds what it calls "the child abuse industry" (Wimberly 1994:47) to be self-serving. This "industry" overdramatizes the problem, seeing child protection workers as zealots trampling the rights of innocent citizens, often "brainwashing" children, and using the courts to engage in hysterical witch hunts against innocent victims. There are also insinuations that the child abuse industry is motivated by economic self-interest. Thus, as Ofshe and Watters (1994:318) note, the pitch for many therapies "ends with two particularly important words: 'insurance accepted.'" Dissociative disorder units, Ofshe and Watters (1994:302) continue, "are profit centers for the hospitals that operate them."

A second theme of the backlash is the relaxed legal protection of the accused. Whereas child protection advocates (Dziech and Schudson 1989; Myers 1994) see a court system that unnecessarily traumatizes and discounts child witnesses in protecting the accused, the backlash holds a diametrically opposed view. They describe nightmares of false accusation, relaxed standards of evidence, and the abrogation of fundamental legal rights (Wexler 1990). This distrust of the judicial system's presumption of the innocence of the child and the lack of protection of the defendant's rights is reflected in Douglas Besharov's statement that society believes alleged child abusers to have "a lesser right to the presumption of innocence" (quoted in Wakefield and Underwager 1988:x). The court system, Victims of Child Abuse Laws (VOCAL) believes, treats those accused of child abuse as if they were guilty. "Once accused of child abuse," Wimberly (1994) contends, "an individual is treated as though he or she is guilty. There is no more presumption of innocence. The burden of proof seems to be on the parents rather than on the state where it belongs" (p. 50).[1] Critics of the child protection movement, such as Wakefield and Underwager (1988), see a corrupt and inept bureaucracy too eager to prosecute the innocent.

A third theme of the backlash is the portrayal of allegations of abuse as a witch hunt. Many critics compare the false allegations from therapeutically induced memories to those made at the Salem witch trials. Indeed, one critic wrote a book titled *Sex Abuse Hysteria: Salem Witch Trials Revisited* (Gardner 1991). Such critics draw parallels between Salem and twentieth-century allegations of abuse. In Salem innocent people were convicted as witches and burned at the stake. Today, critics assert that innocent people are branded as child abusers and punished. In Salem children's testimony was used to convict innocent people of witchcraft. Today, children's testimony is the most important evidence in many sexual abuse cases. Often their testimony is seen to lead to the conviction of innocent people of child abuse. Were these genuine memories, Johnston (1997:8) asks, "or were they another form of spectral evidence, the invisible manifestations of the devil that had condemned Salem's innocent as witches?"

In the backlash literature, hysteria is closely linked with the witch hunt. Hentoff (1992:2) notes that "there is also an increasing, spiraling hysteria, fueled by some parents, therapists, and prosecutors—not unlike the emotional cyclone in 17th century Salem." In *Satan's Silence: Ritual Abuse and the Making of a Modern American Witch Hunt*, Nathan and Snedeker (1995:4) look at ritual abuse cases as "cultural panics," noting that "Belief in ritual sex abuse conspiracies was the stuff of moral panic, not unlike the crusades of the McCarthy era." The villain now was not communists, but "the satanic child molester."

Continual reference to hysteria implies that many professionals are hysterical witch hunters. These recovered memory professionals are compared to other evil doers and doings, such as the Nazi persecutions (Emans 1987:740) and the brainwashing techniques utilized in the Korean War

(Cockburn 1990:190). Among the many of their professional failings are incompetence, zealotry, and corruption. Each professional group—social workers, prosecutors, and therapists—comes in for its share of criticism, but most of the venom is reserved for therapists.

Authors who are highly critical of recovered memory routinely use an extreme example of misused power, an atrocity tale of what they see as the creation of false beliefs by therapists in patients through power or zealous prosecution that results in despair, broken families, and even suicide. Ofshe and Watters (1994) describe the story of Anna Stone, a patient of Dr. Bennett Braun, in which Anna is helped to recall being the high priestess of an international satanic order. The story, Ofshe and Watters (1994:225) conclude, is "an illustration of the harm that can be visited on one woman and her family."

In *The Myth of Repressed Memory*, Elizabeth Loftus and Katherine Ketcham (1994:102–139) have a chapter titled "A Family Destroyed" that recounts how "Fifteen-year old Jennifer Nagle entered therapy with no memories of being sexually abused, but after more than ten months of intensive psychotherapy she suddenly recovered detailed memories of abuse," which resulted in divorce, acrimony, and the complete break-up of a family.

EXPERTS: CLAIMS AS SCIENTIFIC CRITIQUE

It is remarkable how much literature has been generated in a very short time by the controversy between those who subscribe to the construct of delayed recall (Herman 1992; Pope 1994; Terr 1994) and those who claim that false memories are implanted (Howitt 1994; Pendergast 1995; van Til 1997). A number of academic researchers have examined the following question: Is it possible to repress something that is as personally significant as sexual abuse, and to regain access to the memory of it months, years, or decades later? Using the language and methods of science to refute these claims, they focus on the lack of professional and empirical standards in the recovered memory community, the questionable techniques that are used in recovering memories, and the validity of the claims of recovered memory proponents.

In the bitter debate over the practices of recovered memory therapy Richard Ofshe is perhaps the most angry and contentious critic of the recovered memory movement and its practices. Ofshe and Watters (1994:300) claim that the recovered memory movement is "a pseudoscientific enterprise that is damaging the lives of people in need," and that "devastating mistakes are being made within certain therapy settings." The authors contend that "recovered memory therapists are not, as they portray themselves, brave healers but professionals who have built a 'pseudoscience' based on no empirical evidence, out of an unfounded consensus about how the mind reacts to sexual trauma" (p. 5). In the process, "they have slipped the ties that bind their professions to scientific method and sound research" (p. 5). They have, Ofshe and Watters (1994) charge, created an "Alice-in-Wonderland world" in which opinion and ideological preference "substitute for objective evidence." Ofshe and Watters (1994:5–6) go on to suggest:

> that there is now sufficient evidence—within the therapists' own accounts of their techniques—to show that a significant cadre of poorly trained, over-zealous, or ideologically driven psychotherapists have pursued a series of pseudoscientific notions that have ultimately damaged the patients who have come for help.

Thus, Ofshe and Watters conclude that therapists using "pseudoscientific" techniques have committed "gross mistakes in therapy" in which memories and beliefs are produced within the therapeutic encounter. The authors compare the practice of recovered memory to the practice of lobotomy in the 1940s and 1950s in that it harms patients and causes them to suffer.

In the way that recovered memory therapists often train their patients to reexperience their lives, to find rape, sexual abuse, satanic ritual abuse, and other horrors in therapy, Ofshe and Watters (1994) see such therapists as a "new class of sexual predator." Some therapists, they hold, are causing emotional and psychological traumas such as those arising from rape or assault. In effect, Ofshe and Watters (1994:13) argue that "therapy patients might not be victims of their parents, but of their psychotherapists."

Michael Yapko (1994) critically examines the role of therapists in retrieving memories in *Suggestions of Abuse*. Suggestions of abuse, Yapko contends, often occur in a context of therapeutic suggestion. "In almost all of the cases in which I have been involved over the past decade," Yapko (1994) writes, "repressed memories of abuse were 'discovered' only after many therapy sessions and well *after the therapist first introduced it as a possibility*" (p. 126, emphasis added). These suggestive methods include checklists of symptoms, direct communication that a client must have been sexually abused, indirect suggestions, and the redefinition of client's resistance as cooperation.

Indeed, Yapko contends that therapists' unwavering belief in repressed memories of abuse is itself a powerful influence, and that the need for acceptance, support, empathy, and direction places the client in a vulnerable position. While claiming to uncover the truth of their clients' past, these therapists have pursued a treatment regime that persuades clients to accept hypnotically generated images, gut feelings, dreams, and imaginings as valid memories. These therapists have employed methods that blur the already perilously thin line that separates memory from imagination and have unwittingly coerced their patients to mold their beliefs and behaviors to the expectations of the therapy (Yapko 1994).

Yapko goes on to suggest that these "memories" are often little more than the residue of the fertile imagination of a highly suggestible client in the hands of a therapist who uses suggestive techniques to create false memories. Yapko (1994:20) contends that

> In ever-increasing numbers, therapists all across the country are actively or passively encouraging clients to identify themselves as victims of abuse—or, to be "politically correct," as abuse survivors. These clients may be told, "You seem to have the kind of symptoms that suggest you were abused as a child." They do not know that the symptom checklist . . . is general enough that almost any of us could qualify as survivors of abuse. . . . They may even be told, "If you have the feeling abuse occurred, then it did."

"Abuse happens," Yapko (1994:21) writes, "but so do false allegations." He argues that many therapists, without an adequate understanding of memory, repression, or their own power to unwittingly plant suggestions, try to convince their patients that they experienced sexual abuse, and that the symptoms they are having are a result of those early experiences. Clients can be led to believe destructive things that are untrue, recall memories of things that never actually happened, jump to conclusions that are not warranted, and destroy the lives of innocent people.

"It is not an exaggeration," Yapko concludes, "to say that many therapists appear to practice their profession on the basis of sheer myth" (p. 20). The author questions the knowledge of many therapists about memory and memory retrieval. In a survey of over 1000 therapists' understanding of memory (using a Memory Attitude Questionnaire), Yapko found that therapists often held erroneous views on the workings of memory, repression, and hypnosis. Among his findings were the following:

- 43% of respondents believed that if someone doesn't remember much about his or her childhood, it is most likely because it was somehow traumatic;
- almost 33% of respondents agreed that "when someone has a memory of a trauma while in hypnosis, it objectively must have actually occurred";
- one in six therapists did not believe that it was possible to suggest memories;
- 57% of therapists who completed the questionnaire did nothing at all to differentiate truth from fiction.

Some therapists, Yapko observes, hold beliefs about therapy and memory that are not only inadequate, such as the beliefs cited above, but also full of "utter nonsense"—such as the belief that it is possible to summon up actual memories of one's own birth.

Loftus and Ketcham (1994:19) view this situation as "therapy gone berserk." "Something has gone wrong with therapy," the authors contend, "and . . . that something has to do with memory" (p. 30). In many cases it is not trauma that create memories, but memories that create trauma. Loftus, the primary author, is particularly skeptical about the truth-finding function of aggressive therapy when repressed memories are recovered through such questionable techniques of "memory work"—suggestive questioning, guided visualization, age regression, hypnosis, body-memory interpretation, dream analysis, art therapy, rage and grief work, and group therapy.

Loftus is much concerned with the taken-for-granted reliability of claims of recovered memory. Through her research, the author has identified a phenomenon known as the "misinformation effect." In a typical experiment, misleading "post event information"—facts, ideas, inferences and opinion— are credibly made available to witnesses after an event is completely over. Loftus found that witnesses often accepted the suggested information as accurate and incorporated it into their narratives as genuine.

In one informal field experiment Loftus staged a theft of a woman's purse in her university classroom. Loftus quickly took charge and told everyone to stay seated and not go after the thief because "he might be dangerous." She then asked for descriptions of the suspect. One student immediately volunteered her observation of the man's checkered shirt. Loftus quickly confirmed that she saw the checkered shirt, too, and added the misleading information that the man had a beard. Nearly every additional eye witness description of the suspect now included his beard. "Subjects," she observed, "typically resisted any suggestion that their richly detailed memories might have been flawed or contaminated and asserted with great confidence that they saw what their revised and adapted memories told them they saw" (Loftus and Ketcham 1994:62).

Through careful experimental design and controlled studies Loftus attempts to provide a theoretical framework for the creation of recovered memories, showing that it is possible to create an entire memory for a traumatic event that never happened. The technique she used involved a subject and trusted member of the family who suggested that the subject had been lost at the shopping mall. Within a short time the subjects "accepted a false memory and embellished it with details of their own" (p. 95). Loftus repeated this experiment with several individuals. Although she concedes that this experiment is not a large enough sample from which to draw statistically valid inferences, it nevertheless is an important experiment that approximates "real life."

Loftus' suggestibility research was given "real world" application by Richard Ofshe. Ofshe conducted something of a spontaneous field experiment when he was called in as a consultant to examine the validity of Paul Ingram's confessions. After each accusation by his daughters of their father's (Paul Ingram) abuse, Ingram would be able to visualize what he was accused of and confessed that he committed those acts. To test Ingram's suggestibility Ofshe made up a memory and attempted to implant it. He told Ingram that his daughters had accused him of having made them have sex with their brother while Ingram watched. Initially Ingram told Ofshe he had no memory of that particular incident, but the next day Ingram told Ofshe that he could vividly recall what had happened between his daughter and his eldest son. At this point Ofshe interviewed the daughter, asking her if her father ever forced her and one of her brothers to have sex while he watched. The daughter assured him that nothing like that had happened. Paul Ingram had confessed with rich and abundant detail to something that never happened (Wright 1994:144).

Whereas Yapko, Loftus, and Ofshe focus on the recovered memory of adults, Ceci and Bruck (1995) shine the empirical spotlight on the delayed recall of children. They explore the clinical and scientific evidence for children's ability to recall memories of traumatic and suggested events. Their studies indicate that under certain conditions, children make not only omission errors, but commission errors about nonexperienced events involving their own bodies. They also demonstrate the far-reaching influences of the use of some suggestive interviewing techniques on the accuracy and credibility of children's reports.

In *Jeopardy in the Courtroom*, Ceci and Bruck (1995) examine the workings of children's memory. They attempt to generalize their findings to actual forensic and therapeutic interviews using contemporary case materials (Little Rascals, Kelly Michaels, Country Walk, and Old Cutler). For example, Ceci and Bruck conducted several experiments involving repeating questions and repeating interviews and found that such interviews and questions may decrease the accuracy of children's reports. Such techniques, the authors hold (p. 125), "allow an avenue for the introjection of misinformation that, if repeated enough times, may become incorporated by the child." These techniques may also signal to the child the bias of their interviewer, so that the child eventually learns how to answer the questions to provide the information that they feel the interviewer wants to hear. Contextualizing their research in particular cases using transcripts from the Kelly Michaels and Little Rascals cases, Ceci and Bruck (1995:118) conclude that "A consideration of the research findings suggests that if the children had not been abused, this magnitude of repeated suggestive interviewing could have the effect of planting and cementing false reports."

Ceci and Bruck also examined powerful suggestive interviewing techniques such as "stereotype induction," that they feel are more subtle than leading questions. "Stereotype induction" refers to attempts on the part of an interviewer to transmit to a child a negative characterization of an individual or an event, whether it be true or false (p. 127). Ceci and Bruck (1995:137) contend that "as evidenced by the scientific literature, the use of this technique, particularly in the hands of biased interviewers, may seriously tarnish the accuracy of children's reports." They found the interviews in the Michaels case to be "rife with examples of stereotype induction" (p. 135). (The interviewers told the children that Michaels was in jail and she had done bad things.)

In examining interviews in the context of empirical research, Ceci and Bruck found that "supportive statements" by investigators can be implicit or explicit threats, amounting to bribes and rewards that can have the effect of coercing children "to give incorrect information about events for which they have no memory" (p. 141). The effects of letting children know that their friends or siblings have "already told" is a practice that can often "taint reports" (p. 152). Additionally, interviews by high status adults can have "negative effects on the accuracy of children's reports" (p. 153).

Ceci and Bruck question the techniques and practices used to invoke or to validate dramatic and detailed accounts of an alleged early abuse experiences that suddenly erupt into consciousness. Such "repressed" or "delayed" memories of early childhood abuse, they argue, may be the result of positive suggestions that include erroneous constructions based on suggestive therapeutic practices or personal retrieval techniques that seed the growth of recovered memories, conceivably leading clients to imagine that they participated in fictitious scenarios, particularly in childhood. If therapists encourage clients to abandon self-doubts, "coupled with encouragement to use suggestive techniques," Ceci and Bruck (1995:228) are concerned that "some of their clients could develop elaborate pseudo memories that may not be detected as false by either the client or the professional." In essence, suggestive questioning by therapists can generate false memories in children that seem very real, even down to the strong emotions that accompany them.[2]

THE MEDIA: CLAIMS AS PARADIGMATIC TYPIFICATORY ACCOUNT

Katherine Beckett (1996) used content analysis to analyze media coverage of child abuse in four leading news magazines: *Time, Newsweek, U.S. News and World Report,* and *People* covering the years 1980–1994. She found a dramatic transformation of media discourse on child abuse from denial to skepticism during these years. Beckett concluded that the media discussion of child sexual abuse "changed dramatically over the past 15 years," with stories of false accusation dominating the media focus (p. 17). Beckett's study establishes empirically the trajectory and content of media stories but does not examine the claims made in such stories. This section attempts to examine the paradigmatic claims made in media coverage of recovered memories over the past decade.

In its early coverage of abuse charges based particularly on children's memory, the media initially sided unwaveringly with the prosecution's evidence. In a famous child abuse case involving the McMartin preschool, *People* called McMartin "California's Nightmare Nursery." *Time* introduced its coverage of McMartin with a one-word headline: "Brutalized." On ABC's "20/20" news magazine, host Tom Jarriel described the preschool as "a sexual house of horrors," and further inflamed viewers as co-host Hugh Downs asked, "How deeply marred are these children, Tom and will they ever recover from it?" "Psychologically, perhaps never, Hugh," Jarriel replied" (quoted in Nathan and Snedeker 1995:88).

In the mid 1980s the media have shifted their focus from allegations of abuse to critical scrutiny of the claims of abuse. A review of several recent magazine, broadcast stories, and books reveals how the media spotlight transformed the focus from hidden abuse to claims that recovered memory constitutes a social problem. The paradigmatic typification of recent media coverage focuses on lack of evidence, questionable therapeutic techniques, and the validity of recovered memory. Often the media have become what Best (1989) calls a "secondary claims maker," borrowing data from research on recovered memory.

In May 1984, *Newsweek* ran a cover story titled "A Hidden Epidemic: Sexual Abuse of Children is Much More Common than Most Americans Suspect." The article emphasized the surprising extent of child sexual abuse and lamented that "few offenders will be reported to any authority; fewer still will be punished" (May 14, 1984:30). The article presented claims of abuse as valid indicators of a previously ignored social problem.

The April 19, 1993 issue of *Newsweek* contains a close-up of Shirley and Ray Souza, convicted of sexually abusing two of their young grandchildren. Next to them is the headline: "Child Abuse: A court found the Souzas guilty of molesting their grandchildren. They cry witch-hunt. When does the fight to protect our kids go too far?" The cover story is titled "Rush to Judgment," and begins with that statement that "America is now at war against child abuse. But some recent cases suggest we may be pushing too hard, too fast." The story conveys alarm at false allegations and suggests that many innocent people are caught up in a witch hunt:

Woody Allen is accused, day care teachers are jailed, women go on TV to describe their latest memories of childhood victimization. . . . Sometimes, amid all the noise, real sex abusers are identified and convicted. But too often, critics charge, the evidence is flimsy and the pursuit maniacal.

While it is rare for children to invent tales of sex abuse, some experts are convinced that in many instances children describe fantasies generated during months of intense questioning. Psychologists who study the way children remember and recount events are building a huge body of research on how easily children can be swayed. In total the article refers to eight professionals, with the work of six used to raise doubts about the allegations and the memories.

A 1995 segment of "20/20" featured cognitive psychologists Stephen Ceci's and Maggie Bruck's work, which demonstrated how false memories could be created by using simple techniques of persuasion. In the set-up Barbara Walters asks the question "When children tell stories of sexual abuse, should we believe them?" Their answer is, "There is now convincing scientific evidence that the answer is 'not necessarily.'"

In the piece itself Stephen Ceci describes his Sam Stone experiment to show that children's memories can be manipulated through suggestive questions. In the experiment two groups of children were told that Sam Stone was coming soon. This was all one group heard. The other group was told that Sam was clumsy. When Sam finally came to the center, he stayed for two uneventful minutes, then left. Later, on four different occasions over a 10-week period, both groups of children were asked what had happened on the day of the visit. When asked suggestive questions about Sam's clumsiness the children in the first group answered correctly. On the other hand, when the children who had heard stories about Sam's clumsiness were asked questions about his clumsiness, about three-quarters of the children claimed that Sam had committed some kind of clumsy act.

The possibility of false memories of children is shown in the videotaped study by Ceci and Bruck in which 3 year olds visit their pediatrician for a check-up (Ceci and Bruck:164–169). The check-up is shown. There is no genital touching, although the physician does measure wrists and taps feet. Later half of the children incorrectly reported touching. When given anatomically correct dolls, several inserted sticks into vaginal and rectal orifices. Several showed how the doctor had hammered a stick into an orifice.

Ceci and Bruck also found that some of the children in their experiments came to believe that they had actually experienced fictitious events. They conducted an experiment in which preschool children were encouraged to think about actual events that they experienced in their past and fictitious events that they had never experienced, such as getting their hand caught in a mousetrap. Their purpose was to see if repeatedly thinking about fictional events could lead to false beliefs about their reality. During the "20/20" story, John Stossel interviews a boy who has been told by his parents, who believed that the experiment is over, that the mousetrap story was fictitious and had never happened, that it was just in his imagination. Stossel asked the boy if he ever got his finger caught in a mousetrap. The boy states that he remembered this happening, and proceeded to supply a detailed narrative. When Stossel challenges him, asking if it was not the case that his parents had already explained that this event never happened, the child protests, "But it really did happen. I remember it!"

On the September 1996 ABC television program "Turning Point," titled "When Children Accuse: Who to Believe?," allegations of sexual abuse against Scott and Brenda Kniffen by their two sons, 6 year old Brian and 7 year old Brandon, were described. Scott and Brenda Kniffen were each found guilty of 70 counts of child abuse and sentenced to 200 years in jail. The piece described the essentials of the case, largely through the eyes of the prosecutor and the defense attorney, Michael Snedeker. Both of the children recanted their testimony on camera, claiming that their testimony was coerced. Tapes of interviews with the children graphically showed the use of threats, bribes, and rewards. For example, the tapes showed that the children were promised that they could go home with their parents if they told what their parents did to them, and that their sibling had already described incidents of abuse.

The stories cited above follow to some degree the outcomes of court cases (the Amiraults, Kelly Michaels, and Lil Rascals), but they show a clear tilt toward viewing those found guilty of child abuse to be the victims of false testimony and false memories. Editorial comment takes the side of the accused. At the end of the "20/20" episode described above, Stossel asked Maggie Bruck if she thinks that "there are dozens of people in jail who are innocent," to which Bruck answered "Yes, I do." In a 1996 "20/20" piece on the Amirault case, Hugh Downs introduces the audience to the case by noting that "conviction doesn't necessarily mean its true." The piece describes the accusations against the Amiraults, noting that there was no physical evidence, and repeats much of the Ceci and Bruck footage previously described that debunks the idea that children's memories are always accurate. The implication is clearly that the Amiraults have been railroaded. At the conclusion Hugh Downs asks "Is anything being done in this witch hunt atmosphere?" The reporter on the story, noting that the Amiraults are probably innocent, laments "I hope Gerald Amirault gets out."

Perhaps the most notable television coverage of false accusations has been presented in a series of documentaries on the Little Rascals Day Care Center in Edenton, North Carolina, produced by Ofra Bikel for PBS's

"Frontline." This series, "Innocence Lost" (1991), "Innocence Lost: The Verdict" (1993), and "Innocence Lost: The Plea" (1997), details the allegations of child sexual abuse, the children's often fantastic testimony (a child charges the daycare operators with having a shark pond that he puts salt into), problems with the testimony, the jury deliberations, and prosecution claims. These documentaries show how "There had been no conclusive medical evidence, no physical evidence and no eye witnesses" to the alleged memories and testimony of children and claims of parents. (Just prior to the airing of "The Plea" all charges were dropped by the prosecution.) In a 1995 two-part exposé on PBS's "Frontline," Bikel took viewers into therapists' offices and revealed some of the memory recovery techniques in use.

Several book-length exposés of recovered memory by journalists, notably Lawrence Wright's *Remembering Satan* and Debbie Nathan and Michael Snedeker's *Satan's Silence*, make serious claims about the spurious nature of many memories of sexual abuse. Wright's book, *Remembering Satan*, tells the story of Paul Ingram, a sheriff's deputy and chairman of the local Republican Party in Olympia Washington. (The story was also made into a television movie on Fox.) Ingram's accuser was his daughter Ericka, who was 21 years old at the time. On a retreat for women members of a charismatic Christian church, led by "divine prompter" Karla Franklin, Ericka suddenly "remembered" that her father had raped her for years when she was a child as part of a satanic ritual. Ingram's other daughter, Julie, also claimed that she was sexually abused since she was 13. Later, Ingram's son also had recovered memories of abuse. Wright describes how the accusations expanded to include Ingram's wife Sandy, and several other members of the Sheriff's department, Jim Rabin and Ray Risch.

Wright describes how the Ingram case become increasingly bizarre. Ericka, who along with her sister had read books on satanic ritual abuse, began to describe in detail satanic ritual practices to which they had been subjected to by their parents. All in all Ericka estimated that she attended 850 such rituals and had watched 25 babies being sacrificed! And the mother, at the prodding of her pastor, began to visualize such rituals as well. Paul, encouraged by the police investigators, began to produce detailed memories of having perpetrated the sexual abuses. He was assured, Wright says, that if he confessed to the abuse, his memories of the things he confessed would become clearer.

Wright sees the Ingram story as a cautionary tale about the dangers of recovered memories. The Ingram family, he concludes (p. 189), was destroyed by their memories, memories that Wright (1994:200) feels are patently false:

> Whatever the value of repression as a scientific concept or a therapeutic tool, unquestioning belief in it has become as dangerous as the belief in witches.

One idea is modern and the other an artifact of what we like to think of as a credulous age, but the consequences are depressingly the same.

"At no time," Wright maintains, "did the detectives ever consider the possibility that the source of the memories was the investigation itself" (p. 195).

Debbie Nathan's and Michael Snedeker' *Satan's Silence* is a history of what they view as a "cultural panic," an examination of its promoters, an exploration of the accusers, their accusations, and the abuse of defendants in a number of high profile cases during the 1980s. They (1995) note that

> Throughout the decade, a rash of claims would spread, in the popular culture and later among local and national policing agencies, that America's youngsters were gravely threatened by psychopathic murders, kidnappers, occultists, pornographers, and child molesters. These stores were either baseless or grossly exaggerated, but the media, politicians, feminists, psychotherapists, and child-protection professional helped promote and spread them. (p. 7)

Nathan and Snedeker (1995) review the results of the viewpoint "that the accusing children are always to be believed and that adults who demur are always lying" (p. 12). They investigate many of the allegations and accusations, noting the lack of corroborative evidence; lack of medical evidence; questionable interviewing techniques; "architects of the child abuse panic" such as Dr. Roland Summit and Kee MacFarlene; key texts such as *Michelle Remembers*; and the organizational structure of "the ritual abuse industry." The authors conclude that "the psychotic delusions of a few individuals were translated into public policy" in which advocates created a "flawless system, with methods for promoting criminal charges, a patina of science to lend authority, and a rhetoric for explaining away the lack of evidence" (p. 53).

In *Spectral Evidence: The Romona Case*, Moira Johnston (1997) argues that the advocates of recovered memory have ignored justice and the protection of the innocent. In the destruction of Gary Ramona's life, Johnston found a "victim culture and incest fixation that had strewn such havoc through the decade" (p. 386). Reviewing the Holly Romona case, Johnston concluded "that no responsible scientist would dare claim to know if, or how, her memories could be true" (p. 390).

CONCLUSION

Various factors and claimsmakers trigger the construction and evolution of social problems. This examination has focused on the claimsmaking activities of several groups who have made assertions with respect to the problematic status of recovered memory. These claimsmakers have used the rhetoric of politics, the rhetoric of science, and media typifications to bring the problematics of recovered memory to people's attention.

The case of recovered memory demonstrates the successful construction of a new social problem. These claimsmakers have been generally success-ful in combining three elements identified by Lowney and Best (1995:49) as being important to social problem construction: (1) typifying claims, (2) using cultural resources, and (3) developing organizational resources. Each of these elements has been effectively used by the critics of recovered memory.

Typifying Claims

A significant step in social problems construction is linking a troubling event to a problematic pattern and connecting particular incidents symbol-ically and representationally to a larger problem. The attempt is to define an incident as an instance of some larger problem. In the case of recovered memory, this linking of event and pattern has occurred at several points, producing various typifications. Claimsmakers have produced various typ-ifying examples of horrific accusations, most notably of Paul Ingram, Gary Romona, Kelly Michaels, and George Franklin. In these cases and others claimsmakers have illustrated a problem's nature through typifying exam-ples. Academic claimsmakers such as Loftus, Ofshe, and Ceci offered typify-ing examples through their experiments and research of scientific grounds for skepticism.

Cultural Resources

Critics of recovered memory have also related the issue of recovered memory to deep cultural themes. The claims that institutional and profes-sional power was being misused, that the memories of accusers were anoth-er manifestation of the hysteria that had condemned Salem's innocent citizens as witches, and that the advocates of recovered memory ignored the purpose of the quest for truth, justice, and the protection of the innocent, draw on cultural resources that elicit favorable responses. These cultural themes are a key element in the way that claims of "false memory" are presented and "packaged." By linking claims of recovered memory to the misuse of power, witch hunts, and the persecution of the innocent, they become more credible.

Organizational Resources

Prior to the 1980s critical claims about recovered memories lacked significant organizational support. Victims of Child Abuse Laws (VOCAL) was founded in 1984 by parents who had been falsely accused. The False Memory Syndrome Foundation (FMSF) was founded in 1992, also by accused parents. They named distinguished scientists to their advisory board and launched a tenacious campaign to educate the media, professionals, and the public. VOCAL and the FMSF helped to transform a condition that had previously gone unnoticed into an object of concern. Media coverage of recovered memory increasingly cited experts from these organizations. By using their organizational resources to promote the problem of recovered memory, they helped shape the issue for the public and for policymakers.

The claims of critics of recovered memory suggest that this combination of typifying claims, tapping into resonating cultural issues, and developing organizational resources is an important component of successful claimsmaking. Critics of recovered memory have significantly affected the meaning construction and the signification of recovered memory as a social problem. Their claims have redefined recovered memory as unreliable and dangerous.[3]

NOTES

1.   VOCAL was founded in 1984 by parents who claimed to have been wrongfully accused of child abuse (Wimberly 1994:49). VOCAL members argue that the current child protection system is out of control, and that many innocent people are caught up in a web of unfounded and false accusations.

2.   In 1992 the False Memory Syndrome Foundation was founded to promote education and public awareness of the damage recovered memory therapy causes. The Foundation's major role has been to provide a center for the dissemination of scientific research on human memory and to propose the diagnostic category of "false memory syndrome." With the creation of a scientific advisory board (Ofshe and Loftus are members), the Foundation launched a vigorous campaign to educate the media and the public on the dangers of claims based on uncorroborated memories.

3.   What have been the effects of such claims? At this point it is unclear how influential such claims have been on the general public. Polls, although now somewhat dated, show public support for protecting children. Opinion polls (Schulman, Ronca, and Bucuvalas, Inc. 1988) suggest that the public wants more aggressive child protection activity, not less. The public, according to such polls, is more concerned about abusers who go free than about people who are unfairly prosecuted, and is more worried about damage to child witnesses than the protection of defendants' rights. On the other hand, as Beckett (1996) has argued, the media frame has become more skeptical. Several dozen courts have rejected recovered memories

at state appellate and supreme court levels. In May 1996, the U.S. Supreme Court upheld an appeals court finding that abuse allegations in *Borwick v. Shay* were "fanciful . . . far-fetched . . . uncorroborated."

REFERENCES

Beckett, Katherine. 1996. "Culture and the Politics of Signification: The Case of Child Sexual Abuse." *Social Problems* 43 (1):57–76.

Best, Joel (ed.) 1989. *Images of Issues: Typifying Contemporary Social Problems.* Hawthorne, NY: Aldine de Gruyter.

Best, Joel. 1990. *Threatened Children: Rhetoric and Concern About Child-Victims.* Chicago: University of Chicago Press.

Best, Joel (ed.) 1994. *Troubling Children: Studies of Children and Social Problems.* Hawthorne, NY: Aldine de Gruyter.

Ceci, Stephen and Maggie Bruck. 1995. *Jeopardy in the Courtroom: A Scientific Analysis of Children's Testimony.* Washington, D.C.: American Psychological Association.

Cockburn, A. 1990. "Beat The Devil." *The Nation* February 12:190.

Conrad, Peter and Joseph Schneider. 1992. *Deviance and Medicalization.* Philadelphia: Temple.

Dziech, Billie Wright and Charles B. Schudson. 1989. *On Trial: America's Courts and Their Treatment of Sexually Abused Children.* Boston: Beacon Press.

Eberle, P. and S Eberle. 1993. *The Abuse of Innocence.* Buffalo, NY: Prometheus.

Emans, R. 1987. "Abuse In the Name of Protecting Children." *Phi Delta Kappan* 68:740–743.

Gardner, R. A. 1991. *Sex Abuse Hysteria: Salem Witch Trials Revisited.* Cresskill, NJ: Creative Therapeutics.

Hechler, D. 1988. *The Battle and the Backlash: The Child Sexual Abuse War.* Lexington, MA: D.C. Heath.

Hentoff, Nat. 1992. "When Authorities Browbeat Children into a Lie." *The Washington Post,* p. A 19.

Herman, Judith. 1992. *Trauma and Recovery.* New York: Basic Books.

Holstein, J. A. and G. Miller (eds.) 1993. *Reconsidering Social Constructionism.* Hawthorne, NY: Aldine de Gruyter.

Howitt, Dennis. 1994. *Child Abuse Errors: When Good Intentions Go Wrong.* Newark, NJ: Rutgers University Press.

Johnston, Moira. 1997. *Spectral Evidence: The Romona Case.* Boston: Houghton Mifflin.

Loftus, Elizabeth and Katherine Ketcham. 1994. *The Myth of Repressed Memory.* New York: St. Martin's.

Lowney, Kathleen S. and Joel Best. 1995. "Stalking Strangers and Lovers: Changing Media Typifications of a New Crime Problem." Pp. 44–52 in *Sociology: Exploring the Architecture of Everyday Life,* edited by D. M. Neuman. Thousand Oaks, CA: Pine Forge Press.

Myers, John E. B. (ed.) 1994. *The Backlash.* Newbury Park, CA: Sage.

Nathan, Debbie and Michael Snedeker. 1995. *Satan's Silence*. New York: Basic Books.

Nelson, B. 1984. *Making an Issue of Child Abuse*. Chicago: University of Chicago Press.

Newsweek. 1984. "A Hidden Epidemic: Sexual Abuse of Children is Much More Common than Most Americans Suspect." May 14.

Newsweek. 1993. "Child Abuse." April 19.

Ofshe, Richard and Ethan Watters. 1994. *Making Monsters*. Berkeley: University of California Press.

Pendergast, Mark. 1995. *Victims of Memory: Incest Accusations and Shattered Lives*. Hinesberg, VT: Upper Access.

Pfohl, S. J. 1997. "The 'Discovery' of Child Abuse." *Social Problems* 24:310–323.

Platt, Anthony. 1969. *The Child Savers: The Invention of Delinquency*. Chicago: University of Chicago Press.

Pope, K. S. 1994. "Memory, Abuse, and Science: Questioning Claims about the False Memory Syndrome Epidemic." *American Psychologist* 51:957–974.

Prozan, Charlotte. 1997. *Construction and Reconstruction of Memory*. New York: Aronsen.

Public Broadcasting System. 1991. "Innocence Lost."

Public Broadcasting System. 1993. "Innocence Lost: The Verdict."

Public Broadcasting System. 1995. "Divided Memories."

Public Broadcasting System. 1997. "Innocence Lost: The Plea."

Schulman, Ronca, and Bucuvales, Inc. 1988. "Public Attitudes and Actions Regarding Child Abuse and Its Prevention." Chicago: National Committee for the Prevention of Child Abuse and Neglect.

Spector, M. and J. I. Kitsuse. 1977. *Constructing Social Problems*. Menlo Park, CA: Benjamin Cummings.

Terr, Lenore. 1994. *Unchained Memories: True Stories of Traumatic Memories, Lost and Found*. New York: Basic Books.

"Turning Point." ABC. September 1996. "When Children Accuse: Who To Believe."

"20/20." ABC. July 1995. Untitled segment on the Souza case and the work of Stephen Ceci.

"20/20." ABC. June 1996. Untitled segment on the Amirault case.

van Til, Reinder. 1997. *Lost Daughters: Recovered Memory Therapy and the People It Hurts*. New York: Eerdmans.

Wakefield, H. and R. Underwager. 1988. *Accusations of Child Sexual Abuse*. Springfield, IL: Charles C. Thomas.

Wexler, R. 1990. *Wounded Innocents: The Real Victim of the War Against Child Abuse*. New York: Guilford.

Wimberly, Lesley. 1994. "The Perspective From Victims of Child Abuse Laws (VOCAL)." In *The Backlash*, edited by J.E.B. Myers. Thousand Oaks, CA: Sage

Wright, Lawrence. 1994. *Remembering Satan: A Tragic Case of Recovered Memory*. New York: Vintage.

Yapko, Michael 1994. *Suggestions of Abuse*. New York: Simon and Schuster.

The Concept of a "Healthy Person": A Sociological Contribution toward a Truly Revolutionary Psychotherapy

8

John A. Kovach

INTRODUCTION

The concept of a "healthy person" is examined from traditional and radical perspectives in psychology and contrasted with a view informed by critical sociology. The role that the concept of a "healthy person" plays in shaping the therapeutic milieu and goals in therapy is discussed. It is shown that traditionally oriented therapists conceive of the healthy person in asocial, individualistic terms that merely reinforce the status quo. More radically oriented therapists are seen simply to oppose the individualistic focus of traditionalists by emphasizing the primacy of the social. A resolution is presented in discussion of the view of a healthy person that is provided by critical sociology; this perspective involves a dialectical concept emphasizing the *relationship* between individuals and society. The importance of a critical sociological view of individuals as historical rather than social entities is discussed along with current trends in the growing therapeutic community. Through a brief examination of literature in critical sociology, it is shown how categories that are often viewed as economic categories, or as analyses of economic and other social institutions and processes, are indeed discussions about *people* and individual psychological maladies resulting from specific historical relationships between the individual and society.

The purpose of this chapter is to focus discussion and debate on the concept of a "healthy person." The concept is important because whether stated directly or not, assumptions about the nature of a healthy person define the context and trajectory of the therapeutic situation. At the basis of the goals and directions pursued within a therapeutic milieu lies the conception of a "healthy person."

The problem with the concept of a healthy person is that it is defined, albeit usually implicitly, in a manner that reflects the heightened individualism that has been seen as an adjunct to contemporary economic decline. As it guides therapeutic goals, this concept mirrors what has been described by Rubin (1996) as "cultural confusion" where the lines separating what is real from that which is simply a "dramatic reenactment" have become increasingly blurred. In the end, this type of individualism and confusion, which is supported rather than challenged in traditional approaches to therapy, is supportive of the dominant structure of power and privilege in our society. The healthy person is seen by traditional therapists as one who has "adjusted" to his or her life-situation and copes fairly well in his or her professional life. Therapists who consider their approach more radical tend to suggest that it is not people who are mentally healthy or unhealthy but rather it is the social situation to which individuals must adjust that is healthy or "sick." These relationships and differing perspectives demand closer scrutiny in an age when therapeutic intervention has become the first resort for large numbers of the population who suffer silently from problems that manifest themselves in the everyday lives and relationships of individuals, yet appear to be part of larger social trends, issues, or problems.

THE TRADITIONAL VIEW OF THE HEALTHY PERSON

Medical models of health have greatly influenced traditional psychology's conception of a mentally healthy person. For those involved in institutional mental health or those who must work within the managed health care system, the concept of a healthy person is clearly defined by the *Diagnostic and Statistical Manual of Mental Disorders, 4th edition* (DSM-IV). This institutional view of a healthy person rests on the medical model that sees health, be it physical or mental, as a fitness to work. Influenced by psychiatry and institutional psychology, most traditional psychologists tend to see a "healthy person" as one who has accommodated to his or her reality. Traditional therapists are not overly concerned with the dynamics of this social reality; they are more concerned with how well the individual copes with these social circumstances. This approach has been criticized for simply reinforcing a self-blaming view of personal problems and misery (Szasz 1961; Brown 1990; Masson 1994). By presenting the basis of the conflicts that individuals experience in everyday living as being rooted in the unconscious, or through the promotion of "stress management" techniques, these therapists may actually be exacerbating a client's problems by heightening individualism, which is at the core of psychic pain in the first place.

In keeping with an individualistic focus, most traditional psychologists also emphasize the extent to which the healthy person's actions are dominated by the unconscious mind. This focus on the unconscious dynamics of human action has its roots in Freudian approaches to understanding behavior.

FREUDIAN ROOTS

Freud's view of the healthy person was one who is capable of love and work. Interestingly, Freud did take notice of the social origins of illness and health. In one work, he discussed his prescription for a world without many of the social and personal problems (Freud did not see the two as intimately connected) that we see today. Freud described the need for mass therapy so that everyone in society could be helped with their neurosis (Freud 1919). He noted the social link to health and illness when he stated that "We shall probably discover that the poor are even less ready to part with their neuroses than the rich, because the hard life that awaits them when they recover has no attraction, and illness in them gives them more claim to the help of others" (p. 190). Freud's focus, of course, remained highly individualistic. Beyond noticing the possibly different purposes served by neuroses in the rich and poor, he did not recognize the relationship between social stratification in class society and the perception of individual health and illness. He saw nothing political about his therapy or his suggestion of mass therapy for everyone in society. When Freud discussed what form such a mass therapy might take, he said it would assuredly use elements "borrowed from strict psychoanalysis which serves no ulterior purpose" (Freud 1919:190).

Contemporary trends in mainstream psychology continue to promote a context for understanding individual problems that deemphasizes or ignores the relationship between affect, social context, culture, and history (Prilleltensky 1990). Current discussion of the rediscovery, refinement, and popularity of cognitive psychological approaches provides an excellent example of the problem of reification in traditional psychology and psychotherapeutic approaches as well as a continuing example of the apolitical parameters of the field of psychology as a whole that were set by Descartes (Gardner 1985). The dualistic model provided by Descartes is at the root of difficulties that contemporary psychology has in explaining the interaction between mind and body as well as explaining the relationship between mind and social context (Sampson 1983). This model of the "mind" has resulted in the affirmation of an abstracted view of the individual in society—a view that sees the individual as being primarily self-generated (Still and Costall 1987).

To the extent that psychotherapists adopt this Cartesian model, they tend to get caught in the trap of reification, that is, the act of regarding abstractions as real material entities. Cognitive psychologists tend to treat specific instances of phenomena as discrete entities that account for the phenomenon itself; they see cognition that may be involved in the overall phenomenon as distinct events standing on their own or as causative forces of the behavior being explained or examined (Prilleltensky 1990). Interestingly, many so-called "new age" therapies, such as massage, aroma, "rebirthing," and hypnotic regression to "past lives," also suffer from a similar sort of reification. What is lost in all of these approaches is the view of the individual in society that is provided by critical sociology; the individual is not simply a substance or entity that stands alone but a *relation* that cannot be separated from its social and historical context.

To be fair, it should be noted that some traditional therapists who consider themselves enlightened and nonjudgmental would flatly object to the concept of a healthy person. These therapists emphasize functional abilities in an individual rather than concepts of health and nonhealth. They see a fully "functional" individual as one who can set goals and realize these goals, leading to some form of self-actualization (Sobel and Ornstein 1996; Beck 1995). However, this view of a functional individual, as opposed to the concept of a healthy person, is still a view that does not challenge the status quo; this view does not recognize or focus on the larger social structural roots of individual problems. Neither the concept of functionality nor that of the healthy person recognizes that in a class society a sizable portion of the society may perhaps set goals, but social constraints guarantee that this group will not realize these goals. And many of the poorest individuals in our society, suffering the cumulative effects of economic, racial, and sexual oppression, have ceased to set goals beyond those relative to basic daily survival. In the end, the concepts of "functionality" and "goals" as used by therapists who consider themselves progressive are no less racist, sexist, or classist than the healthy person concept as it is applied by other traditional therapists.

THE RADICAL VIEW OF THE HEALTHY PERSON

"Radical therapy" emerged in the 1960s as a response to traditional psychology's overemphasis on the *mind* and the *individual agent* as causative forces related to individual problems in living. As such, radical therapists would not find the concept of a healthy person very useful for setting goals in a therapeutic context. They tend to reject such an individualist, medicalized view of human behavior, and instead, focus on the social structural dynamics impinging on the individual and conditioning the perception of behavior as healthy/unhealthy or normal/abnormal.

The radical approach to the concept of a healthy person was greatly influenced by the work of Szasz over 35 years ago. Szasz, strongly opposed to the medical model of mental health used primarily by psychiatry but also influencing traditional psychology, saw the concepts of mental illness and health as metaphors. To Szasz, psychiatric diagnoses and the categories of abnormal psychology were nothing more than stigmatizing labels (Szasz

1961). Szasz emphasized the need to recognize a wide range of human behavior as normal. He argued that it is when behaviors offend or challenge the status quo that they are labeled as illness, thus allowing the stripping of individual power, the removing of individual responsibility, and the involuntary "treatment" of such a "sick" person. To Szasz, extremes in human behavior were seen as indicative of social or cultural ills. So even though he seemed to reject the concept of a healthy person, Szasz did hold some view of a healthy society. The idea that it is not the individual who is sick, but rather the culture or society, is the basis of most therapies calling themselves radical (see, e.g., de la Cancela 1985; Rosen 1984; Sipe 1985).

It should be noted that most radical therapists would not consider Szasz very radical. Szasz focused on behavior and verbal presentations and how they are perceived, but the subtle role of consciousness is largely absent from his theoretical framework. He does not look at the dynamic role of consciousness as a mediator between the individual and social reality or the political nature of this relationship. Most contemporary therapists who consider their practice to be radical devote much attention to the importance of powerlessness and the processes through which the powerlessness that most people experience in everyday life shapes consciousness and the nature of personal misery or happiness.

Lerner (1987), for example, focuses on the dimension of powerlessness in everyday life. He does not specifically discuss the concept of a healthy person but the implication is that a healthy person is *not* a powerless person. He details how the theory and dynamics of traditional therapy contribute to this problem of powerlessness. Lerner's primary criticism of traditional therapists is that they see a healthy person as one who is well accommodated to reality, as opposed to a person who takes power and acts on his or her reality in an attempt to change it.

A decade ago, Lerner presented what he called liberation therapy. This "radical" approach was geared toward teaching people how their lives are connected to social events. According to Lerner, therapy should be an educative process that helps patients with unresolved conflicts from their past. For example, with issues involving conflict with parents, liberation therapy would aim to help such clients realize how the world of work, the organization of the economy, the legacy of racism and sexism, and the ideology of meritocracy all shaped their parents' experiences.

It is important to note that Lerner's liberation therapy is focused, not unlike traditional therapy, toward *changing the individual* or at least leading the patient to reframe their perception and understanding of their own reality. Not unlike Freud, Lerner saw the need for some sort of mass therapy. However, Lerner's conception of the form that this therapy would take and its goals were quite different from Freud's view. It was the perception of mass neurosis that prompted Freud to discuss the need for mass therapy.

Lerner saw mass therapy as a way to politicize the definition of a healthy person. In essence Lerner, like other so-called radical psychologists of the 1970s and 1980s (e.g., Brown 1974; Rosen 1984), recognized that contrary to the slogan of the 1960s, the personal is *not* political—it must be politicized.

Today, most therapists who consider themselves "radical" practice therapy that involves an element of critical or radical political education. This radical pedagogy is intended to raise the consciousness of the client so that he or she will take power and act on their reality in an attempt to change it. This approach is considered "radical" because it is opposed to the approach of traditional therapists who try to help clients simply accommodate themselves to social reality. The inherent conflict in the therapeutic situation for radical therapists is not between the individual and unconscious motivations or conflicts—as in traditional therapy—but between individuals and social institutions. The goal of radical therapy is development of a radical consciousness where the individual has an awareness of the connections between the dynamics of everyday life and the larger social order. Along these lines, some therapists who have adopted a "postmodern" approach to therapy, and the narrative process through which meaning is constructed within the therapeutic situation, emphasize the need to "relativize experience." This perspective suggests that one way to challenge the hegemonic stance of traditional approaches in therapy is to help clients explore experience from multiple perspectives, thus enabling them to understand the relational context in which behavior is situated (Gergen and Kaye 1992).

A critical issue ignored by many radical therapists that needs to be addressed is exactly how a client is supposed to act on his or her new politicized awareness and understanding. How is the client expected to take any meaningful action that will result in changing the objective, material circumstances that are connected to his or her misery or suffering? It is this element of *praxis* that is the weak link in the framework provided by radical therapists, and it is precisely this understanding of the nature of praxis provided by critical sociology that could be a major contribution to a truly revolutionary view of psychotherapy.

A SOCIOLOGICAL CONTRIBUTION TOWARD
REVOLUTIONARY PSYCHOTHERAPY

What has been referred to here as a "critical" sociological approach is an understanding of social relations that reflects a Marxist worldview. Marx certainly did not set out to develop a psychology of human behavior, but his writings, especially *Capital*, do provide a framework for understanding the socially and historically conditioned nature of the individual in society. The usefulness of this Marxist understanding is seen in the framework that was used by Vygotsky and Luria as they developed a psychology that linked human beings, not merely to society, but to *history*. This "critical" or Marxist approach is fundamental to presenting a holistic view of human nature because it provides a methodology that allows transcendence of the narrow linear focus of traditional psychology. It provides a view of the healthy person that is connected to larger society.

In Marx's early writings he was clear that what makes us individuals is not just the social but the *historical*. Understanding this relationship to history, to broad changes in the social structure, becomes most important in understanding the concepts of the individual and the healthy person as they are informed by this critical sociological perspective. Marx did not oppose the individual or society, nor is there a denial of individual identity in his writings. A Marxist concept of the individual must simply be linked to history. This sociohistorical view of the individual in contemporary society was expressed in Marx's early writings when, in critiquing Feuerbach, Marx wrote that "the human essence is no abstraction inherent in each single individual. In its reality it is the ensemble of the social relations" (Marx 1972:109). The nature of this conditioning relationship in contemporary capitalist society is clearly stated by Marx: "Man [sic] is no longer in a condition of external tension with the external substance of private property; *he has himself become the tension-ridden being of private property*" (Marx 1964:148, emphasis added). This view of the self that is presented by Marx is much more subtle and, at the same time, much more complex than is presented by traditional psychology in its representation of the healthy person in society.

In *Capital*, Marx continued with the view that human beings are not merely social animals, but animals that can become individual only in society. Marx fleshes out his original idea first seen in his critique of Feuerbach, that individuation is a function of social relations (Messinger 1990). The contradictory nature of this view of the individual in society becomes especially fascinating and ironic in contemporary society when, as individuals become more interdependent than ever before in history as well as electronically interconnected, they have at the same time become more atomized and alienated from each other and from their own selves.

Marx's conception of the socially conditioned nature of the individual in society helps to explain why human needs change through history. This view is also useful in providing a sociological critique of the concept of a healthy person. Traditional psychology tends to see needs as static, generated solely by biological and psychological roots that do not extend beyond the individual psyche. Marx's view in *Capital* makes it clear that the way in which need structures are generated and satisfied is conditioned by relationships established in the process of production in our society and the very real market-generated needs (consumption needs) of the capitalist system. There is a reciprocal relationship between production and consumption for Marx; in contemporary society this reciprocal relationship takes the form of individuals getting chained into cycles of work and consumption in a futile attempt to meet self-esteem needs through status competition/consumption. Clearly, the conception of a healthy person within such a social structural reality is radically different from what is provided by traditional psychology with its conspicuous ignorance of the critical importance of these connections of individuals to contemporary social reality. Such a critical or Marxist view of the individual in society was provided, however, by the Soviet psychologist, Vygotsky.

THE PERSPECTIVE OF VYGOTSKY

The psychology developed by Vygotsky is a Marxist psychology—and also one that helps to flesh out the basis for a therapy informed by critical sociology. Vygotsky definitely saw humans as nonpassive, active, and self-regulating in a way much different from the Freudian-influenced view of traditional psychologists. Vygotsky did some ingenious experiments with children in which he showed the socially conditioned nature of language and meaning. Central to his approach was the claim that it is essential to analyze language and signs, which he saw as important mediators in human social and psychological processes (Wertsch 1990). He showed that attention, memory, imagination, and all consciousness are not simply external, innate mental processes. His experiments illustrated how all higher mental functions have their origins in social life. Vygotsky conceptualized consciousness as a product of complex social forms of mental processes. He did not oppose the individual or the social; he recognized the active reciprocal role that the individual plays in creating his or her own consciousness in the process of social intercourse.

In today's terms, Vygotsky could be criticized as being unsophisticated and mechanistic. His conceptions appear to be a vulgar Marxist view that places emphasis on the determination of social factors, rather than highlighting the *relationship* between the individual and society as primary. Vygotsky must be recognized, however, for being the first in modern psychology to suggest the mechanisms by which culture becomes part of each person's nature (Vygotsky 1978). He was a strong advocate of combining experimental cognitive psychology with neurology and physiology; this is probably one of the reasons for his current "rediscovery" by contemporary psychology as the discipline has taken a definite cognitive theoretical bent over the past decade. Most important, by insisting that all areas of study in psychology should be understood in terms of a Marxist theory of the history of human society, he was laying the foundation for the unified behavioral science view that provided the critical approach in sociology.

Luria, building on Vygotsky's theoretical framework, saw the study of psychology as "the science of the socio-historical shaping of mental activity and the structures of mental processes" (Luria 1976:164). These conceptions of Vygotsky and Luria contrast sharply with Freudian notions of the relationship between consciousness, the unconscious, and preconscious. From their perspective, this is simply not how the human mind works. Importantly, Vygotsky and Luria provide the basis for a therapy informed by critical sociology and a model for politicizing the unconscious through their recognition of human development as historical and a process that involves a dialectical relationship between biological processes and higher order psychological ones that are sociocultural in their origin. Human nature, consciousness, and the processes involved in human development are seen as being activist and revolutionary processes. This Vygotskian view successfully incorporates Engels' critique of naturalism by accounting for the dialectical process through which humans change their natural conditions through their own existence, and in this process, change their consciousness and behavior. The implications for a truly revolutionary approach to therapy are profound.

By extending Marxist theory to incorporate a critical view of the formation of individual psychologies within the dynamics of larger society, Vygotsky's perspective is useful for developing a therapeutic model that is radically different from that found in traditional therapy. The individualistic focus illustrated in the concept of a healthy person presented by traditional therapy ignores the fact that what it means to be an individual in society is socially defined and a constantly changing, historically conditioned concept. This conception does not deny that every person is unique, but it recognizes that personality traits are conditioned by what an individual does and the social setting in which this activity is acted out. Schmitt (1987) provides an example when he points out that individual capitalists hold unique personalities but these personalities must include aggressiveness and be money motivated—traits determined by the activities of capitalists and the social setting in which they spend their lives. The important issue here is how this understanding of the sociohistorical essence of human nature, consciousness, and the individual in society can be applied in therapeutic approaches. How can this view be used to construct a truly revolutionary psychotherapy that does not ignore the significance of the unconscious or larger social factors?

A SOCIOLOGY OF THE UNCONSCIOUS

Subjective elements of the unconscious mind, which are of primary importance in traditional therapy, are not ignored in a therapy informed by critical sociology and the insights of Marx. Following from Vygotsky, a sociological view sees the unconscious as activist and revolutionary. It is not seen as a passive component that is a property of the psyche and not of the social relations in which we live. This view of the unconscious is closely tied to the insights of critical sociology because it recognizes, as did Marx in *Capital*, that humans are created not in a separate and individualistic way, but rather are collectively created through a "mode of cooperation"—a social system (Schmitt 1987). Such a view, when applied to therapy, suggests that perhaps therapy should, indeed, be the domain of critical sociologists and social activists whose practice is connected to a larger working class political movement for progressive change.

The model of a sociological view of the unconscious that is being fleshed out here is one that suggests that consciousness is shaped through praxis and what is not produced by theorized political practice is unconscious. This model makes it clear that social relations are embodied in the unconscious and that the goal of a truly radical psychology or therapy should be to politicize the unconscious, that is, reorganize the unconscious through the activity of revolutionary transformation of social relations (Kovach 1988).

A politicized unconscious implies an integrated consciousness. Individuals with an integrated consciousness, collectively, have an integrated practice in which the different social relations are consciously and politically put into relation to each other in a structure that ties together the interconnections of individual psychologies, social institutions, and larger structural forces. This politicizing process is radical and revolutionary because it is precisely what is prevented by contemporary capitalist ideology and the historical development of capitalism (Red Collective 1978). Traditional psychology and therapy simply reinforce capitalist ideology and foster a fragmented consciousness. A truly sociological therapy and view of a healthy person must present a theory and *practice* that ties dissociated social relations together.

Following from a Vygotskian framework, what is being suggested here is that consciousness and the unconscious must be seen as linked in a dialectical relationship to each other and to social structural reality. Relatedly, a fundamental goal of a therapy guided by the tenets and understandings of critical sociology is seen as *politicizing the unconscious*. The important question at this point is, what exactly would such a therapy look like? How does one engage in a therapy informed by Marx and the view of a healthy person provided by critical sociology?

THE PRACTICE OF THERAPY INFORMED
BY CRITICAL SOCIOLOGY

The primary goal of therapy informed by critical sociology would be to "unalienate" the individual. Marx's idea of unalienation is a person who "as a productive social being . . . transforms the world around him in a specific way, leaving his [sic] mark on it" (Meszaros 1970:173). The difference between this sociologically informed therapy and the so-called radical therapy that was developed during the 1970s is the element of praxis. The radical therapists of 25 years ago recognized that critical Marxist insights and an understanding of the world can help to create new psychic forces. The therapeutic approach being developed here, though, emphasizes that to comprehend the world differently, individuals must be involved in the process of changing that world. To become truly revolutionary, therapy must go beyond the critical pedagogy of radical therapy. It must go further than simply enabling individuals to "reconstruct" their reality from different viewpoints that do not involve what Gergen and Kaye (1992) refer to as the "limiting narrative beliefs" of traditional therapy.

The revolutionary approach to psychotherapy being suggested here is curative to the extent that clients become involved in social transformation. This social transformation is seen as possible when the client identifies with a collective social subject and can "conceive of moving from a situation in which the social order is imposed upon us to another in which we seize control of our social nature and direct it for our chosen purposes" (Lichtman 1982:96). To make such a transformation, a client must come to the realization that his or her despair is tied to powerlessness, which is social. The client recognizes the necessity for organizing with others in order to have the power to defeat a social system that makes dehumanization and misery necessary.

An important question is, how is a client to act on his or her newly acquired political awareness and understanding? In the therapeutic model being constructed here, this awareness and understanding should come through experience, that is, praxis. Therefore, in the process of developing this critical consciousness, the client is also working with others to develop strategies for social transformation. This therapy, guided by the insights of critical sociology, goes beyond the so-called radical therapies of the past 25 years because it involves more than simply teaching individuals how consciousness, and all psychological processes such as emotions, intelligence, thinking, and creativity, are social and historical. This truly revolutionary approach involves applying this awareness to change concrete realities in individuals' lives such as racism, sexism, and homophobia. Such praxis is akin to applied critical sociology, guided by Marxist theory. As clients work with others to change social reality, the *relationship* between the client and his or her social world is changing, thus resulting in subjective changes in consciousness as well as objective changes in the client's life relative to problems in living. *History*, and the client's changing role in historical processes, becomes the "cure."

CONCLUSION

Focusing on the concept of a "healthy person" is useful for illustrating the shortcomings in traditional therapy guided by psychological approaches that focus primarily on the individual as the locus of problems in living. Such a perspective mystifies the relationship between individuals and larger social structural reality, thus preventing clients from understanding the ways in which their personal problems are merely reflections of larger social issues and socioeconomic-based trends. In the end, increasing numbers of people are turning to traditional counseling, therapy, and new-age healing practitioners to temper the effects of our flexible global economy that are manifest and experienced at the level of individual families and relationships. The "help" that they receive in most instances results in fostering more self-absorption, more self-blame, and most likely less of an awareness of the need for collective political organizing and action to change the social circumstances that are at the root of their everyday problems.

Good critical sociology makes it clear that what makes us individuals is both the social and the *historical*. This understanding of the relationship between individual psychologies and history is one of the basic goals in the revolutionary model for therapy that has been outlined here.

To speak of sociologists "doing therapy" seems like an anachronism only if one holds a traditional conception of therapy. The conception of a healthy person and therapy guided by the insights of critical sociology presented here is one of people working together in groups, gaining an understanding of the necessity for organizing that replaces misery and suffering with the sense of empowerment and control that people achieve through praxis. Sociologists and other progressive activists seem to be "naturals" for these roles of critical pedagogy and political organizing. They are also best suited for other aspects of a critical therapy that, at any given moment, would be primarily pedagogical and at other moments in history would involve mass political action. The primary task of the "therapist" would become involvement in a continuous analysis in order to understand these historical conjunctures. It would be an understanding of history and change that would guide the action of therapists. This role would be different from contemporary applied clinical sociologists and radical social workers because of the critical sociological understanding, guided by Marxist theory, that clearly shows that in order to be effective in changing the institutions that shape human problems and misery, action must be linked to a *common struggle for working class unity*. Unless "therapy" is linked to a larger political movement, it can result in change that is only reformist at best, with the end result being individuals better adapted to a world that is becoming increasingly dehumanized and less "healthy" for us all.

REFERENCES

Beck, J. 1995. *Cognitive Therapy: Basics and Beyond.* New York: Guilford Press.

Brown, P. 1974. *Toward a Marxist Psychology.* New York: Harper & Row.

Brown, P. 1990. "Toward a Sociology of Diagnosis." *Journal of Mind and Behavior* 11 (3–4):385–406.

de la Cancela, Victor. 1985. "Psychotherapy: A Political Act." *Practice* 3 (3):34–45.

Freud, S. 1919. *Collected Papers of Sigmund Freud,* edited by E. Jones. New York: Basic Books.

Gardner, H. 1985. *The Mind's New Science: A History of the Cognitive Revolution.* New York: Basic Books.

Gergen, K. and J. Kaye. 1992. "Beyond Narrative in the Negotiation of Therapeutic Meaning." Pp. 166–185 in *Therapy as Social Construction,* edited by S. McNamee and K. Gergen. London: Sage.

Kovach, J. 1988. "Politicizing the Unconscious." Paper presented at the Annual Eastern Sociological Society Meetings, Philadelphia, March.

Lerner, M. 1987. "Public-Interest Psychotherapy: A Case for the Pain of Powerlessness." *Utne Reader* (March/April):39–46.

Lichtman, R. 1982. *The Production of Desire.* New York: Free Press.

Luria, A. R. 1976. *Cognitive Development: Its Cultural and Social Foundations.* Cambridge, MA: Harvard University Press.

Marx, K. 1964. *Early Writings,* translated and edited by T. Bottomore. New York: McGraw-Hill.

Marx, K. 1972. "Theses on Feuerbach." In *The Marx-Engels Reader,* edited by R. C. Tucker. New York: Norton.

Masson, J. 1994. *Against Therapy.* Monroe, ME: Common Courage Press.

Messinger, E. 1990. "The Development of the Individual in Marx's *Grundrisse.*" Unpublished manuscript.

Meszaros, I. 1970. *Marx's Theory of Alienation.* London: Merlin Press.

Prilleltensky, I. 1990. "On the Social and Political Implications of Cognitive Psychology." *Journal of Mind and Behavior* 11 (2):27–36.

Red Collective. 1978. *The Politics of Sexuality in Capitalism.* London: Red Collective and Publications Distribution Cooperative.

Rosen, Freda. 1984. "Historical Influences on Social Therapy." *Practice* 2 (2):15–22.

Rubin, B. 1996. *Shifts in the Social Contract: Understanding Change in American Society.* Thousand Oaks, CA: Pine Forge Press.

Sampson, E. 1983. *Justice and the Critique of Pure Psychology.* New York: Plenum.

Schmitt, R. 1987. *Introduction to Marx and Engels: A Critical Reconstruction.* Boulder, CO: Westview Press.

Sipe, Robert. 1985. "Reification in Everyday Life." *Radical Therapy* 1 (3):27–39.

Sobel, D. and R. Ornstein. 1996. *The Healthy Mind, Healthy Body Handbook.* Los Altos, CA: DRx.

Still, A. and A. Costall. 1987. *Cognitive Psychology: In Question.* New York: St. Martin's Press.

Szasz, T. 1961. *The Myth of Mental Illness: Foundations of a Theory of Personal Conduct.* New York: Holber-Harper.

Vygotsky, L. 1978. *Mind in Society.* Cambridge, MA: Harvard University Press.

Wertsch, J. 1990. "The Voice of Rationality in a Sociocultural Approach to Mind." Pp. 111–127 in *Vygotsky and Education,* edited by L. C. Moll. New York: Cambridge University Press.

Toward a Critical Social Interactionism for Counselors

9

Sydney Carroll Thomas

INTRODUCTION

Interactionism has been heralded as part of a new contextualist trend for counseling scholarship. It has been developed in reaction to traditional organismic agestage models of human development that neglected important environmental influences. This chapter will suggest that this "new" interactionism is limited in the same way that earlier organismic theories were in that it ignores a critical analysis of the social context and defines social problems in individualistic terms. Thoughtful attention to the concepts of context and individualism is essential to establishing the criteria that a more adequate theory must satisfy. A Bernsteinian framework will be used to illustrate the macro and micro social linkages important for a critical social interactionism utilizing a school context as an example. The chapter will conclude with a discussion of promising future directions in developing a new metatheoretical approach to interactionism in counseling.

Counseling theorists have identified contextualism as the conceptual basis underlying interactionism in counseling (Pentony 1981; Steenbarger 1991; Thomas 1996). The essential feature of the contextual model of interactionism in counseling is that it views individual behaviors within a systems framework and conceives of changing individual behavior by changing the system of interaction of which it is a component part. This view is sometimes linked to that of symbolic interactionism and the work of Goffman (1959). In this chapter, I will demonstrate that lack of attention to Goffman's critical assumptions as well as those of other important social thinkers has resulted in an ineffective and reductionistic practice that is far removed from the contextualist ideals that it purports to uphold. The concepts of "context" and "individualism" will be analyzed broadly from both logical and ideological perspectives. A logical analysis looks at false beliefs and contradictions, whereas an ideology critique examines the motivation for the persistence of these false beliefs and the interests being served by not challenging them.

AN OVERVIEW OF BASIC INTERACTIONIST
CONCEPTS IN COUNSELING

Claiborn and Lichtenberg (1989) were the first to argue that despite the influence of interactional ideas in counseling and psychotherapy, the integration of these ideas into a coherent framework for theory, practice, and research has been lacking. "Our goal in this article is to correct this state of affairs—to describe the interactional point of view comprehensively and integratively" (p. 356), and "to show that the interactionist view is a unique and valuable perspective for counseling psychology" (p. 355). As such the work of Claiborn and Lichtenberg is a good example of a recontextualization of diverse views deriving from many fields and sources, specifically for the counseling profession. There are, however, other examples of specific concepts and intervention strategies based on interactionist concepts throughout the counseling literature, and these will be cited to illustrate points made by Claiborn and Lichtenberg.

The interactional point of view has been particularly important in specific areas of marriage, family, and group counseling. The concept of interaction is said to have two distinct meanings that are relevant to counseling. The first is from interactional psychology, which refers to the idea that behavior is jointly influenced by person (or trait) and situation (or environment) variables. The second meaning refers to the behavior of people with one another, as in interpersonal interaction. Thus, in an interactional view, behavior is considered "to be simultaneously influenced by the person's view of the world—interpretations, expectations, and choices—and by the world the person is viewing, particularly the behavior of others with regard to the person" (Claiborn and Lichtenberg 1989:356). These variables are said to be causally linked to each other, therefore interventions targeted at either will ultimately impact both the person and the situation.

There are five major areas of interactional thought that are said to be important in describing an interactional point of view: (1) reciprocal causality, (2) communication theory, (3) sequence and patterning in the organization of interaction and the relationship to interpersonal perceptions, (4) relationship formation, and (5) human systems and cybernetic principles (Duncan 1993).

Reciprocal causality is regarded as fundamental to interactionism. It means that person and situation variables affect each other in an ongoing, circular, and multidirectional manner. Persons and situations are said to function as both cause and effect in the interactional process.

In addition, interactional approaches in counseling rely heavily on concepts from *communication theory*. All behaviors (including nonverbal, indirect, and unintended ones) are said to be messages. The focus is on the relation between senders and receivers, and how this process is mediated by communication. Messages are sent simultaneously on content levels and relationship levels. The content level is the literal and semantic meaning of the message; it reports information. The relationship level communicates something about the kind of message that it is. In other words, it qualifies and classifies the content of the message; it indicates expectations in the relationship. For example, a person may say, "I just don't know what to do," and really mean, "Tell me what to do." "Influence on the content level corresponds to the social influence process as commonly understood attitude or behavior change stemming from the content of the influence strategy. Influence on the relationship level, however, makes use of the relationship definition process to produce changes in interpersonal behavior" (Claiborn and Lichtenberg 1989:362). Relationship messages also reflect the kind of relationship the sender and receiver have with one another.

In describing *patterns and sequences of interaction*, Claiborn and Lichtenberg (1989:363) state: "Interactions are not random; they are highly organized exchanges. Their organization emerges as the interaction proceeds, and it is represented not only in patterns of interaction but also in the interactants' cognitive construction of the interaction." As the interaction proceeds, the organization of these interactional patterns emerges. Interactional sequences are stochastic processes—nonrandom chains of events that ultimately affect other events and may constrain or limit their occurrence. This nonrandomness provides stability in forming relationships, providing the "rules" of the relationship or system.

Internal processes are important to the patterning of interactions, "particularly interpersonal perception and interpretation, which results in each person's construction of the interaction" (Claiborn and Lichtenberg 1989:363). People seek confirmation of their internal constructions of the interaction in the interaction itself, "both by behaviorally selecting situations for interaction and by perceptually selecting those aspects of the interaction that correspond to that construction." This functions as an ongoing confirmation of the self, as persons choose situations in which they can be the "other" to others, that they want to be. "In addition, the person, simply by interacting, engages in ongoing self-presentation, wherein she manages others' perceptions of herself in accordance with self-enhancing goals." "All interaction, then, emanates from and returns to the self" (Claiborn and Lichtenberg 1989:363).

Claiborn and Lichtenberg refer to the process of construing these interactional sequences as punctuation. "Punctuation refers to the way interactants perceptually organize events in the sequence (Watzlawick et al. 1967)" (Claiborn and Lichtenberg 1989:362). As an example, they state "the counselor might construe her behavior in the session as taking the initiative, through questions and prompts, to explore an issue with the client. She might correspondingly see the client's behavior as following her lead. The client, however, might see his behavior as taking the initiative in introducing new material, to which the counselor's behavior is a response" (Claiborn and Lichtenberg 1989:364). These punctuations are not deemed incompatible, but are different in terms of what is the stimulus and what is the response. "The more discrepant punctuations become, the greater the likelihood of misunderstanding and conflict in interaction (Watzlawick et al., 1974)" (Claiborn and Lichtenberg 1989:364).

This also results in trait attributions when interactants focus on the other's behavior as abstracted from the interaction itself. The example given here is one of the counselor inferring that clients are resistant, which is a stable attribution, rather than seeing it as part of a process in which they, the counselor, also play a role. This is particularly useful in marriage counseling, the goal being to get spouses to recognize their own roles in the process, and replacing a linear view of their interactions with reciprocal ones.

The concept of *relationship* is the core of interactional thinking. "It could be said to occupy the place that the concept of personality occupies in many theories; it serves to capture, at an abstract level, the more stable properties of interactions" (Claiborn and Lichtenberg 1989:364). Relationships are defined as "redundant patterns of interaction that transcend the particular personalities of the participants"; it is a thing in itself, not simply the sum of two or more persons (Claiborn and Lichtenberg 1989:365). These redundancies are considered to be rules, in the sense that implicit ways of interacting may regulate and stabilize interactions by constraining behaviors. "Whether or not rules are in members' awareness, however, they serve to regulate the interaction by promoting the selective reception of messages (the relationship aspect of messages qualifying the content), the purposive transmission of messages, and the correction of inappropriate messages" (Claiborn and Lichtenberg 1989:365). This relationship definition includes expectations about roles, the position and power members have over one another, and the domain of permissible powers. It regulates the process of interaction and the outcomes of interactions.

As people exchange information on the content level of communication, "they simultaneously negotiate a definition of the relationship on the relationship level" (Claiborn and Lichtenberg 1989:366). Healthy relationships are characterized by clear and stable definitions, in which both parties in the relationship are likely to find their own behaviors validated and confirmed by the impact their behaviors have on the other.

These relationships are also to be considered as *systems*. "The concept of system and accompanying cybernetic concepts like feedback and control have been among the most practically useful of all interactional ideas. They bring the science of information exchange to bear on human behavior and provide a way of keeping the focus on the exchange, rather than the person" (Claiborn and Lichtenberg 1989:369). These concepts are considered especially important for conceptualizing behavior disorders and behavior change.

A LOGICAL AND IDEOLOGICAL ANALYSIS OF CONTEXT AND INDIVIDUALISM IN INTERACTIONISM

At first glance, interactionist assumptions appear to be appropriately contextual and less individualistic than traditional organismic theories. Starting with the assumptions of systems theory, we will see how problematic this incomplete interactionist theory actually is.

Consistent with Claiborn and Lichtenberg, Howard (1985:539) defines a systems perspective as dealing with "notions such a wholeness, holistic, organismic, gestalt, and so forth. These constructs focus our attention on systems of elements in mutual interaction with one another rather than on the summation of a number of causal influences that influence separately, with little evidence of any planfulness in how these summative effects are achieved."

More specifically, Cottone (1991:399) lists some basic propositions of a systemic approach:

1. The focus is on the study of relationships.
2. Relationships can be isolated for study and defined, but only with the understanding that the acts of isolation and definition are relative to the observer and his or her system (relationships) of reference.
3. Cause is nonlinear or circular within the confines of the defined relationships of significance.
4. Therapeutic change occurs through the social relationship.

Circular causality in systems approaches is part of a cybernetic epistemology. In Amatea and Sherrard's (1991) formulation of the Mental Research Institute (MRI) brief therapy model, systems cybernetics is foundational. Human problems and the ways people attempt to resolve them "are viewed as systems of information with negative feedback mechanisms that often produce either chronicity or crisis. . . . According to Watzlawick et al. (1974), 'the principles for understanding human problems are cybernetic: its causality is of a circular, feedback nature; with information its core element; and it is concerned with the process of communication in the widest sense' (p. 127)" (Amatea and Sherrard 1991:341).

In defining the use of cybernetic epistemology and systems theory, Lopez (1989:582) is especially adamant about the concept of power in such a cybernetic epistemology, stating that

Bateson believed that a "true" cybernetic epistemology could never be achieved without a strict adherence to the systemic principle of circular causality, or the assumption that all elements of an interactive system are equally co-responsive. . . . For Bateson, power was a myth, useful perhaps in describing material processes, but irrelevant to understanding form, pattern or organization.

This has important implications for achieving the so-called "double view," the sine qua non of a cybernetic epistemology according to Lopez. "A double view refers to a complex perception that "connects" the two (or more) individual punctuations that together describe a particular relationship pattern" (Lopez 1989:583).

In response to a charge by Zerbe (1988) that the concept of circular causality in family systems does not promote advocacy, Lopez (1989:583) states:

Will our advocacy, as counselors for change in oppressive social structures advance marital and family counseling by improving cybernetic epistemology? No. Let me emphasize here that I am not proposing that such advocacy is inherently wrong or misguided. I am simply saying that it is not defensible as an approach to an improved cybernetic epistemology, because it diverts our attention away from the achievement of a double view.

These examples highlight the fact that interactionist theory, as recontextualized in counseling, is fraught with problems. This view is more concerned with maintaining the integrity of a concept than with helping victims. And there most certainly are victims, especially in instances of spousal abuse. Whether Lopez and Bateson agree with this really does not matter; it is still the truth, people are oppressed and people are victimized. Does interactionism represent a more contextual view of the way humans develop in interaction? Does this view represent an advance in social system awareness? Interactionism in counseling is really more of a method than a theory, and although claims are made that it is rooted in symbolic interactionism, the most important assumptions of this theory concerning the context and the individual have been ignored.

SYMBOLIC INTERACTIONISM

In social psychology, symbolic interactionism has made an important contribution in that it recognizes that perception and interpretation are not just passive processes but are strongly influenced by our social relationships. It is a method that takes experiential reality seriously, and has emphasized a self-consciousness that emerges out of social interaction (Mead 1934). "The self's consciousness and self-consciousness therefore always exist in the context of a fundamental intersubjectivity" (Broughton 1986:143). Broughton, however, notes one central problem in symbolic interactionism is its focus on symbolic levels of discourse and communication as a medium. Thus, it tends "(a) to lose sight of the individual 'I', (b) to confound perception and communication of self with its actual existence, and (c) to obscure the broader *institutional* contexts and concrete *historical* structuring of persons and relations" (Broughton 1986:143). Actually, classical symbolic interactionism does take very seriously the internal subjectivity of individuals (Mead 1934), and provides an important account of the shaping of the self in interaction. Newer forms of interactionism, however, have indeed tended to neglect subjectivity and focus almost entirely on observable communications processes. The obfuscation of institutional contexts and historical structuring does seem to be common to most forms of interactionism.

Few interactionist formulations move beyond microlevel processes. In many, there is almost a complete absence of any concept of structure, in spite of the fact that Goffman (1974) makes explicit use of structural concepts in his analysis of frames (Gonos 1977). Many interactionists, including those in counseling, claim to rely heavily on Goffman's work, yet the concept of frame is completely missing from most formulations, replaced by the vague and empty concept of "situation." Goffman attempted to see behind the everyday constant activity of human beings to the structures (frames) that provided some stable rules of operation. These frames are not to be confused with visible social relations; they constitute a level of reality that is unseen, but on which the laws of social practice and communication depend. "One cannot claim to have reached a scientific understanding of a strip of interaction, says Goffman, unless one has worked out an understanding of the rules of the frame in which this interaction takes place" (Gonos 1977:858).

THE MACRO–MICRO CONTEXT

Questions remain as to what is the context and what does it look like? In a sense, counseling theorists have viewed context only from the standpoint of the effects of interpersonal relationships, not the broader contexts in which we live and work. The way one views the context has important implications for one's view of individualism, which is one criticism of traditional stage theories that contextualist theorists attempt to remedy with their newer formulations.

As an example, it is very important for counselors in educational settings to understand the power and complexity of these institutions. There are few social contexts in which cognition, behavior, and personality are subject to such continuous and multidimensional evaluation and typification (e.g., tracking, sorting, labeling, classifying, and grading). Schools may *create* differences between students on various dimensions that they choose to measure. Systemic demands of educational contexts have a subtle, yet pervasive, impact on developmental outcomes for students allocated to specific school and consequent life-course trajectories.

The following is a brief view of different ways context is conceptualized within the sociology of education. Figure 9.1 illustrates how a critical social

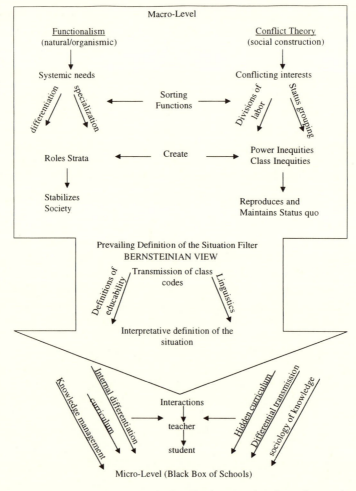

Figure 9.1. Social interactionism, including both macrolevels and microlevels of analysis.

interactionism includes both macro- and microlevels of analysis. Traditionally, sociology of education has conceptualized educational contexts under three umbrella terms: (1) functionalism, (2) conflict theory, and (3) interpretivism (Feinberg and Soltis 1992; Thomas 1996/97).

The functionalist views the educational context as serving a socializing function that helps students adapt to the economic, political, and social institutions within which they must live and work. Risking oversimplification, the functionalist framework, such as the Parsonian view (Parsons 1959), means that as the social environment is like an organism with natural systemic needs, and as an organism functions as a result of differentiation and specialization of its parts, so does society as a whole. Therefore, social roles and strata are necessary for the functioning of the larger organism (society). This view implies that social inequalities are necessary for societal stability and survival. The structured whole is greater and different than the mere sum of its parts. It is very much analogous to classic organismic developmental theory: it is an organismic view of society. Importantly, this view emphasizes connections between education and larger macrostructures such as economic and political systems. However, in sociology of education, functionalist analysis has fallen into some disrepute, and has been criticized for underestimating the importance of power differential, conflict, and ideology, and for legitimating oppressive and destructive forces in society (Karabel and Halsey 1977).

The conflict theorist does not view society as an organism with necessary systemic needs that are natural and benign, but rather views social roles and strata as a result of conflicting human interests, which are then socially reproduced for the purpose of maintaining the status quo. Schooling then is viewed as a set of institutions and social practices that reproduces the existing set of social relations. In a traditional Marxian sense, schools are viewed as instruments of "class domination serving to reproduce the work force and maintain class relationships" (Feinberg and Soltis 1992:7).

Both of these views are concerned with large macrolevel societal processes. Interpretivism, however, is the view of context that school counselors are more familiar with and is the paradigm within which interactionism is located. Interpretivism is concerned with microlevel processes such as interpersonal interactions in school contexts, and comes out of the tradition of symbolic interactionism. It is appealing to counselors because it is a less deterministic view than other alternatives in that it focuses on human agency and self-construction and upholds the idea that people create meaning through negotiation with significant others. It is a step in the critical direction; however, a comprehensive developmental theory must see these microlevel interpersonal and intrapersonal processes not only as private experiences but as entwined with larger institutional arrangements of society and within their historic context.

THE PARADOX OF INDIVIDUALISM:
WHERE IS THE "I" IN INTERACTIONISM?

Critiques of individualism have in common the complaint that excessive focus on the individual leads to self-absorption and narcissism, which tends to devalue social commitment and to encourage unscrupulous competitiveness (Lasch 1977). In addition, a critical theory of context does not focus on the tendency of individualism to denigrate social relatedness; rather it views individualism as paradoxically destructive of the individual, in that it places full responsibility for problems and solutions to these problems on the individual (Thomas 1996/97). In other words, an excessive focus on the individual, as for example in a therapeutic relationship, tends to excuse or at least obfuscate possible deleterious and oppressive social forces that contribute to the problems of the individual.

Individualistic counseling theories have been critiqued from a functionalist perspective. The overarching concern has been that such perspectives have been inimical to social commitment or to a moral order, without usually questioning the social context to which one should be committed. For example, Kelly (1989:341) is concerned with "therapeutic individualism" in which the "ultimate criterion for all valuing, including social commitments, is the individual's self defined self-fulfillment." Although this is a valid critique, it does not address the extensive debate over the destructiveness to individuals themselves of individualism.

Multicultural perspectives in counseling have also critiqued individualism on the grounds that this represents an American, white, middle-class bias, while other cultures may value relatedness and social commitment above the individual. This is also an important critique, but it does not extend to how this "hyperindividualism" actually harms all individuals; it is not just a "values problem." This sort of contextual relativism does not address the totality of ideological and political issues within the critique of individualism in human development and counseling theory. Individualistic theories are not just detrimental to special groups and classes, they are detrimental to human beings generally. A systematic approach to a broad, generic definition of context requires a systematic critique of individualism, not only on the grounds of special bias (e.g., "racism or "sexism"), but on the grounds of a systematic reconsideration of our most basic assumptions of what it means to be human, and how these assumptions inform our practice.

The current interactionist models in counseling retain three questions about human beings that remain unanswered: (1) How much of the self do human beings bring to this interaction? (2) What comprises this self? and (3) How much of the self is actually formed in this interaction? The concept of reciprocal causality would suggest an ahistorical self. "Reciprocal causality also means that explanations of behavior are necessarily based in present, observable functioning, rather than an inferred past, as is characteristic of linear causality" (Claiborn and Lichtenberg 1989:360). If one truly constructs one's self in every interpersonal interaction, then it makes sense that behavior can be explained only as it emerges in the present interaction.

But Claiborn and Lichtenberg also refer to what seems to be a more stable self that brings to the interaction certain self-enhancing expectations and goals; this is what prompts the individual to engage in the activity of managing others' impressions of one's self. Even though there is a "self-facade" that is constructed in a social process of interaction, this does not seem to imply that human beings themselves are malleable or systematically shaped through historical and systematic social processes. Rather, human beings are literally actors, who can choose from among many situations, in the service of managing others' impressions of them. We cannot determine if this "other-directedness" is in the service of the self, is an intrapersonal phenomenon that is organismic, or something that is socially produced, because there is not much attention paid to the self, only to its product, the "self representation."

We are told that meanings determine our behavior, but we are not told how, why, or where these meanings come from. It seems as if they are a product only of the moment, in which case human beings are not susceptible to any profound or systematic shaping of the environment, especially because we are free to choose our situations. But world-openness is not a choice, it is a condition that renders one susceptible to historically and culturally produced meanings, perceptions, and intentions. Focusing on the present should not mean ignoring one's "presently experienced past," but this is precisely what this view is doing.

So we do not really know much about human beings from this view or about any sort of condition of world-openness that would prompt such self-presenting activities, and we do not know how human beings are actually transformed and maintained during the interaction, or if it is just their particular presentation that is changed. By focusing only on the changing self-presentation and not on what constitutes the "self from which all interaction emanates," it is hard to tell if this truly represents a view of human beings as malleable, or if it defaults to an earlier organismic notion of the self. It appears it is the latter, because social processes are important only with respect to the most immediate observable activity. So although the idea that humans are what their behavior shows them to be is contextual in terms of the present, this ahistoricism does not lead one to see the human being as, at least in part, a product of one's culture or society.

As with earlier organismic views, human activity is something that occurs *in* the context, not *of* the context. Furthermore, this view does not get away from the individualism of organismic models, for even though it rejects the idea of problems as being illnesses, it still labels any problems with individuals as "maladaptive behaviors," which does not seem that different or any less individualistic than labeling clients as "immature," "off-time," "stuck," or "deviant." This is ironic because there is no concept of the individual in interactionism. At least organismic theory pays attention to the individual. Indeed the concept of reciprocal causality as used in interactionism, which is an attempt to sidestep issues of power and blame, really turns into blaming the victim.

In a truly contextual model, a discussion of interpersonal interaction and communication cannot be divorced from the larger organizing principles of all social relations. This use of cybernetic explanations of systems processes does not require that a complex model of context be included, because context is not viewed as a systematic powerful force in interaction, communication, or development.

Although interactionism recognizes *relationship systems*, it does not capture the *systems of relationships* within the dominant political/economic structures of our society. It does not ask the question, "Under what historical and political conditions do these interactional processes arise?"

In their description of individuals and contexts, Claiborn and Lichtenberg remain unconscious of the "frame," the invisible web of social relations from which all interpersonal interactions derive, and bring an unexamined prior knowledge of rules to the relationships they have described. Unfortunately, the many interactional concepts Claiborn and Lichtenberg address as relevant to counseling stop short of moving beyond interpersonal, individual level processes and do not take into account the interactions one must have within institutional structures and attendant norms, values, constraints, and resource allocations. Individual "definitions of the situation" are always, to some extent, related to *prevailing definitions of the situation*.

Understanding the prevailing definition of the situation entails a recognition of the set of rules and structured social relations that make the existence of such relationships and human activity possible. For example, in schools, there is a set of structured ongoing relations that are not open to negotiation. In what ways are students transformed by interactional processes and in what ways are they maintained and controlled? Do interactionist counselors view themselves as evaluators of "maladaptive" interpersonal strategies without also addressing the fact that they as well as the larger institutions of schools and society may actually create these problems? Problems cannot simply be relegated to issues of cybernetic feedback processes of communication, or maladaptive interpersonal strategies, and truly be preventative.

In their insistence on upholding a cybernetic epistemology, interactionists have devalued issues of power and control, instead focusing on an endless series of "dysfunctional" sequences of behavior patterns and maladaptive strategies. They have tried to explain away the complexities of social interactions by producing and synthesizing polished techniques of communication and intervention strategies. They either cannot address or refuse to address the broader issues of power and struggle that might not fit the facts of their own "reframing" of these issues. This is consistent with the remarks of Lopez (1989:583) in response to his neglect of power issues: "I am simply saying that it is not defensible as an approach to an improved cybernetic epistemology, because it diverts our attention away from the achievement of a double view." Apparently the fact that cybernetic episte- mology also diverts counselors' attention away from the real, concrete prob- lems of their clients seems to have escaped the interactionists' attention.

A BERNSTEINIAN FRAMEWORK FOR A CRITICAL SOCIAL INTERACTIONISM: LINKING CONTEXTS

One can either hold a functionalist or conflict view of the world and still use interpretivism to explain how macrolevel processes are worked out in microinteractions. Interactionism, as a form of interpretivism, can be ex- tended to provide a macrolevel analysis framework by using criteria put forth by Basil Bernstein (1996).

Bernstein provides outstanding and original criteria for a theory that draws on both normative and interpretivist paradigms to integrate micro- and macrolevels of analysis. As a theory of pedagogic discourse and modal- ities of symbolic control, Bernstein's work represents a persistent effort to account for both structural and interactional aspects of life, and to move beyond what he call the "mystical process of internalisation" of values, roles, and dispositions, to explicate the social structuring of classroom dis- course and the transmission of society's distribution of power and principles of control. In the following, I provide an abbreviated summary of Bernstein's (1996) criteria in a way that makes them applicable to a critical social interactionism.

1. The transition between different levels of theory must be made through the use of concepts, which at each level describe the key relations of the theory as they are realized at each level. The concepts must hold together and specify both interactional and structural rela- tions. That is, macroconstraints must be made visible, by the concep- tual language, in their power to shape interactions. At the same time, the potential of interactions to shape macroconstraints must be capa- ble of being described.
2. The theory must not simply specify its objects at the theoretical level, but must provide the rules for their empirical recognition, descrip- tion, and the different forms the object of analysis can take.
3. The theory must clearly specify not only the contexts that are crucial to its exploration and change, but also the procedure for the descrip-

tions of these contexts and their interpretation. The rules that generate specific descriptions must be capable of apprehending all empirical displays to which the context gives rise.

This third point is particularly important, because counseling theories can become ideological mechanisms for defining situations in such ways that the integrity of the paradigm is preserved, when behavior patterns are treated as a normal part of ontogenetic development rather than as structured by the environment. Most critiques of developmental theory focus on the confusion of a generally accepted "descriptive validity" with the theory's explanatory power. Not much attention has been paid to the criteria for the description itself. Very few developmental or sociological theories are able to provide an unambiguous recognition of the phenomena the theory addresses. Bernstein believes this criterion is crucial to his theory if circularity is to be avoided, in that the theory may construct, at the level of description, only that which lives within its own confines.

4. The substantive issue of the theory is to explicate the process whereby a given distribution of power and principles of control are translated into specialized principles of communication differentially, and often unequally, distributed to social groups and classes.

This last point is specifically relevant to interactionist paradigms in counseling because these theories persistently focus on neutral and benign communication processes without recognizing power differential. For a critical interactionist, an identification of different patterns of cognitive and affective development could be identified as cultural displays of specialized consciousness.

For example, we could ask how an interactionist understands the competitive self. Is this only a product of negotiated meaning constructed within interactions within the "black box" of schools? Or are the schools, as part of the larger macrostructural environment, transmitting implicit or explicit messages about the type of individual needed to be a productive and functioning member in this particular society? Is this transmitted knowledge differentially applied to different classes and groups of students? The addition of macrolevel analysis helps add to the explanatory power of interactionism by moving questions beyond mere negotiation and microlevel pedagogy.

WHAT DOES IT MEAN TO BE HUMAN?

It takes more than an adequate description of social contexts to build a comprehensive theory. Critical assumptions about human beings must be included. Importantly, human beings are malleable (Berger and Luckmann 1967; Dannefer and Perlmutter 1990; Dowd 1990; Thomas 1996/1997). Human beings are "world-open" due to relative plasticity of physical and mental structure as compared to other mammalian species. We are not driven by instincts in the same way as animals; we have to learn from our environments. These anthropological constants mean that human beings are absolutely compelled to get their social and psychological bearings and developmental structuring from the human environment. This dramatic divide between human and nonhuman physiology is indicated by a number of important developmental distinctions.

For example, 65 to 75% of our brain growth occurs outside of the womb, in the environment (Gould 1977): we are neotenous, meaning that half of fetal growth that occurs for other species in the womb occurs for human beings outside of the womb, in interactions with social as well as physical environments (Montague 1989; Portman 1956). The consequence of rapid brain growth outside the womb is accompanied by physiological growth that is retarded compared to other species. We remain more childlike, more dependent, for much longer periods than other animals. This plasticity "is beyond all other traits the most neotenous" (Montague 1989:57). Ironically, plasticity is a fixed genetic characteristic of humans that both facilitates and *requires* that human activity and response patterns be shaped by learning and interaction rather than by genetic programs.

Although human beings are much more malleable than other mammalian species, we are also distinct in our abilities to be self-conscious; we have the capacity to imagine our creations before we create them. Human beings are innovative and creative and are also responsible for creating the powerful social contexts that help create individuals out of human activity. This innovation and creativity are deeply shaped by the environments we create because of our "world-openness." It is a supremely dialectical process, not a onesided one as is most often portrayed in counseling (Thomas 1996).

There are productive capacities in the context that help to explain where the "interactive self" comes from. This goes beyond a recognition of the controlling nature of the social context. It is especially important given that interactionists place so much value on individuals' freedom to choose their situations. Interactionism as presented leads us to believe that individuals are motivated by the natural needs of self-validation and confirmation and can intentionally select aspects of interaction that conform to their own cognitive constructions. Because individuals are naturally dependent on the approval of others, they must continually be engaged in the management of other's perceptions of themselves. But where do these needs come from? Not all interactions are of the same character or motivated by the same needs.

For example, what is the relationship of specific forms of interaction to certain individuals in an alienated society? The concept of alienation need not apply only to the workplace, it can be seen as a fundamental category in social interactional processes in our society.

> If . . . we see alienation as a socially-structured process of fragmentation, in which we each become and are reduced to a specialized and limiting enactment of a social function, then we can begin to see its general applicability. . . . For example, we need not restrict the concept of motivated social interaction to drives for cognitive consistency, maintenance of arousal levels, or social conformity. (Wexler 1983:83)

Wexler denaturalizes the process of social interaction by specifying it as an historically produced condition. Referring to a specific type of interaction, that of interpersonal attraction theory, Wexler states that attraction is usually explained in terms of individualized traits or complementary needs, never in terms of power and wealth.

> Yet, phenomenological descriptions of the earliest stages of love and intimacy are remarkably similar to Marx's descriptions of the expressions of the effects of alienated social relations in religion: of the social psychological efforts to overcome paralysing fragmentation and powerlessness by the idealization of a powerful, mysterious other, whose very completeness reflects the character of our felt inadequacies. Intense attraction can be understood as a manifestation of alienation and the effort to overcome it by valuing and glorifying not only what we do not have, but also what we have learned to believe is beyond our capacity to mutually create in ourselves. (Wexler 1983:84)

Certainly, not all interactions are intense attractions, but interactionists in counseling do place a great deal of emphasis on the need for humans to continually affirm and validate themselves through self-representation in interaction. Not all interactions involve idealizing, but many are motivated to some extent by individuals' felt inadequacies and, as is often argued, the message of all interactions is "validate me." Whether one agrees with Wexler's hypothesis or not, it does provide a good example of how a theory of interpersonal interaction can still be connected to historically specific social organizations and their productive capacity in terms of interactional processes.

Unfortunately, the self-confirmation human beings are seeking by self-presentation and "impression management" is probably not readily forthcoming in many interactions. We live in a culture that pits people competitively against one another and accentuates their alienation. This alienation then compels them to seek more validation from others and makes others more attractive as a means of appropriating what they do not have. In an alienated society, the need for self-validation becomes an insatiable need.

A PROMISING FUTURE

Interactionism in the counseling field loses much of what could be an important contribution by continuing to obscure the persistent problems of human life in contemporary society. The struggles one has with contradictions of American culture, such as living up to the ideals of individualism and autonomy while being pressured to conform, to be unique and to be like others, to be intimate and yet not burdened with obligations and responsibilities, and to maintain integrity in work situations that demand complicity, all could be reflected in a model that captures the human experience of living in a world with incompatible demands. Instead, interactionism is reduced to general laws of communication and behavior, which hide these contradictions, and it fails to address or recognize the struggles of individuals to respond with integrity to conditions that increasingly fragment and disable them.

By addressing the concerns raised in this chapter regarding assumptions about the context and individuals, interactionism could be expanded to provide a much broader scope than is evident so far. Some of the most compelling and exciting new work in cognitive psychology is attempting to bridge social constructionism and cognitive constructivism (Martin and Sugarman 1996). In my view, this is a first step in addressing the criteria set forth by Bernstein for linking the macro–micro views discussed earlier, and for addressing necessary assumptions regarding what it means to be a human being set forth by Thomas. However Martin and Sugarman's theses are specifically focused on psychology and very relevant to a social interactionism.

Social constructionists have been very critical of the cognitive constructivist movement because of its reductionistic and relativistic implications. It is a highly individualistic view that emphasizes subjectivity above all else (Thomas 1996). Furthermore, radical constructivist approaches lead to a relativism that makes it almost impossible to identify real, concrete oppressive social effects. It is ideological in its emphasis on "development-through-crisis" assumptions, by transforming oppression into character building (Duncan 1994; Thomas 1996).

At the other extreme are the radical social constructionists who argue that psychological phenomena are constituted almost entirely by social institutions and practices. This view upholds a nonessential view of the self. This too is problematic as there is no room in such a view for biology, which most certainly plays an important role in human development. There is also no room for enduring human qualities such as spirit, soul, passion, intentionality, and imagination.

Martin and Sugarman (1996) have elegantly presented a view that adopts much of what is good about social constructionism while still maintaining the necessary allowances for human agency, intentionality, essential selfhood, and creativity. They contend that what is needed is a new theoretical approach, one with ontological and epistemological assumptions different from either of the positions to be bridged, namely, social contructionism and cognitive constructivism.

The core ideas of this theory are (1) a *shifting psychological ontology* that describes and explains the gradual emergence of imaginal and memorial capabilities and mediational functions of the human mind and (2) *underdetermination* of these capabilities and functions (and the specific psychologies that arise from them) from their sociocultural and biological origins. "It is precisely because the individual is not an exact replica of, and to some extent can transcend the social, that various kinds of human psychological transformation such as learning, psychological change, and creative innovation are possible" (Martin and Sugarman 1996:294). This statement upholds the necessary assumptions of human development addressed earlier in this chapter, those of malleability, plasticity, and world-openness. What Martin and Sugarman add with their articulation of *shifting ontology* and *underdetermination* is an explanation of how the personal, the psychological, originates in the collective, sociocultural environment, but is not *reducible to these origins.*

The social constructionist view compliments the interactionist perspective in its emphasis on the pivotal role of everyday conversation and other relational practices in the constitution of psychological phenomena. This view is an effective anecdote to the overly individualist constructivist view but is still impoverished in its ability to explain the influence of biology and innate aspects of personality. We still do not know how human beings are able to transcend some aspects of social constraints, how they manifest such variety in knowledge and behavior, and how some accrue such depths of wisdom and strength while others become demoralized. There is little evidence of human intentionality and agency in radical constructionist notions (e.g., Derrida 1978, 1982; Foucault 1972; Gergen 1991). "The problem is that this sort of poststructural social constructionism begs the question of what it is that social influences are acting to constrain. What is happening here is a fundamental confusion about the relations between social structures and human agency" (Martin and Sugarman 1996:297). We are not reducible to social structures any more than we are reducible to mere biology. This is explained by the first principle of underdetermination.

Humans do not become exact blueprints of what cultures conceive them to be because individual experiences are unique. Our interpretations and integrations of experiences are therefore partly responsible for creating an understanding of ourselves that promotes genuine reflexivity and some self-determination. Our *shifting ontological status* of human psychology then is *underdetermined* by sociocultural conventions and structures. Although we may have the freedom to make self-determined choices in life, it is important to remember that these choices are *seldom made within the circumstances of our own choosing.* This loose paraphrasing of Marxist thought nicely illustrates the above developmental bridge proposed by Martin and Sugarman.

These theoretical assumptions relate very well to interactionist theory because of the acceptance of the following assumptions:

1. The fundamental premise from constructivism allows form and organization of thought to be constructed from experiences that are embedded and instantiated in the human psyche from conversational and interrelational practice.
2. Individuals obtain their reflexivity from internalizing conversations and other symbolic relational practices. At the same time, these relational practices are assumed to have unwritten rules that "license" the ways in which human beings related to one another. These conditions are moral and ethical as well as linguistic. This relates to Goffman's unique version of symbolic interactionism (dramaturgy).
3. Human beings, as a result of these encounters, develop personal theories about their experiences. These theories are interpreted personally and as part of the prevailing interpretations of the surrounding culture. This relates very much to interpretivism.
4. Human beings have the capacity for imagination and memory. These capacities allow us to reflect on our past and reconstruct its significance in the present, as well as project ourselves into the future. The fact that we are quite possibly the only species that can foresee our own deaths has a profound impact on our meaning-making of the past, present, and future. This relates to assumptions by Thomas (1996) and others regarding a critical interactionist theory.

These assumptions help us to define and clarify the ways in which socioculturally produced cognitive capacities are mediated by individual capacities of memory, imagination, and agency. Certainly, in education these will help us look at students' creative learning capacities in a more balanced and contextualized way. It adds the important assumptions necessary to articulate the psychological questions of self-definition as well as the philosophical questions of how we are to live in a world filled with contradiction. When people come to realize that much of everyday life is produced by people instead of seeing it as natural and inevitable, they can more easily question the current order and develop alternative ideas and approaches to problems. This sociological and psychologically informed contextualism is a counseling that is geared toward realizable possibilities in the future as well as the realities of immediate day-to-day struggles in an often overwhelming environment.

ACKNOWLEDGMENTS

I wish to express appreciation to Jim Chiavacci for his invaluable assistance in the design of Figure 9.1 and to Walter McIntire for his constructive comments.

REFERENCES

Amatea, E. and P. Sherrard.1991. "When Students Cannot or Will Not Change Their Behavior: Using Brief Strategic Intervention in the School." *Journal of Counseling and Development* 69:341–344.

Berger, P. and T. Luckmann. 1967. *The Social Construction of Reality: A Systematic Treatise in the Sociology of Knowledge.* New York: Anchor.

Bernstein, B. 1996. *Pedagogy, Symbolic Control and Identity: Theory, Research and Critique.* London: Taylor and Francis.

Broughton, J. 1986. "The Psychology, History and Ideology of the Self." In *Dialectics and Ideology in Psychology,* edited by K. Larsen. Norwood, NJ: Ablex Publishing.

Claiborn, C. and J. Lichtenberg. 1989. "Interactional Counseling." *The Counseling Psychologist* 17 (3):355–453.

Cottone, R. 1991. "Counselor Roles According to Two Counseling Worldviews." *Journal of Counseling and Development* 69 (5):398–401.

Dannefer, D. and M. Perlmutter. 1990. "Development as a Multidimensional Process: Individual and Social Constituents." *Human Development* 33:108–137.

Derrida, J. 1978. *Writing and Difference,* translated by A. Bass. Chicago: University of Chicago Press.

Derrida, J. 1982. *Margins of Philosophy,* translated by A. Bass. Chicago: University of Chicago Press.

Dowd, J. 1990. "Ever Since Durkheim: The Socialization of Human Development." *Human Development* 33:138–159.

Duncan, S. 1993. "A Critical Analysis of the New Contextualism in Counseling." Doctoral dissertation, University of Rochester.

Duncan, S. 1994. "The Trouble with the New Contextualisms." *Collected Original Resources in Education* 18 (1). University Microfiche No. 2EO1.

Feinberg, W. and J. Soltis. 1992. *School and Society,* 2nd ed. New York: Teachers College Press.

Foucault, M. 1972. *The Archeology of Knowledge,* translated by A. M. Sheriday Smith. London: Tavistock.

Gergen, K. 1991. *The Saturated Self: Dilemmas of Identity in Contemporary Life.* New York: Basic Books.

Goffman, E. 1959. *The Presentation of Self in Everyday Life.* Garden City, NY: Doubleday.

Goffman, E. 1974. *Frame Analysis.* New York: Harper & Row.

Gonos, G. 1977. "'Situation' versus 'Frame': The 'Interactionist' and the 'Structuralist' Analyses of Everyday Life." *American Sociological Review* 42:854–867.

Gould, S. 1977. *Ever Since Darwin.* New York: Norton.

Howard, G. 1985. "Can Research in the Human Sciences Become More Relevant to Practice?" *Journal of Counseling and Development* 63:539–544.

Karabel, J. and A. H. Halsey (eds.) 1977. *Power and Ideology in Education.* New York: Oxford University Press.

Kelly, E. 1989. "Social Commitment and Individualism in Counseling." *Journal of Counseling and Development* 67:341–344.

Lasch, C. 1977. *Haven in a Heartless World.* New York: Harper & Row.

Lopez, F. 1989. "Is Society 'Sick'? Comment on Zerbe Enns Article." *Journal of Counseling and Development* 67:582–584.

Martin, J. and J. Sugarman. 1996. "Bridging Social Constructionism and Cognitive Constructivism: A Psychology of Human Possibility and Constraint." *Journal of Mind and Behavior* 17 (4):291–320.

Mead, G. H. 1934. *Mind, Self and Society from the Standpoint of a Social Behaviorist.* Chicago: Chicago University Press

Montague, Ashley. 1989. *Growing Young.* New York: McGraw-Hill.

Parsons, T. 1959. "The School Class as a Social System: Some of Its Functions in American Society." *Harvard Educational Review* 29:297–318.

Pentony, P. 1981. *Models of Influence in Psychotherapy.* New York: Free Press.

Portman, A. 1956. *Zoologie und das neue Bild vom Menschen.* Hamburg: Rowohlt.

Steenbarger, B. 1991. "All the World Is Not a Stage: Emerging Contextualist Themes in Counseling and Development." *Journal of Counseling and Development* 70 (2):288–296.

Thomas, S. 1996. "A Sociological Perspective on Contextualism." *Journal of Counseling and Development* 74:529–536.

Thomas, S. 1996/97. "Context and Individualism: Critical Issues for Contextualist Counselors." *International Journal for the Advancement of Counselling* 19:101–110.

Watzlawick, P., J. Beavin and D. Jackson. 1967. *Pragmatics of Human Communication: A Study of Interactional Patterns, Pathologies, and Paradoxes.* New York: Norton.

Watzlawick, P., J. Weakland and R. Fish. 1974. *Change: Principles of Problem Formation and Problem Resolution.* New York: Norton.

Wexler, P. 1983. *Critical Social Psychology.* Boston: Routledge and Kegan Paul.

Zerbe, E. 1988. "Dilemmas of Power and Equality in Marital and Family Counseling: Proposals for a Feminist Perspective." *Journal of Counseling and Development* 67:242–248.

The Family under Siege ———————————— **10**

James J. Chriss

INTRODUCTION

There is a vague sense in some parts of the United States, and perhaps across the West more generally, that people are losing control of their lives, and that they are no longer able to withstand the encroachment of experts and other systems or organizations as they conduct their day-to-day affairs. To better comprehend any number of issues arising in modern American society today, it is helpful to articulate certain master trends or themes that might plausibly explain a myriad of phenomena that may at first glance appear unrelated, but that nevertheless share a lineage with this issue of the encroachment of the system, or "expertocracy."

Jurgen Habermas (1984, 1987, 1996) calls this the "colonization of the lifeworld," that is, the process by which systems steering media—such as power from the polity, money from the economy, or even "cognitive ratio-nality" from education—infiltrate and systematically distort the day-to-day life and communicative conduct of a people. One social institution in partic-ular, the family, has become the locus or battleground for such activities. The ongoing colonization of the lifeworld, in conjunction with certain con-temporary American trends concerning adolescence, has given rise to new, peculiar cultural codes, which in turn has led to new, sometimes perplexing forms of behavior.

These new forms of behavior are not so noticeable at the level of the lifeworld, or rather, of everyday life. That is, across a variety of informal social gatherings or contexts—family dinners, dates, waiting queues, anony-mous public doings—the nature of face-to-face interaction between familiar or unfamiliar others remains rather stable and predictable. It is at the level of institutions, that is, the behavior of whole organizations or organizational actors, that new forms of conduct are evident.

As a consequence of all this, a perception has been growing, both among lay audiences and social scientists alike, that the family as we once knew it is on the decline. The twin trends of rising divorce rates and increasing numbers of women in the full-time work force have led some observers to suggest that parental care and oversight of children have been eroded sub-stantially.[1] Divorce often leads to one parent (usually the mother) attending to the socialization and supervision of children. Also, as more women are away from home pursuing advanced degrees or working full-time, the sentiment is that the quality of child care is diminished, either because children are placed into the care of secondary, formal institutions (e.g., daycare centers), or simply because it is assumed that women are better (read "natural") caregivers who should be at home attending to their young children. In other words, according to this "essentialist" argument, even a stay-at-home dad is a poor substitute for the expressive and empathetic qualities that mothers bring to child rearing.[2]

UNCERTAINTY PATHOLOGIZED

As the family institution appears to come under siege, other institutions and organizational concerns come to the fore and implicate themselves in the day-to-day struggles of modern family life.[3] Many of these extrafamilial structures and activities emerge and gain sustenance from the therapeutic state. These may appear in the form of either direct interventions by the state (via family and welfare policy or other statutes), or more indirectly via moral entrepreneurship (Becker 1963) on the part of business, charitable organizations, and concerned citizens (e.g., victims rights or self-help groups; see Weed 1995).

For many adults working hard to raise children in today's world, commonsense understandings of how to go about this task seem less and less adequate. That is to say, there appears to be high levels of uncertainty among parents about how to raise their children given all the horror stories they hear about inadequate parenting and other problematic accounts of modern society. These problems would include high divorce rates, drug and alcohol abuse among adolescents, gangs and violence, teen smoking, the recent and well-publicized string of school shootings by youth, teenage pregnancy, children suffering from attention deficit disorder (ADD) or attention deficit hyperactivity disorder (ADHD), child abuse, and child abductions and kidnappings.

Although this brief list of maladies is certainly alarming, I would suggest that the rising concern about society and childrearing today is more a reflection of the impact of the therapeutic ethos on persons' commonsense notions of reality, rather than of any actual or putative increase in the rate of such problems. The Enlightenment program of science promised to deliver more certitude about the world and greater predictability and control of human affairs. In this era of the information age and the counseling boom, more and more persons are offering their services as "experts" to help parents overcome their fears or uncertainties about particular areas of family life. In other words, uncertainty itself has become pathologized, especially with regard to the psychotherapeutic dictum that people should seek "professional help" for even minor disturbances or troubles in their lives.

Marriage and family therapists or counselors are the front line of professionals providing information to parents grappling with what they may believe to be unacceptably high levels of uncertainty or suffering in their lives (see, e.g., Gavazzi and Law 1997; Gubrium 1992; Patalano 1997). As the sentiment continues to proliferate that parents are doing a poor job of raising their children, more experts in fields such as marriage counseling and child protective services are suggesting that couples be licensed before they are allowed to have children, thereby further eroding the autonomy and authority of the family. The issue of parental licensing also goes hand in hand with the notion that parents need handbooks purporting to provide expert guidance in child rearing. In fact, one such handbook (Briesmeister and Schaefer 1998) has taken the therapeutic ethos so far as to suggest that parents ought to be "co-therapists," in alliance with certified mental health professionals, in diagnosing and treating children's behavior problems.

One important function of socialization historically has been that children develop a sense of self as they begin to understand how others see them and respond to their actions or utterances. Ideally, the deep and abiding attachments that children form with agents of primary socialization—most importantly, their parents[4] —create need-dispositions within the child that direct the child to comport his or her behavior to the desires, wishes, or expectations of his or her significant others. In other words, if things work right, kids act in ways that please parents. If parents are pleased, they give positive and reassuring feedback to their kids. The family system thus produces children with positive senses of self, and so healthy, vibrant self-esteem is ensured.[5]

STEPPING IN FOR EMBATTLED FAMILIES

What happens, then, when children are neglected, or their socialization is impoverished by the absence of one or both parents over significant portions of their youth? Formal agents of social control often step in to take up the slack for parents who have supposedly abrogated their responsibilities for raising and supervising their children. For example, legal and medical (that is, psychological or psychiatric) oversight of adolescents has expanded enormously at about the same time the alleged decline of the family has occurred. The American Psychiatric Association's *Diagnostic and Statistical Manual of Mental Disorders*, 4th edition (DSM-IV), has come up with yet another category of "mental illness" that just happens to apply particularly to the behavior of adolescents. This category is oppositional defiant disorder (ODD). What are some of the diagnostic criteria that may suggest that a child is suffering from ODD?

The DSM-IV (pp. 93–94) states the diagnostic criteria as follows: "A pattern of negativistic, hostile, and defiant behavior lasting at least 6 months, during which four (or more) of the following are present:

1. often loses temper
2. often argues with adults
3. often actively defies or refuses to comply with adults' requests or rules
4. often deliberately annoys people
5. often blames others for his or her mistakes or misbehavior
6. is often touchy or easily annoyed by others
7. is often angry and resentful
8. is often spiteful or vindictive.

This is an incredible turn of events in the history of society's—or rather, of select groups supposedly acting in the best interests of society's—attempt to control the behavior of its children. Aside from the inexact language of these so-called "criteria" (how often is "often," for example?), this new attempt to further drive children's everyday, informal behaviors or misbehaviors into the formal realm of control—whereby experts (counselors, psychologists, psychiatrists, doctors, social workers, law officers, the courts) intervene on behalf of parents and teachers allegedly swamped with the rigors of work and other pressing concerns—reeks with the stench of narrow economic interest. That is, as much as anything, the ODD category has been created to expand the areas of expertise that can be claimed by doctors, counselors, lawyers, and whomever else wants a piece of the action of controlling children. After all, it is a huge and growing industry, with many economic payoffs to be had (see Armstrong 1993; Armstrong 1995; Caplan 1995; Heitzeg 1996; Livingston 1997).

KIDSVOTING USA

Another example of secondary organizations stepping in to rescue embattled kids who, it is assumed, are not receiving adequate attention or supervision from parents, teachers, or the community is KidsVoting USA. A recent self-description I received from this organization states that KidsVoting USA is "a private, nonpartisan, nonprofit, grassroots organization, in the schools and community, dedicated to educating America's youth about the importance of an informed electorate and about voting to sustain democracy and to increase voter turnout now and in the future. Kids go to official polling sites to cast their own ballot, accompanied by their parents or guardians."

This sounds fine as a statement in an organizational manifest. But think about the conditions or perceptions that had to be present to bring to fruition such an organization. Apparently three Arizona businessmen visited Costa Rica in 1987 and noticed that that country's voter turnout hovers impressively around 90%. Troubled by the United States' historically low levels of voter turnout—the 1996 presidential election pulled in less than 50% of registered voters, for example—the businessmen sought to apply the successful Costa Rican strategy—a tradition whereby youths apparently accompany parents to the polls in great numbers—to the United States. After several years of implementation and continuing expansion of the program across the United States, research by Dr. Bruce Merrill of Arizona State University indicates that adult voter turnout has risen about 3% at those polling sites where the Kids Voting program has been implemented.

But why do we need yet another organization to do this? As far as I know, schools have always held mock elections for kids in the classroom, and this has always been a sufficient little exercise in democracy toward the ultimate goal of teaching about and socializing children into civic participation. I volunteered to man a Kids Voting booth at a voting precinct in Wichita, Kansas during the last presidential election. What I saw left me with grave doubts about how worthwhile or meaningful it is to drag kids to polling places on election day.

For example, at one point during my 2 hours of manning the booth, a very young, perhaps kindergarten-aged, child came up to the table who could not even sign his name to the register. His mother stood behind him and said, "That's okay, he just wants to pretend like he's voting." I gave the child a ballot and pencil, and he dutifully scurried off to the makeshift voting booth to "vote." On exiting the voting booth, the youngster proudly proclaimed "I voted for everyone with 'D' names!" (The mother, a Bob Dole supporter, knew full well that her child had no idea what he was doing, and conveniently used the 'D' name bit to get her child to vote for Dole, unwittingly of course.) Everyone within earshot smiled and made comments like "How cute," but I just sort of sunk back in my chair and thought to myself, "Something is terribly wrong here."

What is terribly wrong is that many children who came and participated in the mock vote simply were too young to understand what they were doing, and it is likely that they were not helped at all by the exercise. Social scientists and philosophers have shown that the cognitive ability of children is quite limited before the age of 8, and that there is simply not much of lasting beneficial value to be gained from having children go through such exercises (see, e.g., Mead 1962; Piaget and Inhelder 1969).

The desire to have kids experience voting at such an early age is symptomatic of a pervasive "pop" psychology culture that emphasizes the importance of self-esteem, the "warm fuzzies," and being included or participating in activities as an end in itself (see Hewitt 1998; Tallman 1997). In the "good old days," children's self-esteem was ensured by the warm coziness of a stable, nuclear family and safe neighborhoods and decent schools in which children could be kids and did not have to be taught about all the nasty things that awaited them on being released to make their way through a rough and tumble world. Now, with the perception of the breakdown of the family, with poor schools and teachers who have lost their will and have given over direct assessment and supervision of their classes to counselors and other gurus perpetuating the myth of out-of-control ADD- or ADHD-afflicted children, and with the perception of unsafe, crime-ridden neighborhoods, children are viewed as victims of impoverished lifeworlds in which self-esteem is tenuous at best. Why? Because they live in a fragmented, postmodern world in which shared visions of the good life no longer seem to apply or even make sense. In other words, the days of informal raising of children is over. First-line agents of socialization, such as parents, teachers, and other community leaders, have not gotten it done, or so the sentiment goes. So it is time for agents of formal social control to do the work of supervising and controlling children.

With regard to KidsVoting USA, my position is that there was never a need to systematize kids voting in elections. If you want to increase adults' rates of voter participation, there are probably better ways to do it than using children as pawns in a newfangled enterprise.

ARE KIDS GROWING UP TOO FAST?

Also, it appears that in so many ways kids are being pushed into adult roles too quickly, not for the sake of the kids, but for the sake of adults. More organized sports, such as pee-wee basketball leagues and T-ball, are being offered to very young children (younger than 8) who have no understanding of what they are doing out on the court or on the field. Kindergarten and elementary school students are even being given diplomas and are walking through graduation ceremonies with robes and full academic regalia. Young children are competing in beauty pageants and representing schools, communities, and even states, carrying the title of Little Miss This or That. This is ersatz community building at its best (see Klapp 1991).

Kay Hymowitz (1998), in an editorial that recently appeared in *Wall Street Journal*, lamented the ongoing vulgarization of social life and the fact that children are becoming streetwise and precocious at rates never before seen in American society. Although the idea that children are growing up too fast in today's society may have merit, it should also be remembered that before the advent of industrialization children were pushed into adult roles quite rapidly as well. In fact, in earlier times children were not really differentiated from adults at all, and when they got old enough they were expected to help out on the family farm or business, or in some other capacity (Aries 1962). It was not until the advent of industrialization and the massive expansion of education that children were viewed as somehow different from adults. Indeed, the teenage years, a concept most westerners take for granted these days, was invented only recently as a concomitant to the many changes taking place in the economy and society, which have already been discussed (see Felson 1994:75–91).

What is different about the way children used to be pushed into the adult role and how they are being pushed into adulthood today is that in earlier times the family was still primary and maintained direct and overt supervision of the young. Granted, in preindustrial society children had to work hard as soon as they were physically able, but they were doing so for the direct benefit of their family. Today, children are being pushed into adult roles often with little or no input or supervision from their parents.

As the family recedes as the primary agent of socialization and as the major source of social integration for the broader society, other persons, organizations, or activities arise to pick up the slack. One such activity promising greater social integration and a greater sense of community is amateur singing in karaoke bars (see Drew 1997). Because modern social life seems more and more fragmented and because people are dealing with anonymous others on a routine basis, the interaction rituals signaling good manners, deference, and accommodation between strangers are being twisted into perverse forms that in effect serve to feed and stroke fragile self-esteem [Chriss 1993a, 1993b, 1995a, 1995b; Durkheim 1984 (1933); Goffman 1967, 1971]. In an earlier time, it was unthinkable that a rank amateur would even consider going up to the mike before a group of anonymous others and singing his or her favorite songs, however flat, however out of tune, however weak or untrained the voice. The old, perhaps now outdated, idea was simply that there were some genuinely talented, privileged folks out there who had good voices and who could legitimately entertain audiences, and that most other persons should remain on the sidelines and not make others endure their feeble attempts at singing. After all, back then, in real communities, with real people who knew you and cared about you, there were plenty of places to go to get your ego stroked. Now, anonymous others go willingly to karaoke bars to sing and to be sung to by people who, like them, are searching for a moment in the sun, the expressive act giving comfort to egos that otherwise might not have access to what most of us understand as "real" connections, feelings, emotions, attachments, or community. (This is also symptomatic of the "cult of participation" that underlies the KidsVoting phenomenon, as well as most underage sports activities.)

It is vital that we reverse such trends as ersatz community building and the increasing presence of business or other formal organizations (systems) in everyday life, and simply let the schools or the parents do what they are supposed to do with respect to the socialization of our children. Too many outside groups are moving in to strip away the functions of our major social institutions, especially those of the family. We do not need yet another organization, such as Kids Voting USA, steering the everyday lifeworld activities of the home, school, or community.

A similar thing has happened, for example, in the case of the "malling of America" where enclosed shopping malls are taking on more and more of the functions and activities of the community (see Kowinski 1985). For example, more and more malls advertise that on Halloween parents can bring their kids to the mall so they can trick or treat in a safe environment in which merchants will gladly hand out all sorts of goodies. Also, malls are increasingly advertising themselves as safe havens in which elderly citizens in particular can do their daily walking so they will not have to negotiate dangerous neighborhood streets. To accommodate this group, malls often open early and even mark off a walking route with signposts for every eighth or quarter mile. Above all else, though, there is a decidedly consumerist flavor to the malls' seemingly altruistic act of stepping in for embattled communities. That is, as more and more persons long for connectedness in a fragmented, postmodern world, counterfeit claims to community are being offered by those promoting economic agendas or who operate under the altruistic guise of the therapeutic ethos (Freie 1998).

A NEW TRIBALISM?

If indeed modern society is producing more and more children who are coming out of fragmented families and communities and who are growing up to become bitter adults suffering from low self-esteem who tend to be cynical about almost everything in life (especially government, the mass media, police, law, medicine, and science), we should not compound the problem by allowing, even encouraging, persons or entities to come forth to offer services or to otherwise feed off their misery by providing false indicators of a world they may have longed for but which is now only a dim memory. At its very essence, social life *must* be built on the hard work of going out and meeting people, of making friends, of getting involved in communities and civic groups, of forming dating dyads that evolve into families with supportive kinship networks that are interlocked with other kinship networks (see Putnam 1996).

But I also know that pressures of anonymity and cynicism toward the other are running high, especially in modern mass society, and that these tend to mitigate against such an easy fix. In a restaurant I recently overheard two women talking about their failed love lives. They complained that finding a good man and building a relationship was tough work, perhaps more work than it was worth. One women told the other that she was getting up in years, and that she would not wait around any longer. She pulled a pamphlet about sperm banks from her purse, and then displayed a computer-generated list of donors with accompanying age, occupation, height, weight, and hair color descriptions. She said she had already made her choice, and told her friend that she ought to consider going the sperm bank route as well. This is just one example of the problem of modern life: It is simply too easy to sidestep the admittedly hard work of relationship building, or neighboring, or making friends, or being involved in community.

The postmodern loss of certitude has pretty much set the stage for a regression of sorts, in which we have lost faith in the Enlightenment-inspired ideal of the universal and the hope that truth and knowledge are discoverable "out there" just so long as we remain true to objective, systematic analysis and follow the prescripts of the scientific method.[6] All signs seem to be pointing in the other direction, however, namely, the sentiment that truth resides only in local circumstances, and that justice and solidarity and community are to be found in the tribe, among people who share similar characteristics, such as race, ethnicity, gender, social class, disability, sexual orientation, or age (see Maffesoli 1996). Tribalism is something that humankind fought long to overcome. But whereas many of us are content now to huddle in our tribes like scared little animals scurrying from the sights and sounds of a world we do not understand, there are people and groups out there mining the situation for all it is worth.

They are the custodians of the therapeutic welfare state. They are the experts of the growing expertocracy. They step in and tell us that we do not understand how to raise our kids, or that a child is hyperactive or is suffering from some other "disease," mental or physical. Lawyers, doctors, law enforcement officials, social workers, and a myriad of other formal agents are busily at work defining and redefining social reality for us. What are we to do as a society about the increasing encroachment of systems imperatives into previously informally regulated arenas of social life? Are we fated to live in an expertocracy in which collective understandings forged through voluntary cooperation between members of a citizenry are being replaced by the formalized rulings of legal bureaucrats and the cost–benefit analyses of efficiency experts or other technocrats?

These questions are difficult to answer, and I have no easy solutions. The first step in tackling this problem is simply talking about it, and this polemic is offered in that spirit. But polemics must lead to fuller, more robust discussions if they are to contribute to real-world solutions to pressing dilemmas faced by free democracies such as ours. It is hoped that the discussion engaged in here concerning the family under siege, as well as the various issues raised by the other contributors to this volume, will indeed contribute to a rethinking of social policies and serious reflections on those (individuals or organizations) purporting to act in the name of social justice and in the best interests of society.

NOTES

1. These are but two of the salient features of the "family decline" thesis. For a more detailed summary of the family decline literature, see Amato and Booth (1997), Coppock (1997), Giele (1996), and Kain (1990).

2. This is not to imply that the absence of fathers is not equally damaging to children. Recent research on fatherlessness has documented the grim reality of an American culture that has tended to view fathers as irrelevant or, at best, only loosely connected to their children's lives and sense of well-being (see, for example, Blankenhorn 1996; Popenoe 1996).

3. I am indebted to much of Christopher Lasch's work, which touches on similar issues regarding the family under siege and the cultural conditions of modernity, especially the rise of the therapeutic state, that support the continuing erosion of family authority and autonomy. See especially Lasch (1977, 1979).

4. Although even this age-old notion, that parents are the most important agents of socialization in the lives of their children, has fallen out of favor among some in the helping professions and human sciences of late. For example, psychologist Judith Harris (1998) claims that the "nurture" assumption, this being that parents, and especially mothers, have the most direct bearing on how their children turn out, is wrong, and that in the modern world, other agents of socialization, especially same-age peers, are at least as important as parents in influencing and determining child outcomes.

5. Although the importance of positive self-esteem in ensuring healthy and well-adjusted citizens has become a taken-for-granted assumption among a great majority of social scientists and laypersons alike, it must also be recognized that self-esteem itself has become a cottage industry, thereby being subject to the same sorts of distortions and illegitimate usages that other popular ideas or fads are prone to suffer. For a brilliant summary of the abuse and inappropriate extension and application of the concept of self-esteem in modern society, see Hewitt (1998).

6. Nowhere has the flight from the universal to the specific become more obvious than in the area of sexual harassment law. As the language of rights and entitlements becomes more and more narrowly defined along the lines of personal or group attributes or social status (for example, in terms of race, ethnicity, disability, sexual orientation, age, or, in the case of sexual harassment law, gender), the general ideas of "citizen" and "community" continue to erode and lose their meaning (see Chriss 1997; Weed 1995).

REFERENCES

Amato, Paul R. and Alan Booth. 1997. *A Generation at Risk: Growing Up in an Era of Family Upheaval.* Cambridge, MA: Harvard University Press.

Aries, Phillipe. 1962. *Centuries of Childhood,* translated by R. Baldick. New York: Random House.

Armstrong, Louise. 1993. *And They Call It Help: The Psychiatric Policing of America's Children.* Reading, MA: Addison-Wesley.

Armstrong, T. 1995. *The Myth of the A.D.D. Child.* New York: Dutton.

Becker, Howard. 1963. *Outsiders: Studies in the Sociology of Deviance.* New York: Free Press.

Blankenhorn, David. 1996. *Fatherless America: Confronting Our Most Urgent Social Problem.* New York: Harper Collins.

Briesmeister, J. M. and C. E. Schaefer (eds.) 1998. *Handbook of Parent Training: Parents as Co-Therapists for Children's Behavior Problems.* New York: Wiley.

Caplan, Paula J. 1995. *They Say You're Crazy.* Reading, MA: Addison-Wesley.

Chriss, James J. 1993a. "Durkheim's Cult of the Individual as Civil Religion: Its Appropriation by Erving Goffman." *Sociological Spectrum* 13 (2):251–275.

Chriss, James J. 1993b. "Looking Back on Goffman: The Excavation Continues." *Human Studies* 16 (4):469–483.

Chriss, James J. 1995a. "Habermas, Goffman, and Communicative Action: Implications for Professional Practice." *American Sociological Review* 60:545–565.

Chriss, James J. 1995b. "Some Thoughts on Recent Efforts to Further Systematize Goffman." *Sociological Forum* 10 (1):177–186.

Chriss, James J. 1997. "Public Harassment, Sexual Harassment, and the 'Reasonable Woman' Standard: Some Limitations of Legal Rationality." Pp. 121–141 in *Perspectives on Social Problems,* Vol. 9, edited by C. B. Gardner. Greenwich, CT: JAI Press.

Coppock, Vicki. 1997. "'Families' in 'Crisis'?" Pp. 58–75 in *"Childhood" in "Crisis"?,* edited by P. Scraton. London: UCL Press.

Diagnostic and Statistical Manual of Mental Disorders, 4th edition. 1994. Washington, DC: American Psychiatric Association.

Drew, Robert S. 1997. "Embracing the Role of Amateur: How Karaoke Bar Patrons Become Regular Performers." *Journal of Contemporary Ethnography* 25 (4):449–468.

Durkheim, Emile. 1984 [1933]. *The Division of Labor in Society,* translated by W. D. Halls. New York: Free Press.

Felson, Marcus. 1994. *Crime and Everyday Life.* Thousand Oaks, CA: Pine Forge Press.

Freie, John F. 1998. *Counterfeit Community: The Exploitation of Our Longings for Connectedness.* Lanham, MD: Rowman and Littlefield.

Gavazzi, Stephen M. and Julie C. Law. 1997. "Creating Definitions of Successful Adulthood for Families with Adolescents: A Therapeutic Intervention from the Growing Up FAST Program." *Journal of Family Psychotherapy* 8 (4):21–38.

Giele, Janet Z. 1996. "Decline of the Family: Conservative, Liberal, and Feminist Views." Pp. 89–115 in *Promises to Keep: Decline and Renewal of Marriage in*

America, edited by D. Popenoe, J. B. Elshtain, and D. Blankenhorn. Lanham, MD: Rowman and Littlefield.

Goffman, Erving. 1967. *Interaction Ritual*. Garden City, NJ: Doubleday Anchor.

Goffman, Erving. 1971. *Relations in Public*. New York: Basic Books.

Gubrium, Jaber F. 1992. *Out of Control: Family Therapy and Domestic Disorder*. Newbury Park, CA: Sage.

Habermas, Jurgen. 1984. *The Theory of Communicative Action*, Vol. 1, translated by T. McCarthy. Boston: Beacon Press.

Habermas, Jurgen. 1987. *The Theory of Communicative Action*, Vol. 2, translated by T. McCarthy. Boston: Beacon Press.

Habermas, Jurgen. 1996. *Between Facts and Norms*, translated by W. Rehg. Cambridge, MA: MIT Press.

Harris, Judith R. 1998. *The Nurture Assumption*. New York: Free Press.

Heitzeg, Nancy A. 1996. *Deviance: Rulemakers and Rulebreakers*. Minneapolis: West.

Hewitt, John P. 1998. *The Myth of Self-Esteem*. New York: St. Martin's.

Hymowitz, Kay S. 1998. "Kids Today Are Growing Up Way Too Fast." *Wall Street Journal*, Wednesday, October 28, p. A3.

Kain, Edward L. 1990. *The Myth of Family Decline: Understanding Families in a World of Rapid Social Change*. Lexington, MA: Lexington Books.

Klapp, Orrin E. 1991. *Inflation of Symbols*. New Brunswick, NJ: Transaction.

Kowinski, W. S. 1985. *The Malling of America*. New York: Morrow.

Lasch, Christopher. 1977. *Haven in a Heartless World: The Family Besieged*. New York: Basic Books.

Lasch, Christopher. 1979. *The Culture of Narcissism*. New York: Norton.

Livingston, Ken. 1997. "Ritalin: Miracle Drug or Cop-out?" *Public Interest* 127:3–18.

Maffesoli, M. 1996. *The Time of the Tribes: The Decline of Individualism in Mass Society*. London: Sage.

Mead, George H. 1962. *Mind, Self, and Society*. Chicago: University of Chicago Press.

Patalano, Frank. 1997. "Developing the Working Alliance in Marital Therapy: A Psychodynamic Perspective." *Contemporary Family Therapy* 19 (4):497–505.

Piaget, Jean and B. Inhelder. 1969. *The Psychology of the Child*. New York: Basic Books.

Popenoe, David. 1996. *Life Without Father*. New York: Free Press.

Putnam, Robert D. 1996. "The Strange Disappearance of Civic America." *The American Prospect* 24:34–48.

Tallman, D. A. 1997. "Why I Quit Teacher's Education to Go Back to Law School." *The Long Term View* 3 (4):62–69.

Weed, Frank J. 1995. *Certainty of Justice: Reform in the Crime Victim Movement*. New York: Aldine de Gruyter.

Biographical Sketches of the Contributors _____

James J. Chriss is Associate Professor of Sociology at Newman University, where he also serves as Chair of the Social Sciences. His main areas of research are sociological theory, law, management and organizations, and the social organization of the helping professions. His latest book is *Alvin W. Gouldner: Sociologist and Outlaw Marxist* (Ashgate, 1999).

John A. Kovach is Assistant Professor of Sociology in the Department of Anthropology and Sociology at Kutztown University in Kutztown, Pennsylvania. He has also served as Assistant Director at the Temple University Center for Research in Human Development and Education, and as a consultant to the Philadelphia Psychiatric Center and the School District of Philadelphia. He conducts short-term therapy in his own private practice.

Philip Manning is Associate Professor of Sociology at Cleveland State University. His research interests concern the development of sociological theory, particularly theories of agency. He has published papers on ethnomethodology, social constructionism, and Goffman's use of ethnography. With Gary Fine, he has also recently completed a long review article on Goffman's contribution to sociology.

Roger Neustadter is Professor of Sociology at Northwest Missouri State University in Maryville. He has authored articles on the status of childhood in social theory and in American culture, temporality, the therapeutic state, and responses to technology. He currently is writing on the memoir boom.

James L. Nolan, Jr. is Assistant Professor of Sociology at Williams College. His most recent book is *The Therapeutic State: Justifying Government at Century's End* (NYU Press, 1998).

John O'Neill is Distinguished Research Professor of Sociology at York University, Toronto, a Member of the Centre for Comparative Literature at the University of Toronto, and a Fellow of the Royal Society of Canada. His most recent book is *The Poverty of Postmodernism* (Routledge, 1995). Currently, he is working on the political economy of child suffering, welfare state theory, and civic practice.

Roger Sibeon is Director of masters courses in the Department of Sociology at the University of Liverpool, UK. His teaching and research interests center on the application of sociological theory to public policy and contemporary governance.

Sydney Carroll Thomas is Associate Professor of Educational Counseling at the University of Maine in Orono. She recently published "The Soul of a Teacher" in *Journal of Maine Education*. She is primarily interested in educational counseling and in examining ideological assumptions of developmental theories that support unethical and oppressive practices in school.

James Tucker is Associate Professor of Sociology at the University of New Hampshire. He has published several articles on conflict and social control in organizations and a book on therapy in the workplace titled *The Therapeutic Corporation* (Oxford University Press, 1999).

Index